Anonymous

Reports on the Extent and Nature of the Materials available for the Preparation

Of a medical and surgical History of the Rebellion

Anonymous

Reports on the Extent and Nature of the Materials available for the Preparation
Of a medical and surgical History of the Rebellion

ISBN/EAN: 9783337212674

Printed in Europe, USA, Canada, Australia, Japan

Cover: Foto ©ninafisch / pixelio.de

More available books at **www.hansebooks.com**

CIRCULAR No. 6.
WAR DEPARTMENT,
SURGEON GENERAL'S OFFICE,
Washington, November 1, 1865.

REPORTS

ON THE

EXTENT AND NATURE OF THE MATERIALS

AVAILABLE FOR THE PREPARATION

OF A

MEDICAL AND SURGICAL HISTORY

OF

THE REBELLION.

PRINTED FOR THE SURGEON GENERAL'S OFFICE
BY
J. B. LIPPINCOTT & CO.
PHILADELPHIA.
1865.

SURGEON GENERAL'S OFFICE,
WASHINGTON, D. C.,
November 1st, 1865.

The following Circular is published for the information of the Medical Officers of the Army.

JOSEPH K. BARNES,
SURGEON GENERAL.

ERRATA.

Page 9, fifth paragraph, for 604 read 704.

Page 41, fifth paragraph, for "fractured wounds" read "*punctured* wounds."

Page 43, line fifteen, for "internal carotid" read "internal *maxillary*."

reports of the medical officers engaged in it, and of illustrations of these reports in the shape of pathological specimens, drawings, and models. The documentary data are of three kinds: first, the numerical returns, in which the number alone of the different forms of wounds, accidents, injuries, and surgical diseases is given; secondly, what may be called the nominal returns, in which are furnished the name and military description of each patient, and the particulars of the case, with more or less of detail; and thirdly, the miscellaneous reports. To the first class belong the "classified return of wounds and injuries" which every medical officer has been required to furnish immediately after every engagement, the "tabular statement of gunshot wounds," and the portion of the "monthly report of sick and wounded" referring to surgical diseases and accidents. The second class comprises the "quarterly reports of wounded" and the "quarterly reports of surgical operations" required of all general and post hospitals, the quarterly "sanitary reports" of regimental surgeons, the "nominal lists of wounded" forwarded by medical directors after every general engagement, and extracts from "case books." In the third class are included the reports of medical directors of armies

SURGEON GENERAL'S OFFICE,
WASHINGTON, D. C.,
November 1st, 1865.

The following Circular is published for the information of the Medical Officers of the Army.

JOSEPH K. BARNES,
SURGEON GENERAL.

CIRCULAR NO. 6.

SURGEON GENERAL'S OFFICE,
WASHINGTON, D. C,
October 20th, 1865.

BREVET MAJOR GENERAL JOSEPH K. BARNES,
SURGEON GENERAL U. S. ARMY.

GENERAL:—

IN response to your inquiries relative to the nature, extent, and value of the surgical data that have accumulated in the department of your office under my charge, and in regard to the progress that has been made in arranging these materials, I have the honor to make the following report:

The materials in the office relating to the surgery of the late war consist of the reports of the medical officers engaged in it, and of illustrations of these reports in the shape of pathological specimens, drawings, and models. The documentary data are of three kinds: first, the numerical returns, in which the number alone of the different forms of wounds, accidents, injuries, and surgical diseases is given; secondly, what may be called the nominal returns, in which are furnished the name and military description of each patient, and the particulars of the case, with more or less of detail; and thirdly, the miscellaneous reports. To the first class belong the "classified return of wounds and injuries" which every medical officer has been required to furnish immediately after every engagement, the "tabular statement of gunshot wounds," and the portion of the "monthly report of sick and wounded" referring to surgical diseases and accidents. The second class comprises the "quarterly reports of wounded" and the "quarterly reports of surgical operations" required of all general and post hospitals, the quarterly "sanitary reports" of regimental surgeons, the "nominal lists of wounded" forwarded by medical directors after every general engagement, and extracts from "case books." In the third class are included the reports of medical directors of armies in regard to the operations of the Medical Department, and the succor given to the wounded; reports and dissertations on new methods and modes of treatment, and modifications of surgical apparatus and appliances; pathological researches on morbid processes pertaining to surgery, as hospital gangrene, osteomyelitis, pyæmia, and the like; plans for ambulance organization, and the transportation of the wounded by land and water.

The extent of these materials is simply enormous. The returns are of as huge proportions as the armies that have been engaged in active operations for the last four years. The great body of the medical officers have made the reports required of them with commendable diligence and promptitude, and their zeal is the more deserving of praise when the engrossing nature of their field duties is considered. The result has been the accumulation of a mass of facts and observations in military surgery of unprecedented magnitude.

It is as yet impracticable to determine with accuracy the number of wounds received in action during the late war, though data for a near approximative estimate are accessible. But a comparison of a portion of the returns with the complete statistics of other armies will sufficiently indicate the vast numbers that are dealt with.

In the British Army in the Crimea, during the entire war there were 12,094 wounded and 2755 killed, or a total of 14,849.*

In the French Army in the Crimea, of a total effective force of 309,268, according to the report recently made by M. Chenu, there were 39,868 wounded and 8250 killed, or a total of 48,118, although in his report of injuries of different regions M. Chenu records but 26,681 cases.†

In the late war, the monthly reports from a little more than half the regiments in the field give, for the year ending June 30th, 1862, an aggregate of 17,496 gunshot wounds. The reports from rather more than three-fourths of the regiments, for the year ending June 30th, 1863, give a total of 55,974 gunshot wounds. The battle-field lists of wounded for the years 1864-65 include over 114,000 names. But these returns are to be completed by collating with them the reports of general hospitals, where many wounded were received whose names the recorders of field hospitals or regimental medical officers failed to obtain, and by adding the names of those killed in battle.

In comparing the numbers of cases of some important injury, as, for example, gunshot fractures of the femur, it is found that in the French Crimean Army there were 459 such injuries, and in the English Army 194, while over 5000 such cases have been reported to this office. Or if one of the major operations is selected for comparison, as excision of the head of the humerus, the Crimean returns give 16 of these excisions in the British, and 38 in the French Army, but the registers of this office contain the detailed histories of 575 such operations.

---

* Medical and Surgical History of the British Army which served in the Crimea, during the war against Russia, in the years 1854, 1855, 1856. London, 1858. Vol. ii. p. 259.

† Rapport au Conseil de Santé des Armeés sur les Résultats du Service Médico-Chirurgical aux Ambulances de Crimée et aux Hôpitaux Militaires Français en Turquie pendant la Campagne d'Orient en 1854, 1855, 1856. Par J. C. Chenu, D.M., Médecin Principal, Bibliothécaire de l' cole Imperiale de Médecine Militaire, Officier de la Légion d'Honneur, etc. Paris: Victor Masson et Fils, 1865.

INTRODUCTION. 3

The surgical specimens of the Army Medical Museum number 5480; and not only in specimens of recent injuries, but in illustrations of reparative processes after injury, of morbid processes, of the results of operations, and of surgical apparatus and appliances, this institution is richer, numerically at least, than the medico-military museums of France or Great Britain.

The value of these materials has been foreshadowed in referring to their nature and extent. It may be emphatically said that they throw much light on some of the great moot points in surgery; that they comprise on some subjects, as, for example, on the question of the propriety of excising the head of the femur for injury, fuller data than are now extant in the entire range of surgical literature; and that it may be hoped, without temerity, that they include the elements for the solution of many grave surgical problems.

To render intelligible an account of the progress that has been made in collating and classifying the surgical records of this office, and the collections of the Army Medical Museum, it is requisite to review briefly the measures that have been adopted by the Medical Department to gather and preserve the observations of the medical officers of the Army, and to compile, in an available form, the results of their inquiries and of their vast surgical experience in the late war.

In 1861, and during the first eight months of 1862, the "case book" and "register," made obligatory by regulations, the monthly and quarterly reports of sick and wounded, and the sanitary reports required of regimental surgeons, and of the surgeons in charge of hospitals, were the channels through which medical officers communicated such professional facts as they desired to place on record. These sources of information have been decried in some quarters, and in an official report to this office,[*] in July, 1863, it was declared that previous to September, 1862, "the surgical statistics of the war were absolutely worthless," and that "the only information procurable is such as can be derived from the examination of a mass of reports, all of which present merely certain figures under the vague and unsatisfactory heading, 'Vulnus sclopeticum.'"

That the surgical records of a period including the casualties of the first and second battles of Manassas, the battles on the Chickahominy, Ball's Bluff, Cedar Mountain, and Shiloh, and in which the returns from about one-half of the regiments in the field give an aggregate of over thirty thousand cases of gunshot injury, were deserving of such emphatic censure would be a source of grave regret, and it is gratifying to be able to state that a careful re-examination of these records proves that they contain a large amount of material that is far from valueless. The reports of the Washington, Fort Monroe, Baltimore, and Philadelphia hospitals of the treatment of the wounded from the Peninsular campaign, are replete with interest; the reports of the hospitals at Alexandria give voluminous materials in regard to the wounded from Cedar Mountain and the second Bull Run. The surgical records of the Fort Donelson campaign are very complete. The returns of the casualties incurred in the operations in North Carolina are satisfactory. The extracts from the case books of Surgeons Page and Clements, and Assistant Surgeons Peters and Billings, of the Army, and of Sur-

---

[*] Consolidated Statement of Gunshot Wounds. Washington, July 1, 1863. Octavo, pp. 11.

geons Neill, Bontecou, and Bently, of the Volunteers, give a multitude of observations that throw light on some of the most important subjects in military surgery.

On May 21st, 1862, it was enjoined upon medical officers, by a circular order from the Surgeon General's Office, to enter upon the monthly reports details in regard to the surgical cases that came under their care, and to forward pathological specimens to the Surgeon General's Office, with the view to the establishment of an Army Medical Museum.

In June, 1862, a "tabular statement of gunshot wounds" was appended to the monthly report of sick and wounded. A consolidation of these tables for the months of September, October, November, and December, 1862, was published. The tabular statements of the first two quarters of 1863 have been consolidated also, but it has not been deemed expedient to publish them, because materials are on hand in which fewer sources of error exist.

On March 25th, 1863, Circular No. 4, of the Surgeon General's Office, established the "classified return of killed and wounded in battle."

On November 4th, 1863, by General Order 355, War Department, medical directors of armies in the field were directed to forward to this office duplicates of their reports of killed and wounded; and, in promulgating this order, you instructed medical directors to detail suitable officers to collate and prepare all obtainable statistics and data in connection with past or future operations in the field that might be useful in the accurate compilation of the medical and surgical history of the war, and you directed the attention of all medical officers to this subject, and urged their co-operation in the work.

Circular 26, of November 26th, 1863, S. G. O., called the attention of medical officers in charge of general hospitals to the importance of preserving representations of the results of surgical operations for the Army Medical Museum.

It was found that the details in regard to wounds, accidents, and injuries, inserted in the monthly and quarterly reports of sick and wounded, were insufficient, and that, although the defects in the reports were supplied by those officers who diligently recorded their cases in the registers and case books, yet such fidelity was not universal, and the histories of many cases were meagre or imperfect, or omitted altogether. It was considered that the register in use was too bulky for field service, and too small for the requirements of general hospitals. A board of medical officers was accordingly directed to recommend a new form of register. The recommendations of the board were approved, and small portable registers were issued to medical officers in the field, while to each general hospital two large folio volumes were distributed, one as a register of sick and wounded, the other as a register of surgical operations. These registers contained minute directions as to the form in which cases should be entered under appropriate headings. The form of the register of sick and wounded is illustrated in the portion of this report that refers to injuries of the head, and the form of the register of surgical operations is given in connection with the subject of excisions of the head of the femur. To assist in the compilation of these registers, a new form of bed-card was adopted. Blank forms of quarterly reports of wounded and of surgical operations corresponding with the registers were prepared, and, on December 26th, 1863, by a special circular from this office, the officers in charge of general hospitals were

INTRODUCTION.

required to fill up these forms for the months of October, November, and December, 1863. In January, 1864, the new registers were introduced in all the general hospitals, the "consolidated statement of gunshot wounds" was discontinued, and a quarterly transcript from the registers of all cases of wounds or of operations was required. The new system has been found to work well, and the surgical records of the last quarter of 1863, and for 1864–65, are believed to possess a higher degree of statistical accuracy than has heretofore been attained.

Early in 1864, the new forms of reports of wounds and operations began to arrive at this office, and the work of transcribing and classifying their contents began. The cases of wounds were recorded in ten books, the new hospital registers being used for this purpose. The classification was as follows: nine volumes of gunshot injuries, viz.: 1. Wounds of the Head and Face. 2. Wounds of the Neck and Chest. 3. Wounds of the Abdomen, Back, and Spine. 4. Wounds of the Perineum and Genito-Urinary Organs. 5. Fractures of the Upper Extremities. 6. Fractures of the Lower Extremities. 7. Flesh Wounds of the Upper Extremities. 8. Flesh Wounds of the Lower Extremities. 9. Wounds of Arteries, Veins, and Nerves; and a tenth volume embracing Sword, Bayonet, and Miscellaneous Wounds. The cases of operations were recorded in five books, viz.: 1. Amputations in the Continuity. 2. Amputations in the Contiguity. 3. Excisions. 4. Ligations. 5. Miscellaneous Operations. On September 1st, 1864, there had been transcribed upon these registers the histories of 30,435 wounds, and of 1179 operations.

It was objected to this mode of registration, that injuries of the gravest and most trivial nature were confounded, and that the great mass of materials contained in the special reports, which medical officers had been encouraged to forward, was entirely omitted from the records. The least important cases received as much attention as the most serious, or even more, because the patients with trifling wounds were more likely to be transferred from hospital to hospital, and their histories were traced with greater difficulty. Moreover, the registers, though well adapted to the requirements of hospitals, were unsuitable for permanent records, the space being inadequate for the requisite details of important cases, or for summaries of the treatment and results in cases protracted through several quarters.

It was therefore determined that an effort should be made to arrange the records in a form more convenient for reference and study. In the first place, the early returns of the war were examined, and cases of the more important injuries were gleaned from them, and tabulated upon the new form of surgical reports. This work was of necessity performed by medical officers, or by clerks possessing a competent share of surgical information. In October, 1864, suitable books of record having been procured, the task of revising the surgical records began. It was decided to make numerous subdivisions, and, while avoiding impracticable refinements, to group together similar classes of injuries. On the new registers were entered, in the first place, the cases extracted from the early reports. Then the registers in use were examined, and the category in which each case should be placed was indicated; or, if from lack of precision in the report this was impossible, additional information was sought from the source from which the report had originated. Thus the cases recorded in the register of gunshot wounds of the head and face were distributed in six registers, viz.: those of Fractures of the Cranium, of Fractures of the Bones of the Face, of Fractures of the Vertebræ, of Scalp Wounds, of Flesh Wounds of the Face, and of Flesh Wounds of the Neck. Especial attention was given to collecting all the information on file in the office in relation to gunshot wounds of the three great cavities, gunshot fractures of the femur, and the less common surgical operations. The histories of several thousand specimens at the Army Medical Museum, that had been forwarded prior to the adoption of the new system of reports, were tabulated upon the proper forms and transcribed upon the records; and, on the other hand, the records were found to furnish histories for many later specimens that had been forwarded without memoranda. An endeavor was made to co-ordinate and harmonize these data.

The following classification of wounds and their results and of operations was finally adopted. It is less elaborate than that employed in the British statistics of the surgery in the Crimea, and more detailed than that followed by M. Chenu, in the French surgical report of the Crimean war. The appended figures give the number of cases of each class that were revised and corrected upon the new registers on September 30th, 1865.

Classification of Wounds and Injuries, and their Results, followed in the Division of Surgical Records S. G. O.		Classification of Surgical Operations followed in the Division of Surgical Records S. G. O.	
Gunshot Fractures and Injuries of the Cranium	1108	Amputations of the Fingers	1849
Gunshot Fractures of the Bones of the Face	1579	Amputations at the Wrist-Joint	46
Gunshot Fractures of the Spine, not involving the Chest or Abdomen	187	Amputations of the Forearm	992
		Amputations at the Elbow-Joint	19
Gunshot Fractures of the Ribs, without injury of the Thoracic or Abdominal Viscera	180	Amputations of the Arm	2706
		Amputations at the Shoulder-Joint	437
Gunshot Fractures of the Pelvis, not involving the Peritoneal Cavity	397	Amputations of the Toes	802
		Amputations of the Foot (Partial)	160
Gunshot Fractures of the Scapula and Clavicle, not implicating the Thoracic Cavity	389	Amputations at the Ankle-Joint	78
		Amputations of the Leg	8014
Gunshot Fractures of the Humerus	2408	Amputations at the Knee-Joint	132
Gunshot Fractures of the Radius and Ulna	785	Amputations of the Thigh	2684
Gunshot Fractures of the Carpus and Metacarpus	790	Amputations at the Hip-Joint	21
Gunshot Fractures of the Femur	1957	Excisions of the Head of the Humerus	575
Gunshot Fractures of the Tibia and Fibula	1220	Excisions of the Elbow	315
Gunshot Fractures of the Tibia and Fibula	1056	Excisions of the Wrist	34
Gunshot Fractures of the Tarsus and Metatarsus	629	Excisions of the Ankle	22
Gunshot Penetrating Wounds of the Chest, and injuries implicating the Thoracic Viscera	2303	Excisions in the Continuity of the Upper Extremities. { Shaft of Humerus.. Radius. Ulna. Radius and Ulna.. }	695
Gunshot Penetrating Wounds of the Abdomen, and injuries involving the Abdominal Viscera	565		
Gunshot Scalp Wounds	8942	Excisions of the Shafts of the Tibia and Fibula. { Tibia. Fibula. Tibia and Fibula. }	220
Gunshot Flesh Wounds of the Face	2588		
Gunshot Wounds of the Neck	1329		
Gunshot Wounds of the Thoracic Parietes	4759	Excisions of the Knee	11
Gunshot Wounds of the Back	5195	Excisions of the Shaft of the Femur	68
Gunshot Wounds of the Abdominal Parietes	2181	Excisions of the Head of the Femur	32
Gunshot Wounds of the Genito-Urinary Organs	468	Excisions of Bones of the Face or Trunk	101
Gunshot Wounds of the Upper Extremities	21,248	Trephining	221
Gunshot Wounds of the Lower Extremities	25,152	Ligations of Arteries	404
Gunshot Wounds of Arteries	44	Extractions of Foreign Bodies	726
Gunshot Wounds of Veins	3	Operations for Surgical Diseases	443
Gunshot Wounds of Nerves	76	Operations not included in other categories	28
Sabre Wounds	106		
Bayonet Wounds	143		
Simple Fractures, and Miscellaneous Wounds and Injuries	2983		
Cases of Tetanus	303		
Cases of Secondary Hæmorrhage	1035		
Cases of Pyæmia	754		
Total	87,822	Total	17,125

Some observations on each of these classes will be offered in another portion of this report.

The several circulars requesting medical officers to forward preparations to the Army Medical Museum met with very general and liberal responses, and, in January, 1863, a numerical list of 1248 surgical specimens was published by this office. Shortly afterwards, a suitable building was procured, and cases were erected in it for the reception of specimens. Several artists were engaged: a colorist to prepare illustrations of surgical pathology and representations of remarkable injuries; a draughtsman to make maps and plans; and two engravers. The requisite workshops were connected with the Museum. A medical officer was detailed to describe and classify the preparations. In short, this branch of the office was rapidly augmenting in importance. At the end of 1864, the number of specimens had quadrupled. Among the later specimens a large proportion of illustrations of reparative and morbid processes and of the results of operations were included. A valuable collection of drawings had been accumulated; draughtsmen having been sent to battle-fields and hospitals to portray the effects of recent wounds, or the results of surgery. A photograph gallery was now established at the Museum. Typical specimens were reproduced, and the photographs, accompanied by brief printed histories, were distributed to medical directors, to be shown to the medical officers serving with them, in order that the knowledge to be obtained from a study of these instructive examples might be generally disseminated. Other preparations were photographed for the use of the engravers. Many of them are reproduced in this report. Numerous patients in hospitals were photographed, and the Museum now possesses four quarto volumes, with over a thousand photographic representations of wounded or mutilated men. Meanwhile the work of describing and classifying the collections at the Museum has been steadily pursued, and the descriptive catalogue is now nearly ready for publication.

To state, then, in brief, what the records of the surgery of the late war are, and what progress has been made in their arrangement, over 40,000 monthly regimental reports of sick and wounded are on file, which furnish, under Class V.,* the total number of wounds, accidents, and injuries in the army, and the resulting mortality, as ascertained by the regimental medical officers, and which, having served their purpose of informing military commanders, month by month, of the extent of the losses in their commands, by the casualties of war, are now available for estimating the entire losses of the army from diseases and wounds. These reports have been consolidated for the first two years of the war and for the greater portion of the third year. But, as a certain number of regimental medical officers failed to make the required reports, it is necessary to correct these results by other numerical returns. Prior to September, 1862, these are only to be sought in special reports and case books of hospitals, and in the reports by medical directors of battles and minor engagements. It is found that these supply the deficiencies of the regimental returns to a satisfactory degree. For the latter part of 1862, and the whole of 1863, the "tabular statements of gunshot wounds" give the number of such injuries, separated according to regions, and the

---

* The form of the Report of Sick and Wounded being printed in the accompanying Report on the Medical Statistics of the War, it is not inserted here.

number of operations to which they gave rise. These tabular statements have been consolidated for the entire period, and the results for 1862 have been published. After March, 1863, consolidated classified returns of wounds and injuries were rendered, after every engagement, by the medical directors of armies or detached commands. This series is very complete. It serves as a check upon the monthly reports, and as a basis for estimating the frequency and fatality of wounds according to regions, and the total losses of the army in killed and wounded for the period covered by the returns. These results are not yet worked out, although satisfactory progress has been made towards their attainment. Throughout the war, many medical directors had transmitted to this office nominal lists of the wounded in battle; but after November 4th, 1863, this was made obligatory. After October 1st, 1863, all general hospitals reported by name all wounded men received, and gave full details of their injuries. From these two sources nearly complete lists of the wounded for the last two years of the war have been procured; for the names of those who died before reaching the base or general hospitals are found on the battle-field casualty lists. The progress that has been made in classifying and collating these returns has been already indicated. It will appear, hereafter, that the additional information afforded by case books and special reports has not been neglected.

The formal reports of medical directors of armies give a general view of the operations of the Medical Department. For the Army of the Potomac, the reports of Medical Directors Tripler, Letterman, and McParlin furnish a connected narrative of the services rendered by the medical staff. For the Western armies, the reports of Medical Directors McDougall, Murray, Cooper, Perin, Moore, and Hewit afford similar information. These papers will guide the future historiographer of the surgery of the war, and enable him to put in evidence the immensity of the task that devolved on the Medical Department, and to vindicate its achievements, in showing the extent of the succor given to the wounded in despite of almost incredible obstacles. Besides these authoritative documents, there are on file in the office, to serve as supplementary reports, individual narratives of observations in active service from each member of the regular or volunteer medical staff. The remaining papers for reference are the reports of boards on surgical improvements and appliances, or methods of transport for the wounded; 17,000 descriptive lists of surgical cases; 4200 reports from the manufacturers of artificial limbs of cases of recovery after amputation; and the surgical essays and dissertations that have been contributed. All of these have either been bound, or indexed and filed in a convenient and accessible form. Lastly, the great treasures of the Army Medical Museum, comprising over five thousand illustrations of military surgery, have been so far classified and arranged as to be available for scientific inquiry.

ON SPECIAL WOUNDS AND INJURIES.

It is now proposed to review briefly the records of special wounds and injuries, of some of their complications, and of the operations which they have rendered necessary.

GUNSHOT INJURIES OF THE HEAD.

In this important class of injuries, the utmost pains has been taken to secure completeness and accuracy in the records. The registers have been copied by experienced clerks, and have been supervised by a medical officer. Exclusive reliance has not been placed upon the field and hospital reports; but in a large proportion of cases, specific inquiries in regard to the extent and results of individual injuries have been made by letter.

All, or nearly all, cases of gunshot injuries of the head that have been reported to the office from the commencement of the war to October 1st, 1864, have been entered in the records. They number 5046, and have been recorded in two classes: first, the gunshot fractures and injuries of the cranium, including the perforating and penetrating and depressed fractures, the fractures without known depression, and the contusions of the skull resulting in lesions of the encephalon; and, secondly, the simple contusions and flesh wounds of the scalp.

It is quite possible now to establish subdivisions in the first class; but to have attempted this heretofore, would have been premature, and likely to produce confusion.

In the first class 1104 cases are recorded. Of 604 of them, of which the results have been ascertained, 505 died and 199 recovered. In 107 of those terminated cases the operation of trephining was performed, of which 60 died and 47 recovered. In 114 cases fragments of bone or of foreign substances were removed by the elevator or forceps, without the use of the trephine; and of these 61 died and 53 recovered. When operative procedures were instituted, the recoveries were 45·3 per cent. But it must be apprehended that this favorable exhibit will be materially modified when a larger number of results are ascertained, and that a great proportion of the field operations of trephining, in which the results are stated to be undetermined, were lost sight of, and terminated fatally. In the 483 cases treated by expectancy, the ratio of recovery is only 20·5 per cent. But the latter group of cases includes nearly all of the penetrating and perforating fractures, and it would be unwise to base on these figures an argument in favor of operative interference.

The gunshot contusions and wounds of the scalp that have been entered on the records number 3942, of which 103 terminated fatally. It is altogether probable that in all of these fatal cases some undiscovered injury was done to the cranium or its contents; or that the pericranium was removed, with death of bone ensued, with consecutive lesions of the encephalon. The histories of many of these cases are now under investigation. So far as ascertained, the fatal results have depended upon concussion or compression of the brain, or upon the formation of abscesses in the liver or lungs, in consequence of inflammation in the veins of the diploe. Compression has resulted either from extravasation of blood, or inflammation of the brain or its membranes, or from suppuration. The following is an example of a scalp wound, followed by inflammation of bone and meningitis:

FIG. 1.—Section of a cranium, exhibiting five trephine perforations for the evacuation of pus, the result of a gunshot contusion of the right parietal. Spec. 2000, A. M. M.

Private Joseph R——, Co. E, 151st New York Vols., received, in a reconnoissance near the Rapidan, November 27th, 1863, a gunshot wound of the scalp. The nature of the missile was unknown. The patient was removed to Fairfax Seminary General Hospital near Alexandria. There were no cerebral symptoms at the time of his admission, and it was hoped that the pericranium had escaped uninjured. He was up, and apparently well on December 13th, 1863, when he was suddenly seized with convulsions, which were followed by coma. Surgeon D. P. Smith, U. S. Vols., laid bare the calvaria at the seat of injury, and finding the bone diseased, applied the trephine. Matter was found immediately beneath the bone and oozing from the diploe. It was thought expedient to make five perforations with the trephine, in order to remove the diseased bone and to give free exit to pus. Convulsions did not recur, but the comatose condition continued, and the case terminated fatally twelve hours after the operation. The autopsy revealed diffuse inflammation of the arachnoid and of the dura mater.

The foregoing case illustrates the fallacy of Pott's views in relation to trephining for pus under the skull-cap; and yet, under such circumstances, the best modern authorities advise the use of the trephine as affording the patient the only chance of recovery. The records attest how slight this chance is, and corroborate the observation of Mr. Hewett, that "the successful issue of a case of trephining for matter between the bone and the dura mater is almost unknown to surgeons of our own time."*

The Army Medical Museum furnishes very ample illustrations of almost every variety of gunshot injury of the skull and its contents. The number of osteological specimens relating to this class of injuries is 246, of wet preparations 22, of drawings, photographs, engravings, and plaster casts 97.

There are 22 specimens of gunshot contusion of the cranium. In these, either necrosis has taken place, with exfoliation of the external table only, or of the entire thickness of the bone, or else inflammatory suppuration has occurred in the diploe or between the skull and dura mater.

The Museum possesses eight examples of that rare and interesting variety of gunshot fracture of the cranium, in which the external table is unbroken, while the vitreous table is fissured and sometimes depressed. One of the most perfect of these specimens (No. 1568, A. M. M.) is figured in No. 94, Photographic Series, S. G. O. An abstract of the case is subjoined:

FIG. 2.—Section of skull-cap, exhibiting a depressed fracture of the vitreous table. Spec. 1568, A. M. M.

Private David P——, Co. C, 35th Wisconsin Vols., was wounded at Tupelo, Mississippi, July 18th, 1864, by a musket-ball, which struck the skull obliquely, and apparently inflicted a scalp wound merely, between the sagittal suture and the left parietal protuberance. There were no signs of cerebral disturbance. The wound was dressed simply, and the patient was conveyed to Memphis, Tennessee, and admitted into the Adams U. S. General Hospital on July 23d. He was then perfectly rational and free from head symptoms. Two days subsequently, indications of compression of the brain were observed, and on the afternoon of the 25th they had rapidly become aggravated. The pulse was slow, the respiration labored, the pupils dilated, the sphincters relaxed. A very careful exploration of the wound was made, but, of course, no cranial fracture could be detected. The treatment was limited to cold applications to the head, scarified cups to the nucha, and brisk purging. On the 26th, the patient gradually became comatose. The discharges from the bowels and bladder were involuntary.

---

* A System of Surgery, Theoretical and Practical, in treatises by various authors, edited by T. Holmes, M.A. Cantab. London, 1861. Vol. ii. p. 101.

GUNSHOT INJURIES OF THE HEAD. 11

The patient continued to sink on the 27th, and died at 1 A.M. on the 28th of July. At the autopsy the internal table of the left parietal was found to be fractured and depressed at a point corresponding with the wound in the scalp. The dura mater was wounded, and there was a large abscess in the left cerebral hemisphere.

In a specimen which is believed to be unique, without any apparent lesion of the external table, a fragment of the vitreous plate of the frontal bone was found to be completely detached and depressed upon the dura mater. The history in this case is unfortunately imperfect.

Private A—— L——, Co. C, 78th New York Vols., was wounded by a conoidal musket-ball, at the battle of the Wilderness, May 6th, 1864, and entered Armory Square Hospital, at Washington, on May 12th. He was in a comatose condition when admitted, and died on May 24th, eighteen days after receiving the injury. No further particulars of the case could be obtained. At the autopsy a fracture was discovered of the inner table of the frontal bone, near the coronal suture, to the left of the median line. There was no solution of continuity in the outer table; but it was softened where the pericranium was destroyed by the ball. A fragment, an inch and a half in length and half an inch broad, was completely detached from the vitreous table. The specimen was forwarded by Surgeon D. W. Bliss, U. S. Vols.

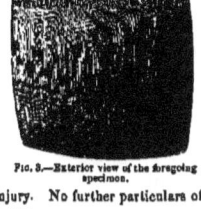

FIG. 3.—Exterior view of the foregoing specimen.

In a case which was observed by Surgeon Bontecou, U. S. V., who had examined the specimens above referred to, the probability of a depression of the vitreous table was inferred, and the diagnosis was verified, during life, by the application of the trephine. Unhappily, an abscess had formed in the brain, and the operation, though performed as soon as evidence of compression existed, was too late to save the patient.

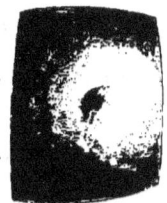

FIG. 5.—Exterior view of the foregoing specimen.

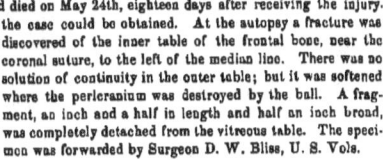

FIG. 4.—Fracture of the vitreous table of the frontal bone, without fracture of the external table. Spec. 2313, A. M. M.

Private D—— S——, Co. E, 2d Virginia Cavalry, aged twenty-one, was wounded at Appomattox Court House, April 6th, 1865, and admitted to Harewood Hospital, at Washington, on April 19th, with a gunshot wound of the scalp, just below the coronal suture. The bone was denuded of its pericranium, but there was no apparent fracture. Prior to his admission, the patient had chills, which recurred at intervals of twelve hours, until April 25th, quinia having no appreciable influence upon the paroxysms. There was no pain in the head nor disturbance of the cerebral faculties until April 26th. On the 25th, inflammation of the lower lobe of the right lung was observed, and on the 26th, there was endocarditis. At 10 P.M. of the 26th, the patient became unconscious. Shortly afterwards he was trephined. When the external table was passed, pus exuded from the cells of the diploe. A depressed fracture of the inner table was discovered, and the detached fragments were removed. The patient did not arouse from his comatose state, and died the next morning, April 27th, 1865. A photograph of this patient, prior to the operation, was preserved at the Museum. (Photo. Surg. Cases, vol. i. No. 58.)

FIG. 6.—Section of cranium, showing a depressed fracture of the vitreous table. There was a contusion only of the outer table. Spec. 4346, A. M. M.

Specimens 3639, 3406, 622, 1922, and 646, A. M. M., afford other examples of this rare form of injury, to which S. Cooper,* Guthrie,† Hennen,‡ Hewett,§ Williamson,‖ and Legouest¶ allude, illustrating their observations by a case examined by Mr. Dean, of Cambridgeshire, a specimen in the Dupuytren Museum, which is figured in M. Legouest's work, and specimen No. 2893 of the Netley Collection.

---

* S. Cooper, Dictionary of Practical Surgery. † Guthrie, Commentaries, paragraph 262.
‡ Hennen, Military Surgery, p. 326, ed. 1829. § Holmes' System of Surgery, vol. ii. p. 114.
‖ Williamson, Military Surgery, pp. 29, 30.
¶ Legouest, Traité de Chirurgie d'Armée, p. 283. See also Compendium de Chirurgie, t. ii. p. 573.

12   ON SPECIAL WOUNDS AND INJURIES.

It is believed that this accident results, in most instances, from a small projectile striking the cranium very obliquely, or possibly, in some cases, from a comparatively slight blow from a body with a large plane surface.

Closely allied, clinically, to the foregoing cases are those in which a ball produces linear fissure of the external table with displacement of the inner table. Specimen No. 24, of the Army Medical Museum, affords an excellent illustration. The following is an abstract of the case:

Private M. L. H——, Co. E, 21st Virginia (Rebel) Regiment, aged twenty years, was wounded and taken prisoner in one of the later engagements prior to the capitulation of the Army of Northern Virginia, and was admitted into the Lincoln General Hospital, at Washington, on March 25th, 1865, with a wound over the left supra-orbital ridge, inflicted apparently by a glancing musket-ball. There were no cerebral symptoms when the patient was admitted, and he seemed to be doing well for several days, being quite free from pain or any febrile movement. The pulse was normal and the bowels in good condition. On April 1st, he complained of a dull

Fig. 7.—Section of the frontal bone exhibiting a fissure over the left supra-orbital region. Spec. 24, A. M. M.

Fig. 8.—Internal view of the foregoing specimen, showing the extensive splintering of the vitreous table.

deep-seated pain over the left eye. Later in the day he was feverish and restless, his countenance was pale, and his pulse slow and weak. On April 2d, he failed rapidly. On the night of the 3d, he was delirious. On the 4th, there was violent raving, which continued until his death, on the afternoon of April 5th, 1865. At the post-mortem examination, a fissure was found extending into the right orbit, and upwards beyond the left frontal prominence. The vitreous table beneath was largely depressed. There was a small abscess in the anterior lobe of the left cerebral hemisphere.

Fig. 9.—Gunshot fracture of right temporal. Spec. 183, A. M. M.

Of fractures without depression, the cases in which the mastoid process is knocked off by a ball afford examples. Specimen 183, A. M. M., is a very perfect illustration of this accident. The mastoid cells were opened. After a fortnight, meningitis supervened. Specimen 3451 was furnished by a fortunate case of recovery after a fracture of the mastoid process.

Private William F——, Co. G, 98th Pennsylvania Vols., was wounded near Fort Stevens, Washington, July 12th, 1864, by a glancing shot from a conoidal musket-ball, and was admitted into Mount Pleasant Hospital on the following day. A little above the right auditory meatus was a scalp wound an inch and a half long. A piece of the mastoid process was chipped off, and a fracture extended into the petrous portion of the temporal. The patient did well with simple dressings and rest and gentle cathartics till the 20th of July, when the wound began to slough. Applications of nitric acid, creosote, etc., failed to arrest the sloughing, which presently gave rise to repeated hæmorrhages from branches of the temporal artery. The gangrene continued to spread until August 9th, when the eschars separated, leaving a space five inches in diameter on the right lateral region of the head, denuded of integument, fascia, and muscles. During this long period, the patient complained of no inconvenience at the seat of fracture, though there was at times acute frontal pain. Early in September, it was evident that the exposed portions of the temporal and parietal bones were necrosed, and on September 6th a fragment of the squamous portion of the temporal was removed. Two days subsequently other fragments were detached and extracted. After this the wound began to cicatrize rapidly, and on December 3d, 1864, the patient was reported to be entirely out of danger, and in fact nearly well.

Fig. 10.—Exfoliation from the right parietal and temporal, resulting from gunshot injury. Spec. 3451, A. M. M.

Several cases of undepressed fracture are reported in which a ball gouged out a small portion of the external table. A number of instances are recorded in which con-

GUNSHOT INJURIES OF THE HEAD.

siderable portions of the calvaria have been removed by explosions of shell, without depression. Very rarely a musket-ball produces the same effect, as in the following remarkable case. The patient is represented in Photograph No. 58, A. M. M.:

Private Edson D. Bemis, Co. K, 12th Massachusetts Vols., was wounded at Antietam by a musket-ball, which fractured the shaft of his left humerus. The fracture united kindly, with very slight angular displacement and quarter of an inch shortening. Promoted to be corporal, Bemis received, May 5th, 1864, at the battle of the Wilderness, a wound from a musket-ball in the right iliac fossa. He was treated in the Chester Hospital, near Philadelphia. There was extensive sloughing about the wound, but it ultimately healed entirely, leaving a large cicatrix, parallel with Poupart's ligament. Eight months after the injury, Bemis returned to duty with his regiment. On February 5th, 1865, Corporal Bemis was again severely wounded at the engagement at Hatcher's Run, near Petersburg, Virginia. Surgeon A. Vanderveer, 66th New York Vols., reports that the ball entered a little outside of the left frontal protuberance, and passing backwards and upwards, removed a piece of the squamous portion of the temporal bone, with brain substance and membranes. When the patient entered the hospital of the 1st Division of the 2d Corps, brain matter was oozing from the wound. Respiration was slow ; the pulse 40; the right side paralyzed; insensibility total. On February 8th, the ball was removed from the substance of the left hemisphere. In a few days paralysis disappeared. The patient was transferred to Fort Richmond, New York Harbor. ·He recovered perfectly, and on July 15th visited Washington, and was photographed at the Army Medical Museum. The wound in the head was then nearly healed. There was a slight discharge of healthy pus from one point. The pulsations of the brain could be felt through the integument. The mental and sensory faculties were unimpaired. The corporal had been discharged from service, and recommended for a pension.

From the numerous instances of fracture with depression of both tables of the skull, a very few are selected. The first is an example of a common class of cases, in which symptoms of compression of the brain depend upon extravasation of blood, or inflammation of the membranes, and come on tardily.

Private Leonard L——, Co. F, 74th New York Vols., was wounded at the battle of Williamsburg, May 5th, 1862, and was admitted into Broad and Cherry Streets Hospital, at Philadelphia, May 13th, 1862. A musket-ball had struck near the left parietal eminence, and, producing a slight depression of the outer table, had lodged under the scalp, whence it had been removed by a surgeon on the field. The wound had a healthy aspect when the man was admitted, and there was no cerebral disorder. This favorable condition continued unaltered till May 20th, when a febrile movement set in, accompanied by nausea and vomiting ; drowsiness and stupor followed, and the patient died comatose on May 23d, eighteen days after the injury. At the autopsy, a small clot was found beneath the depressed portion of the vitreous plate ; the dura mater was uninjured ; the arachnoid, near the seat of injury, was opaque, and studded with deposits of lymph ; the gray matter of the brain was softened.

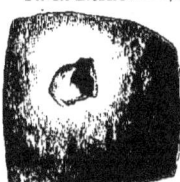

Fig. 11.—Portion of left parietal, showing a slightly depressed fracture of the outer table. Spec. 224, A. M. M.

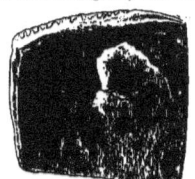

Fig. 12.—Interior view of the foregoing specimen, exhibiting extensive splintering of the vitreous table.

Private George V——, Co. C, 84th New York Vols., was wounded at Chancellorsville, May 3d, 1863, and admitted into Carver Hospital, at Washington, D. C., on May 7th, 1863. His injury was supposed to be a simple scalp wound from a musket-ball. It was situated over the right parietal protuberance, and, on admission, was granulating kindly. Ten days subsequently, the patient, after a walk out of doors, had headache and nausea, and the wound gaped, and its edges ulcerated. On the 18th of May, the probe detected denuded bone ; but no fracture was discovered. There were no febrile or cerebral symptoms. On May 20th, a depression of the outer table of the skull was detected. At night there was delirium, and the following day the pulse became feeble and irregular, the stomach irritable, the tongue heavily furred. The patient died on May 22d, 1863, being conscious and rational to the last. At the autopsy, extensive inflammation of the dura mater was observed, and softening of the middle lobe of the right cerebral hemisphere.

Fig. 13.—Gunshot fracture of the right parietal bone. Spec. 1257, A. M. M.

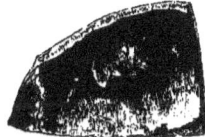

Fig. 14.—Interior view of the foregoing specimen.

The next case is an example of the classical "punctured" gunshot fracture of systematic writers.

Private James K——, Co. G, 6th New York Cavalry, was wounded at the battle of Gettysburg, July 3d, 1863, by a pistol-ball, which produced a punctured fracture of the os frontis. He was conveyed to a hospital at Baltimore, and from thence to Carver Hospital, at Washington, on July 24th. He stated that, at Baltimore, he walked about and felt no inconvenience from his wound. On July 27th, he had a convulsion. The wound, which was nearly healed, was laid open, and depressed bone being detected, an effort was made to elevate it. Several small necrosed fragments were removed, and a small quantity of fetid pus escaped. The patient had become comatose, and the operation had no influence in relieving the symptoms. Death took place a few hours subsequently.

FIG. 15.—Fracture of the frontal bone by a pistol-ball. Spec. 1673, A. M. M.

FIG. 16.—Interior view of the foregoing specimen.

At the autopsy, the extended depression of the inner table was discovered, and a large abscess of the brain.

Instances were not uncommon of the splitting of round musket-balls in striking the skull at an acute angle. The following is an example:

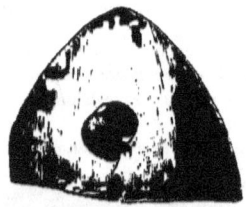

Corporal John N——, aged eighteen years, Co. H, 159th New York Vols., was struck on the left side of the forehead, on April 14th, 1863, at an engagement at Irish Bend, Louisiana, by a round musket-ball. He was admitted to the University Hospital, at New Orleans, on April 17th. The ball had been removed on the field. Several depressed fragments of bone were removed, and cold water-dressings were applied. The case progressed without a bad symptom until April 30th, when there were clonic spasms, which, after a few hours, were followed by a semi-comatose condition, which continued until death, on May 2d, 1863. A necroscopic examination revealed extensive meningitis, and a large abscess of the left cerebral hemisphere. The lateral ventricles were filled with sero-purulent matter. The surfaces of the pons Varolii and of the medulla oblongata were covered with lymph. The specimen was forwarded by Assistant Surgeon P. H. Conner, U. S. A.

FIG. 17.—Section of a frontal bone, with a split musket-ball. Spec. 1264, A. M. M.

Conoidal balls were less liable to split after this fashion, yet such instances were occasionally observed.

Private C. C. W——, Co. I, 6th Wisconsin Vols., aged twenty-one years, was wounded at Spottsylvania, May 12th, 1864, and was admitted to Douglas Hospital, in Washington, four days subsequently. It was ascertained that the cranium was fractured, but the symptoms were not urgent, being limited to slight paralysis of the right upper extremity, and operative interference was deferred. On May 31st, a conoidal musket-ball and several fragments of the left parietal were removed by Assistant Surgeon Wm. F. Norris, U. S. A. One large fragment of the vitreous plate was pressing on the dura mater; this was elevated and removed. The next day symptoms of compression of the brain were manifested. An exploration of the wound was made and a quantity of pus evacuated. On June 4th, 1864, twenty-three days after the injury, the case terminated fatally. At the autopsy, the arachnoid was found little altered. There was an abscess in the posterior lobe of the left hemisphere near the longitudinal sinus, of the size of a walnut. Its walls were of a greenish-yellow color. It communicated with the lateral ventricle. The right ventricle was filled with sero-sanguinolent fluid. There was a deposition of lymph at the base of the brain, extending from the medulla oblongata to the bifurcation of the optic nerves. The specimen and facts connected with it were contributed by Assistant Surgeon William Thomson, U. S. A.

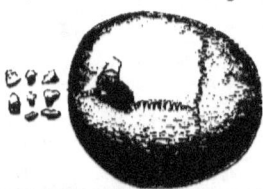

FIG. 18.—Skull-cap, exhibiting gunshot fracture near the vertex, by a conoidal musket-ball which has split against the lamina of the left parietal. Spec. 3543, A. M. M.

The depressed fractures produced by cannon-balls, or by the explosion of large shells, were commonly attended by frightful comminution and disjunction of the sutures, and were almost always immediately fatal, and hence had little surgical interest. A single example is given:

GUNSHOT INJURIES OF THE HEAD.   15

A Confederate soldier was wounded in the demonstration on Washington, July 17th, 1864, by a shell from one of the large guns of Fort Stevens, and was admitted into Lincoln U. S. General Hospital, on that day, and died two hours after admission. Over the anterior superior angle of the left parietal bone there was an extended scalp wound. On reflecting the scalp, multiple depressed fractures of the vault of the cranium came into view. The point of greatest depression is an inch to the left of the median line, near the coronal suture. The depressed fragments measure from before backwards two inches, and from right to left three inches, and involve both parietals and the os frontis. A fissure runs through the squamous portion of the left temporal, and all the sutures of this bone are separated.

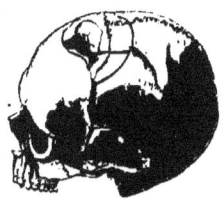

FIG. 19.—Cranium fractured by the explosion of an 11-inch shell. Spec. 2871, A. M. M.

There have been a very few extraordinary and exceptional recoveries after penetrating and perforating fractures of the cranium, and, in rare instances, the fatal termination has been long delayed. In the following curious case, the presence of a ball within the cranial cavity was unsuspected:

Corporal G. W. S——, 12th Massachusetts Vols., aged twenty-nine years, was wounded at the battle of Fredericksburg, December 13th, 1862, and was admitted to Camden Street Hospital, Baltimore, six days subsequently. The humors of the right eye had been evacuated by a ball, which had likewise inflicted a slight wound of the lower lid. The left eye was observed to be unnaturally prominent, but its functions were undisturbed. The patient did not complain of pain or any inconvenience, except a slight headache. There were no cerebral symptoms, and no one suspected that the projectile had entered the brain. The wound healed kindly, and, after three weeks, the man walked about the city habitually, with a hospital pass. He appeared to be well, except that he had an occasional pain over the left eye, until February 6th, 1863, when he had a chill, followed by a febrile reaction. No marked cerebral disorder supervened, however, until February 10th, when delirium was noticed at night. On the following day the patient was comatose, and at midnight of February 15th, he died. The autopsy revealed a conoidal musket-ball wedged between the sphenoid and the left orbital plate of the frontal bone, and lying in contact with the dura mater. The orbital plate was pressed inwards and fractured, and a fissure extended through the superciliary ridge. Over the ball, at the base of the anterior lobe of the left hemisphere, was an abscess containing two drachms of pus. The ball was incrusted by callus, and the opening it had made in entering through the walls of the right orbit was greatly diminished by osseous deposition.

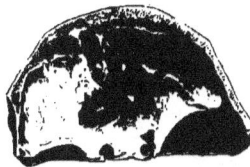

FIG. 20.—Conoidal ball embedded between the sphenoid and parietal bones. Spec. 1148, A. M. M.

FIG. 21.—Exterior view of the foregoing specimen.

In the next case, half of the ball had deeply penetrated the brain:

Sergeant J. N. H——, Co. K, 19th Maine Vols., aged thirty-six years, was struck on the right side of the head, by a musket-ball, in a skirmish at Morton's Ford, on the Rappahannock, February 6th, 1864. The ball was smoothly cut in two, one-half lodging under the scalp, and the other passing into the brain. The patient was perfectly rational until February 11th, when his mind wandered at times. On the 12th, Surgeon Justin Dwinelle, 101st Pennsylvania Vols., extracted the fragment of the ball which had buried itself in the brain. Its track communicated with the right lateral ventricle. The other portion of the ball had been removed from under the scalp immediately after the injury. When the patient recovered from the influence of the chloroform, he was rational, and continued so for twenty-four hours or more. Coma gradually supervened, and death took place on February 15th. The left ventricle was found filled with pus.

FIG. 22.—Section of right parietal on which a conoidal musket-ball has split. Spec. 2121, A. M. M.

A very remarkable case of perforating fracture of the skull, with recovery, is represented by No. 16 of the Surgical Series of Drawings, S. G. O. The ball entered a little to the right of the occiput, and passed out somewhat below and to the left of the vertex. The intervening bridge of bone was about three inches wide. There had been a cerebral hernia at the wound of exit, and, when the drawing was made, four months after the reception of the injury, there was still a small tumor, covered by half-formed cicatricial tissue. There was a firm depressed cicatrix at the aperture of entry. There were no evidences of impairment of the cerebral faculties. At the time the drawing was made, the man was employed as an orderly.

The next case illustrates Mr. Erichsen's remark that the greater splintering of the inner table does not depend exclusively upon its greater density and brittleness, but partly on the direction of the fracturing force. At the aperture of exit, the outer table is splintered more than the inner. In the same specimen the bones forming the right orbit are fractured by contre-coup:

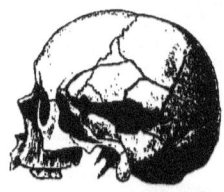

FIG. 23.—Skull, exhibiting an extensive fracture by grapeshot. Spec. 1316, A. M. M.

A soldier of Longstreet's Corps was killed in a charge upon a Union battery, in the second battle of Manassas, August 29th, 1862, by a grapeshot at short range. The cranium was picked up a year subsequently by Surgeon F. Wolfe, 39th New York Vols., under an abatis near the stone bridge over Bull Run. The missile entered the left parietal near the lambdoidal suture, and made its exit through the squamous portion of the temporal.

According to Mr. Teevan's experimental inquiries,* the aperture of exit in gunshot perforations of the cranium is always larger than the aperture of entry, because it is made by the ball *plus* the fragments of bone driven out from the proximal table and the diploe.

While the number of fatal results after trephining are very great, the examples of success are yet numerous. The data are not sufficiently complete to admit of fair comparative analysis; still it is difficult to avoid the impression that a larger measure of success has attended this operation in the late war, than the previous experience of military surgeons would have led us to anticipate. Surgeon D. W. Bliss, U. S. Vols., alone has reported eleven successes after the use of the elevator or trephine. Even in those almost hopeless cases in which compression of the brain follows a gunshot injury of the skull at a late date, instances of recovery are reported.

In the following case it is not likely that suppuration had occurred, a complication that has rarely presented itself prior to the fifteenth day after the injury; but it can hardly be doubted that meningitis was averted or relieved by the opportune employment of the trephine:

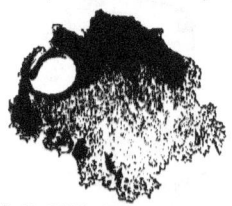

FIG. 24.—Exfoliation from the right parietal bone. Spec. 3452, A. M. M.

Private John McK——, Co. H, 105th Pennsylvania Vols., was wounded at Petersburg, Virginia, June 14th, 1864, by a conoidal musket-ball, which struck the right side of the skull very obliquely, and produced a slightly depressed fracture of the right parietal bone. He was admitted to Mount Pleasant General Hospital, Washington, on June 24th, with the report that the progress of the case had been so far eminently satisfactory. After admission, he was found to be insensible, and a few hours subsequently, convulsions supervened in rapidly recurring paroxysms. Twelve ounces of blood were taken from the temporal artery without apparent benefit. A trephine was then applied to the seat of fracture, and, upon the removal of a button of bone, a portion of the inner table was found slightly depressed. This was elevated, and the patient soon afterwards regained consciousness. On the 28th of June, the wound in the scalp became erysipelatous, and before the inflammation subsided, there was extensive loss of substance of the integuments and pericranium, denuding a large portion of the parietal bone. Necrosis ensued, and embraced the whole thickness of the bone. In September, 1864, a portion of the parietal, three inches by four, had become so much loosened that it was readily removed. After this, cicatrization went on rapidly, and, at the date of the last report, December 2d, 1864, the wound had contracted to an ulcer less than an inch in diameter. The patient's mental faculties were impaired somewhat, the ward physician thought, but not to a great extent. The specimen was contributed by Assistant Surgeon C. A. McCall,

---

* British and Foreign Medico-Chirurgical Review, vol. xxxiv. p. 205.

GUNSHOT INJURIES OF THE HEAD. 17

U. S. A. A colored drawing was made representing the appearance of the parts prior to the separation of the exfoliation. (No. 74, Surgical Series of Drawings, S. G. O.)

The occurrence of hernia or fungus cerebri is mentioned in connection with 18 cases of gunshot fracture of the skull, complicated by lacerations of the dura mater and brain. In 4 of these cases, recovery took place without operative interference with the protruding fungous mass, which, in these instances, gradually contracted, was then covered by granulations, and finally cicatrized. In those cases in which bandaging and compression were resorted to, cerebral oppression was soon manifested, and stupor and coma eventually supervened. In those in which the tumor was sliced off, as usually recommended, at the proper level of the brain, it was commonly speedily reproduced, and death from irritation ensued.

Charles T——, Co. H, 63d New York Vols., aged seventeen years, was admitted to Hospital No. 1, Frederick, Maryland, on September 28th, 1862, with a fracture of the skull. He was wounded at Antietam, September 17th, 1862, by a conoidal musket-ball, which struck at the lower anterior angle of the right parietal, fracturing both tables of the cranium, and lodged under the scalp in the occipital region. The scalp was lacerated, and a dark pulsating mass protruded in the wound. The left side of the body was paralyzed. The patient's mental faculties were unimpaired. On September 29th, flaps of integument were reflected by a T-shaped incision. The ball and a number of fragments of bone were removed, some of the latter being embedded in the brain substance. The inner table was found badly splintered, but the fracture of the external table was still more extensive. The protruding cerebral mass was shaved off. The rough edges of the fractured bone were smoothed by cutting forceps. The following day, the paralysis was more complete than before the operation. There was severe headache. The pulse was slow and weak. On October 3d, the fungus was sprouting and sloughing. The left arm was powerless; the paralysis of the left leg was less complete. On October 4th, the hernia was again sliced off, and gentle compression was applied. There was great irritability and restlessness. On October 21st, the patient had improved. His appetite was voracious. He was less irritable, and the hemiplegia was much less complete. He was very sensitive to cold. The temperature of the left side was lower than that of the right. The fungus was of the size of a pigeon's egg. On November 17th, a dilatation of the left pupil was first noticed. Sensation in the left leg, and partial control of the muscles had returned. Since the last report the tumor of the brain had continued to grow and slough away, so that it remained of about the same size. On December 7th, the report states that little change had taken place, except a gradual amelioration of the hemiplegia, and improvement in regard to the fretfulness and irritability. On this day there was a severe chill. After this, the patient never regained his accustomed readiness and clearness of mind. The discharge from the wound became watery, unhealthy, and more copious. There was an exacerbation of fever every afternoon. On December 17th, there was a severe convulsion, which lasted half an hour, and was terminated by death.

At the autopsy, an irregular portion of the right parietal, four inches in diameter, was found to be necrosed and detached. The dura mater was much thickened in the vicinity of the fracture, and was adherent to the margins of the healthy bone. Except in the immediate vicinity of the hernia, the brain matter appeared to be in a healthy state.

FIG. 25.—Gunshot fracture of right parietal, followed by necrosis. Spec. 3869, A. M. M.

In looking over the registers of gunshot injuries of the head, two general facts are noticed: First, that in the after-treatment of scalp wounds, a multitude of surgeons did not consider spare diet, perfect rest, and antiphlogistic measures as of essential importance; and, secondly, that in the treatment of cranial fractures, the general tendency was to the practice recommended by Guthrie in regard to operative procedures, rather than the more expectant plan insisted upon by the majority of modern European writers on military surgery. The interest of the material and the importance of the subject alike invite extended comment; but in this brief and cursory review, the motto of Montaigne, je raconte, je ne juge pas, must be rigorously adhered to. A few more cases of gunshot injuries of the head are appended, to illustrate the form of the register of wounds now in use in the army.

3

ON SPECIAL WOUNDS AND INJURIES.

Hospital.	NAME.	Rank.	Co.	Regiment.	Age.	When admitted.	From what General Hospital Transferred.	From what other source admitted. From Field, from Field Hospital, etc.	DIAGNOSIS. In Surgical Cases, state Seat and Character of Wound or Injury.	On what occasion Wounded. Date.
Hygeia Hospital, Old Point Comfort, Va.	Burd, Charles W.	Lieutenant.	F	4th Maine Volunteers.	28	Feb. 20, 1862.		Prison in Richmond	Gunshot fracture of both tables of os frontis at left frontal eminence. Penetration of the substance of the brain by a portion of the ball.	Bull Run, July 21, 1861.
National Hospital, Baltimore, Maryland.	Stallman, John	Private.	A	4th Penn. Cavalry.	21	Sept. 8, 1864.	Sandy Hook, Maryland.		Missile entered at the right temple, and emerged at the opposite side of the head.	Winchester, Va., July 24, 1864.
Cuyler Hospital, Philadelphia, Penn.	Stallman, John H.	Private.	A	4th Penn. Cavalry.	21	Dec. 11, 1864.	National, Baltimore.		Missile entered the right side of the frontal bone near its superior margin. Evidently passed through the brain, and emerged on the opposite side.	Winchester, July 24, 1864.
Mower Hospital, Philadelphia, Penn.	Stallman, J. H.	Private.	A	4th Penn. Cavalry.	21	May 10, 1865.	Cuyler, Phila., Penn.		Ball passed through brain, carrying away anterior portion.	Winchester, July 24, 1864.
Armory Square Hospital, Washington, D. C.	Kennedy, Charles	Lieutenant.	I	28th Penn. Volunteers.	25	May 7, 1863.	Hospital Transport.		Missile removed the superior angle of the occipital bone and the dura mater beneath.	Chancellorsville, Va., May 2, 1863.
1st Division Hospital, Annapolis, Md. 13,254.	Kennedy, Charles	Lieutenant.	I	28th Penn. Volunteers.	25	Nov. 14, 1863.	Armory Square.	From furlough.		
U. S. A. General Hospital, Frederick, Md.	W——, Charles	Private.	E	14th Virginia Infantry.	22	Sept. 17, 1864.		Field.	Missile entered the left temporal bone one inch from the meatus auditorius externus, and penetrated the cavity of the skull, lodging on the side of the sella turcica.	Berryville, Sept. 3, 1864.
Grafton Hospital, West Virginia. 785.	W——, Charles	Private.	E	14th Virginia Infantry.	22	Nov. 2, 1864.	Frederick, Maryland.			

GUNSHOT INJURIES OF THE HEAD. 19

IN SURGICAL CASES ONLY.		RESULT.							
Nature of Missile or Weapon. Round or Conical Bullet, Solid Shot Bayonet, Sword.	TREATMENT. Amputation...Date of Excision........ " " Other operation............ " " Simple dressings....... ' "	Returned to duty. — Date.	Transferred to Veteran Reserve Corps. — Date.	To other General Hospital, State or City. — Date.	Furloughed. — Date.	Deserted. — Date.	Discharged from Service. — Date.	Death. — Date.	Readmitted from Furlough or Desertion. — Date.	REMARKS. Here state cause of death, of discharge, or of transfer to Veteran Reserve Corps.
Musket Ball.	A portion of the ball was removed, from under the integument, on the field. Seven months afterwards the fistulous orifice of the wound was dilated, depressed bone was removed, and a portion of the ball from within the cavity of the cranium.	March, 1863.								During his imprisonment he suffered from pain in the head, but had no delirium, coma, or paralysis. Was perfectly well when he rejoined his regiment. (Vide Special Report from Surgeon R. B. Bontecou, U.S.V. General Index A, No. 59.)
Musket Ball.	Simple dressings.			Dec. 10, 1864, to Cuyler Hospital.						When admitted, his bowels were constipated, and nausea was almost constant. His pulse was slow and feeble. His pupils were constantly dilated. When discharged his mental operations seemed slow and uncertain, but there was no aberration of mind, and his memory was unimpaired. (See Report of Assistant Surgeon Schell, U.S.A.)
				May 10, 1865, to Mower Hospital, Phila., Pa.						
								May 23, 1865.		
Probably a piece of shell.	May 7th. Hair shaven, water-dressings, cathartics, injections and anodynes, leeches to temples and behind the ears. May 13th. A splinter of bone removed.				June 20, 1863.					On admission, substance of brain protruded about one inch and a half; wound was about two inches long and one inch wide; pulsation was distinct; total loss of vision; pulse 60; inclined to sleep but could not; mind dull; partial paraplegia. May 11th. Rests quietly but cannot sleep; has not slept from date of injury; no nivine evacuation. May 12th. Not so much pain. May 13th. Had four dejections. May 15th. Fungus retracted somewhat, with a healthy granulating surface; vision partially restored. June 16th. Sitting about ward, talking and laughing; fungus retracted entirely, but pulsation distinct; vision restored; pulse and bowels regular; sleeps well; intellect perfect; no pain. The wound is represented in Nos. 26 and 27 Surgical Series of Drawings, S. G. O.
									Jan'y 12, 1864.	
Conoidal Musket Ball.	Part of ball extracted from under the scalp in the frontal region, by forceps. This fragment was about one-third of the ball.			To Grafton, Nov. 2, 1864.						When admitted, patient had paralysis of 2d, 3d, 4th, 5th, 6th, and 7th nerves of the left side. No pain in the head. General health of patient was good. His pulse, skin, and bowels were natural. His consciousness perfect. His articulation was thick, but improved, and after the extraction of the ball became almost natural. There was a free evacuation of pus after the operation, the pupil of the left eye diminished in size, and vision partially returned. Oct. 10th, 1864. Was so far recovered as to walk about and assist in nursing in the ward. If, however, he exerted himself too much he suffered from headache. While being transferred to Grafton, Va., he drank a large quantity of whiskey. The day after his arrival he had a violent chill, followed the next morning by convulsions, and strabismus of right eye; these continued during the day, and coma succeeded on the following morning, and he died without reaction. Post-mortem showed the larger portion of a conoidal musket-ball resting against the sella turcica. The encephalon was extensively disorganized; the ventricles, and nearly the whole base of the brain, bathed in pus. (Med. Des List, from J. H. Bartholf, A. A. Surg. U.S.A.)
								Nov. 6, 1864.		

GUNSHOT WOUNDS OF THE FACE.

Of 4167 gunshot wounds of the face transcribed from the reports from the beginning of the war to October, 1864, there were 1579 fractures of the facial bones, and 2588 flesh wounds. Of the former 891 recovered, 107 died, and the terminations are still to be ascertained in 581 cases.

Secondary hæmorrhage has been the principal source of fatality in these injuries. It is a frequent complication in gunshot fractures of the facial bones; and the difficulties in securing bleeding vessels in this region are very great. Recourse has often been had to ligations of the carotid, with the result of postponing for a time the fatal event.

Owing to the great vascularity and vitality of the tissues in this region, gunshot wounds of the face have commonly healed rapidly, and many creditable plastic operations for the relief of deformities following such injuries have been accomplished. Such operations are illustrated at the Army Medical Museum by numerous casts and photographs. An interesting example is the case of Private Rowland Ward, Co. E, 4th New York Heavy Artillery. A fragment of shell removed the anterior portion of the lower jaw within one inch of the ramus on both sides, destroyed the genio-hyoglossus and genio-hyoid muscles, and afforded the occasion for a very successful cheiloplastic operation by Surgeon J. C. McKee, U. S. A. (See Photographs of Surgical Cases, S. G. O., vol. iii. p. 1, *et seq.*)

GUNSHOT WOUNDS OF THE NECK.

Of the 1329 cases of this category that have been entered on the records, the ultimate results have been ascertained in 546 cases only. Time has not been found to trace the histories of many of the remaining cases. In the terminated cases, the mortality is 14 per cent.

Several instances are recorded in which large grapeshot, on striking the hyoid bone, were deflected, and buried themselves in the supra-spinous fossa of the scapula, or among the muscles of the back. These patients died from laryngitis or œdema of the glottis, and might have been saved, perhaps, by tracheotomy; but they died suddenly, when surgical assistance could not be immediately procured.

Wounds of the neck, with lesions of the vertebræ, are classified with fractures of the spine.

There are eight examples of gunshot perforations of the larynx or trachea among the specimens at the Army Medical Museum. The series of surgical drawings includes several curious illustrations of the escape of the great blood-vessels of the neck from injury, when balls have traversed the neck directly in their course.

Cases in which the great vessels were injured are classified with wounds of the arteries.

GUNSHOT WOUNDS OF THE BACK AND SPINE.

In this class have been included the fractures of the vertebral column which were not complicated by penetrating wounds of the chest or abdominal cavity, and flesh wounds of the region covered by the trapezius, latissimus dorsi, and gluteal muscles.

Of 187 recorded cases of gunshot fracture of the vertebræ, all but 7 proved fatal. Six of these were fractures of the transverse or spinous apophyses. The seventh case is that of a soldier wounded at Chickamauga, September 20th, 1863, by a musket-ball, which fractured the spinous process of the fourth lumbar vertebra, and penetrated to the vertebral canal. The ball and fragments of bone were extracted at a Nashville hospital. The patient was transferred to Louisville, thence to Jefferson Barracks, Missouri, thence to Madison, Indiana, and finally, on July 26th, 1864, to Quincy, Illinois. The last report states that he was likely to recover.

Gunshot lesions of the vertebræ and spinal cord are illustrated at the Army Medical Museum by 66 specimens.

An engraving of one of these is subjoined.

Private Frederick L——, Co. H, 8th New York Vols., aged twenty-six years, was wounded at Cold Harbor June 3d, 1864, and admitted into Carver Hospital, at Washington, D. C., June 11th, 1864. A conoidal musket-ball had entered the right side of his back and penetrated the vertebral canal, shattering the transverse and articular processes of the eighth and ninth dorsal vertebræ. The patient stated that, immediately upon the reception of his injury, he lost all sensation and power of motion below the wound. On admission, he was in a very feeble state; his pulse was slow, his respiration labored, his skin cool, clammy, and cyanosed, his excretions involuntary. In this wretched condition he lingered till the 27th of June, when symptoms of extreme gastric irritability supervened, and every form of nourishment was promptly rejected by the stomach. He died July 2d, 1864. At the autopsy, the spinal cord appeared to have been completely severed at the seat of injury, and was disorganized above and below.

FIG. 26.—Eighth, ninth, and tenth dorsal vertebræ, with a conoidal ball in the vertebral canal. Spec. 2939, A. M. M.

Five thousand one hundred and ninety-five gunshot flesh wounds of the back have been recorded, of which a large proportion are injuries from shell. Troops being often ordered to lie down under a shell fire, this region becomes particularly exposed.

GUNSHOT WOUNDS OF THE CHEST.

Of 7062 gunshot wounds of the chest that have been examined and transcribed from the reports belonging to the period prior to July, 1864, there were 2303 that either penetrated the thoracic cavity or were accompanied by lesions of the thoracic viscera. The results have been ascertained in 1272 of these, and were fatal in 930, or 73 per cent. The 4759 flesh wounds presented a very small ratio of mortality. It was observed, however, that they were commonly long in healing, in consequence, no doubt, of the mobility of the thoracic parietes.

The cases of wounds of the lung by the sharp edges of the fractured ribs, or of contusion of the lung by non-penetrating gunshot injuries, have been recorded with the penetrating wounds.

In the treatment of penetrating wounds of the chest, venesection appears to have been abandoned altogether. Hæmorrhage was treated by the application of cold, perfect rest, and the administration of opium. These measures seem to have proved adequate generally, and no instances are reported of the performance of paracentesis or of the enlargement of wounds for the evacuation of effused blood. Hæmorrhage from the vessels of the costal parietes has been exceedingly rare, and, in the few instances recorded, was a secondary accident. Hence the management of bleeding from wounded intercostal arteries has presented theoretical rather than practical difficulties.

ON SPECIAL WOUNDS AND INJURIES.

It has been the common practice to remove splintered portions of fractured ribs, and to round off sharp edges that were likely to wound the pleura or lung. After this, with the exception of extracting foreign bodies whenever practicable, and performing paracentesis when empyema was developed, it has been usual to leave these cases to the natural process of cure.

The records of the results of the so-called method of "hermetically sealing" gunshot penetrating wounds of the chest are sufficiently ample to warrant an unqualified condemnation of the practice. The histories of the cases in which this plan was adopted have been traced, in most instances, to their rapidly fatal conclusion. The following case is the only recorded exception:

Corporal Peter Welker, Co. A, 1st U. S. Sharpshooters, was admitted July 30th, 1863, into Mount Pleasant Hospital, at Washington, having received, at Manassas Gap, July 23d, 1863, a gunshot wound of the chest. The missile entered near the nipple, between the fourth and fifth ribs, traversed the lung, and emerged at the inferior border of the scapula, fracturing the sixth rib. Treatment: Opiates and stimulants, the wound being hermetically sealed. When admitted, the patient had much pain in the chest, and dyspnœa. The latter increased almost to suffocation, and was accompanied by fever. On July 31st, the posterior wound gave way, and a profuse discharge of clotted blood and purulent matter escaped. The next day the anterior wound was opened, and a pint of matter of similar character escaped, after which the patient became much better. He continued to improve until furloughed. On December 13th, 1863, when readmitted, he had entirely recovered.

Few examples of recovery are recorded where the track of the ball passed near the root of the lung. The cases in which there was a fracture of the rib at the wound of entry were very dangerous. The established opinion, that penetrating wounds with lodgement of the ball are more fatal than perforating wounds, was amply illustrated. But very few recoveries with balls lodged in the lung are recorded, and the histories of such cases are less explicit and complete than could be desired.

Private John H. Prouty, Co. G, 27th Illinois Vols., was admitted into the Sherman U. S. General Hospital, at Nashville, Tennessee, from the Field Hospital at Chattanooga, Tennessee. with gunshot wound of the thorax. He was struck in the left chest at Dallas, Georgia, May 25th, 1864, by a musket-ball, which lodged in the substance of the left lung, and was not extracted. The case progressed favorably, and on July 14th, 1864, the patient was furloughed and went to his home.

Private Isaac Miller, Co. B, 139th Pennsylvania Vols., was admitted into the Haddington General Hospital, at Philadelphia, on the 3d of August, 1864, from Fort Schuyler Hospital, New York Harbor. He was wounded at the battle of the Wilderness, May 5th, 1864, by a musket-ball, which entered at the left shoulder, and passed downwards and inwards, and lodged in the left lung. . He was fairly convalescent when admitted to Haddington Hospital, and ultimately regained his usual health almost, and on May 3d, 1865, was transferred to the Veteran Reserve Corps.

In the following case the ball was believed to have lodged in the body of one of the upper dorsal vertebræ:

Private Daniel Rich, Co. B, 55th Pennsylvania Vols., aged twenty-one, was wounded at the battle of Pocotaligo, October 22d, 1862, and was admitted to Hospital No. 1, at Beaufort, South Carolina, on October 24th. The ball had entered at the left sterno-clavicular articulation, traversed the apex of the left lung, and lodged in the vertebral column. Immediately after his injury, he had hæmoptysis. He was able to walk from the field of battle to the hospital steamer, six miles distant. He stated that the wound bled very freely. When admitted to the hospital his face was dusky, his pulse accelerated, and crepitant rales were audible in the left chest. There was partial paralysis of the arms. He was ordered ⅛th of a grain of tartarized antimony every two hours, low diet, and perfect quiet. On October 25th, there was less vascular excitement and less dyspnœa. The medicine had nauseated and purged the patient. There was great tenderness of the spine in the upper dorsal region, and the vertebral column was perfectly rigid. The patient would allow no one to touch him anywhere but on the head. He was lifted by his head into an upright position, like a stick. The antimony was continued till October 31st. At this date an abscess pointed over the sternum, and was evacuated by a free incision. The wounds were poulticed. On November 13th, he was allowed to sit up a portion of the time, and was much less troubled by a cough in this position. On November 20th, he began to walk about the ward, and the wounds discharged but little. On December 1st, a necrosed bit of the sternum was removed. Cerate dressings were applied to the wounds. On December 20th, erysipelas attacked the wounds and spread over the chest. On December 28th, the patient had recovered from the erysipelas, the wounds were nearly healed, but the immobility of the spine continued. He was this day sent to a Northern hospital, on the steamer "Star of the South." He ultimately recovered, and was transferred to the First Battalion of the Veteran Reserve Corps. A photograph of the recent wound is preserved. (See Photographs of Surgical Cases, S. G. O., vol. i. No. 47.)

In the next case the ball was extracted. Nature made an effort to repair the fractured ribs, but the wound of the lung was followed by fatal suppuration.

Private S—— B——, Co. A, 83d New York Vols., was wounded at the battle of Fredericksburg, and was admitted into the Lincoln Hospital, at Washington, December 23d, 1862. He had been struck by a conoidal musket-ball in the back of the right chest, the ball entering over the attachment of the eleventh rib, and passing forwards. The ball was extracted and simple dressings were applied. Pleuro-pneumonia ensued, and resulted in empyema. On January 3d, 1863, a pint of pus was evacuated from the pleural cavity. The case terminated fatally on January 21st, 1863. The specimen was contributed by Surgeon H. Bryant, U. S. Vols., and the particulars of the case were furnished by Surgeon J. Cooper McKee, U. S. A. At the point of fracture, necrosed splinters are seen, attached by large irregular formations of callus.

FIG. 27.—Portions of the eleventh and twelfth ribs of the right side, exhibiting gunshot fractures of the shafts with attempts at reparation. Spec. 845, A. M. M.

A remarkable recovery is recorded, in a case in which the anterior mediastinum was opened.

Private Charles P. Betts, Co. I, 26th New Jersey Vols., aged twenty-two, was struck by a three-ounce grape-shot, on the morning of May 3d, 1863, in a charge upon the heights of Fredericksburg. The ball comminuted the sternum, at the level of the third rib, on the left side, and tore through the costal pleura. It remained in the wound and was removed by the patient. On the following day, Betts entered the hospital of the Second Division of the Sixth Corps. Through the wound the arch of the aorta was distinctly visible, and its pulsations could be counted. The left lung was collapsed. When sitting up there was but slight dyspnœa. Several fragments of the sternum were removed, and the wound soon granulated kindly. On May 10th, a colored drawing of the wound was made. (No. 19, Surgical Series of Drawings, S. G. O.) On July 5th, the patient was transferred to Washington, convalescent. He ultimately recovered perfectly.

The result was less favorable in the next case.

Private Patrick H. B——, Co. C, 147th Pennsylvania Vols., was wounded at Chancellorsville, May 2d, 1863, by a conoidal musket-ball, which entered between the second and third ribs, on the right side, two inches from the median line, fractured the sternum, and lodged beneath it. The wound bled profusely, but the hæmorrhage was arrested by pressure. The patient was conveyed to Douglas Hospital, at Washington, on May 8th, and died the following day. He had hæmoptysis and the symptoms of traumatic pneumonia.

Only four cases are recorded of gunshot wounds of the heart that came under treatment. The specimens from these four cases are preserved in the Army Medical Museum. The patient that lived longest after a gunshot wound of the heart survived twelve hours (Spec. 837, A. M. M.). In this case a small pistol-shot entered the left ventricle and passed out through the right auricle.

FIG. 28.—Sternum, showing a gunshot fracture by a musket-ball. The misshapen, battered ball is attached. Spec. 1073, A. M. M.

Not a few cases are recorded of gunshot wounds involving both the thoracic and abdominal cavities. Among them occur the following remarkable instances of recovery from this formidable kind of injury:

Lieutenant Daniel B——, 63d New York Vols., was wounded at Gettysburg, July 2d, 1863, by a conoidal musket-ball, which passed through the belly of the biceps of the right arm, entered the chest, traversed the base of the right lung and diaphragm, wounded the intestines, and passed out above the anterior superior spinous process of the left ilium. When admitted to the field hospital, he had dyspnœa and bloody sputa, and there was a fæcal discharge from the wound of exit. He was treated by large doses of opium, and, at the end of three weeks, convalescence was fairly established. In the course of a few months his wounds had entirely closed, and he rejoined his regiment for duty.

Captain Robert S——, Co. A, 29th New York Vols., was wounded at Chancellorsville, on the 2d of May, 1863. A round musket-ball, fired from a distance of about one hundred and fifty yards, entered the eighth intercostal space of the left side, at a point nine and a half inches to the left of the extremity of the ensiform cartilage, and fractured the ninth rib. Without wounding the lung apparently, the ball passed through the diaphragm, and entered some portion of the alimentary canal. Captain S—— walked a mile and a half to the rear, and entered a field hospital. On examining his wound, the surgeons found a protrusion of the lung of the size of a small orange, which they unavailingly attempted to reduce. The wound was enlarged, and still it was impracticable to replace the protruded lung. On May 3d, the field hospital where Captain S—— lay was exposed to the enemy's fire. He walked half a mile further to the rear, and was there placed in an ambulance, and taken across the Rappahannock, at United States Ford, to one of the base hospitals. Here fruitless efforts were again made to reduce the hernial tumor, after which a ligature was thrown around its base and tightened. A day or two subsequently the patient passed into the hands of Surgeon Tomaine, who removed the ligature from the base of the tumor. A small portion of gangrenous lung separated and left a clean granulating surface beneath. On May 7th, the ball was voided at stool. On May 8th, the patient was visited by Surgeon John H. Brinton, U. S. Vols., who found him walking about the ward, smoking a cigar. There was an entire absence of general constitutional symptoms; no cough, no dyspnœa, no abdominal pain; the bowels were regular and appetite good. The protruding portion of the lung was carnified, and there was a dullness on percussion and absence of the respiratory murmur in a zone an inch and a half in width around the circumference of the base of the tumor. Surgeon Tomaine stated that the hernia had been gradually diminishing in volume. It was at this date half the size of an egg, and covered with florid granulations. On May 10th, a drawing of the parts was executed by Mr. Stauch, artist of the Army Medical Museum. On June 2d, Captain S—— was transferred to Washington. There was an elastic partly reducible tumor, over which was an oval granulating surface, an inch and a half by three-quarters of an inch. The vesicular murmur was perfect throughout the lung, except in the immediate vicinity of the tumor. Compression of the tumor was advised. After a furlough of sixty days, Captain S—— was again examined. The wound had entirely healed; the respiratory sounds were normal; there was still a slight hernia of the lung. The general health of the patient was excellent. At this date a second drawing was executed.

Private B. S. Sheridan, Co. A, 9th Massachusetts Vols., was wounded at Malvern Hill, July 1st, 1862, by a musket-ball, which entered the right side between the ninth and tenth ribs, and passed out a little to the right of the xyphoid cartilage. Soon after the reception of the injury, a portion of the lung protruded from the anterior wound, and from the posterior wound there was a constant dripping of bile. On July 4th, Sheridan walked from the ambulance station to James River, a distance of a mile and a half, with the hope of getting on board of a gunboat. He was disappointed, and was taken prisoner and conveyed to Richmond. No dressings were applied to the hernia of the lung. It was uncovered, and the patient occasionally washed it. He suffered little pain or dyspnœa, and there was an amazing absence of shock or prostration. On July 25th, the bile had ceased to dribble from the posterior wound, and the hernia of the lung had greatly receded. The imperfect field notes state that the patient ultimately recovered, and was exchanged.

Private Latimer Whipple, Co. H, 73d New York Vols., was wounded at Bristoe Station, Virginia, August 27th, 1862, and admitted to the First Division Hospital, at Alexandria, on August 31st. A musket-ball struck him on the right side, four inches above the crest of the ilium, and six inches from the spine, passed upwards and inwards, and lodged. On admission, the patient had cough, with bloody expectoration, and crepitant rales in the lower lobe of the left lung. There was a profuse discharge of bile from the wound. There was acute pain and tenderness in the hepatic region, but no evidence of peritonitis. At the end of a week the symptoms of acute inflammation of the lung subsided, but a cough, with purulent expectoration, persisted for months. Early in October the discharge of pus and bile from the wound began to diminish, and in November the pain ceased in the hepatic region, and was referred to the immediate vicinity of the orifice of the wound. The patient now began to walk about the ward. Throughout the treatment there was great tendency to constipation, which was obviated by enemata. In the middle of December the cough had nearly disappeared, and there was but a scanty discharge from the wound. On January 12th, 1863, the wound was entirely healed, and the patient was discharged from service.

GUNSHOT WOUNDS OF THE ABDOMEN.

Of 2707 gunshot wounds of the abdomen reported from the beginning of the war to July 1st, 1864, there were 2164 flesh wounds, and 543 cases in which the peritoneal cavity was penetrated or the abdominal viscera injured. Among the flesh wounds, 114 fatal cases are recorded, which were, in most instances, cases of sloughing from injuries of the abdominal parietes by shells. Of the 543 penetrating wounds, the results have been ascertained in 414, and were fatal in 308, or 74 per cent. The number of recoveries is unexpectedly large, but includes only cases in which the reports showed, beyond question, that the abdominal cavity had been involved. Abstracts of several such cases are subjoined:

Private John Barr, Co. E, 76th New York Vols., aged forty-five years, was admitted into Douglas Hospital, at Washington, May 18th, 1864, with a penetrating gunshot wound of the abdomen, received on May 9th, at the battle of the Wilderness. A conoidal musket-ball had entered at the junction of the left twelfth rib with its cartilage, and, passing downwards, backwards, and outwards through the ilium, lodged in the gluteal muscles, whence it was removed by incision. On admission, the wound copiously discharged a thin translucent fluid, resembling diluted bile, which evidently came from the small intestine, for, among other reasons, it had no fæcal odor. Were further proof of the origin of the discharge required, it would be furnished by the fact that three ascarides lumbricoides escaped from the wound during the second and third weeks of the treatment. The discharge, for nine days prior to admission, was, according to the patient, similar to that above noted. The patient was kept perfectly quiet in a recumbent posture. The discharge from the wound was facilitated by large masses of charpie being used to absorb it. For several weeks the patient was nourished solely by milk, milk-punch, and beef tea. His appetite was poor, his sleep much disturbed by cough. But there was no abdominal pain or tenderness, and at no time, throughout the treatment, was there any symptom of peritoneal inflammation. On May 22d, a soap and water enema was administered without result. Nothing more was attempted in this direction, as the patient was doing well, and nature seemed competent to meet every indication. On June 3d, the discharge had entirely ceased, and the patient was much improved. On June 6th, he had a large alvine evacuation, the first since May 9th. On June 11th, with the aid of an enema, he had another large dejection. From this time he improved rapidly. On August 16th, a fragment of necrosed bone, that could be recognized as a portion of the ilium, was removed from the wound in the gluteal region. About the same period bits of necrosed cartilage were taken from the fistulous orifices opening near the wound of entrance. The bowels were disposed to costiveness, and flatulence was troublesome. Early in October there was an attack of dysentery, which lasted one week. On May 5th, 1865, a needle-shaped bit of bone escaped from the wound of entrance. On May 8th, both wounds were entirely healed. On July 16th, the patient was photographed at the Army Medical Museum. He was then in good health.

Private George H. Bowers, 8th Illinois Cavalry, was wounded in a skirmish near Frederick, Maryland, September 13th, 1862, by a musket-ball, which entered two inches above the umbilicus, an inch to the left of the linea alba, and made its exit beneath the tenth rib, three inches to the left of the spinous process of the tenth dorsal vertebra. Immediately after he was shot, he vomited blood copiously until syncope supervened. Hæmatemesis recurred frequently for seven days, and blood was passed at stool. Acute peritonitis ensued. The medical attendants had no doubt that the stomach was perforated. Liquids taken into the stomach passed freely through the anterior wound. The case was treated by opium in large doses. In May, 1863, the patient was transferred to the hospital at Stewart's Mansion, in Baltimore. The wound had healed, and the digestive organs had resumed their normal action. But the body was bent forward by intra-abdominal adhesions. The patient was subsequently discharged from service.

In many instances fæcal fistulæ were produced. They commonly closed after a time, without operative interference, reopening at intervals, and then healing permanently.

Sergeant Lewis E. Morley, Co. F, 61st New York Vols., was wounded at Gettysburg, July 1st, 1863, by a conoidal musket-ball, which entered a little below the umbilicus and to the left of the linea alba, and passed directly through the body, dividing the intestine in its passage. When brought to the field hospital he was in a state of collapse. Fæces escaped from the wound. There was excessive tenderness and pain. Opiates were freely administered, and the symptoms of peritonitis gradually abated. On July 10th, the patient was in a condition to be removed to Baltimore. The discharge of fæces from the wounds continued until September 28th, when there was an evacuation by the rectum. The wounds soon afterwards closed, and on October 27th, the patient was sent home on furlough.

Private A. J. Marker, Co. I, 4th Maine Vols., aged eighteen years, was wounded at Centreville, September 1st, 1862, by a conoidal musket-ball, which entered the left hypochondriac region, between the eighth and ninth ribs, and lodged under the skin a little to the left of the spinous process of the second lumbar vertebra. He entered Epiphany Hospital, at Washington, on the following day, and the ball was removed by an incision. There was immediately a copious fæcal discharge through the incision. It was ascertained that the ninth rib was fractured, and fragments of it were removed. On September 5th, a portion of gangrenous omentum presented at the posterior wound and was excised. A sphacelated portion of the descending colon was also removed. The fæcal fistula persisted until May, 1863, when the discharge from the anterior wound became sero-purulent. A month afterwards both wounds healed up soundly, and the patient was sent to his home in Belfast, Maine. In November, 1863, while the wounds were still discharging stercoraceous matter, a colored drawing was made, which is No. 15 of the Surgical Series of Drawings, S. G. O.

Private John Harm, Co. I, 20th Indiana Vols., was wounded at the battle of Fair Oaks, May 31st, 1862, by a musket-ball, which entered three inches to the right of the spine and one inch above the crest of the ilium, and, passing upwards across the abdominal cavity, made its exit in the left hypochondriac region. He was admitted to Broad and Cherry Streets Hospital, in Philadelphia, on July 29th, 1862. He stated that there was free hæmorrhage from the wounds at first, and subsequently a discharge of fæces. At the date of his admission, the wound of exit had closed; but fæces and flatus still escaped by the posterior wound. At the end of October, 1862, this wound also closed; but it reopened a few weeks subsequently, and a fragment of flannel was extracted from it. After this it healed soundly, and the patient was discharged from service.

Private Franklin Harsh, Co. G, 7th Ohio Vols., was wounded at Chancellorsville, May 3d, 1863, by a conoidal musket-ball, which entered the abdomen six inches to the right of the umbilicus, and passed out posteriorly, having wounded the ascending colon and the crest of the right ilium. He was admitted to Armory Square Hospital, at Washington, and remained there for a long time with a fæcal fistula. On September 13th, 1863, the anterior wound had closed, and the discharge from the posterior wound was much diminished. Ultimately the fistula closed, and the patient was discharged from service. Early in the history of the case, a colored drawing of the patient was made. (Nos. 21 and 22, Surgical Series of Drawings, S. G. O.)

Sergeant Joseph E. Fletcher, Co. D, 8th Connecticut Vols., aged twenty, was struck at the battle of Antietam, September 17th, 1862, by a musket-ball, which entered six inches to the left of the umbilicus, and, passing somewhat downwards, emerged an inch and a half to the left of the spine. The ball opened the descending colon, and when the patient was examined by Surgeon T. H. Squire, 89th New York Vols., there was a profuse fæcal discharge from the wound of exit. The ensuing peritonitis was circumscribed, and the patient was transferred to Frederick, a few weeks subsequently, in a satisfactory condition. The fæcal fistula finally closed and the patient recovered.

Lieutenant G. P. Deichler, Co. I, 69th Pennsylvania Vols., aged twenty-two years, was wounded by a conoidal musket-ball, at Hatcher's Run, Virginia, in March, 1865. The ball entered the right iliac region, and, passing through the ascending colon, made its exit a little to the left of the last dorsal vertebra. The patient was taken to a field hospital, and from thence to Armory Square Hospital, at Washington, where he was admitted on April 1st, in an exhausted condition, with grave symptoms of peritonitis. There was a copious fæcal discharge from both wounds. Appropriate dressings were applied, a fourth of a grain of sulphate of morphia was ordered to be given every second hour, and stimulants were directed. On April 7th, sloughs separated from both wounds, and left a clean granulating surface. A large piece of sphacelated omentum was removed from the anterior wound. The opiate treatment was continued till April 27th, when there was a fæcal evacuation by the anus, for the first time since the injury. On June 12th, the discharge from the wounds was very slight. The edges of the wounds were now refreshed and approximated by adhesive strips. On August 10th, the anterior wound was firmly healed. There was a small fistulous sinus at the posterior wound, discharging pus scantily. On this day, a photograph was taken at the Army Medical Museum, from which the plate opposite is copied, and the patient left the hospital for his home in excellent general health.

Private Robert Brierly, Co. A, 1st Delaware Vols., aged twenty-two, was wounded at the battle of Antietam, by a conoidal musket-ball, which entered a little to the left of the umbilicus, and lodged under the muscles near the anterior superior spinous process of the right ilium. There was great prostration, with nausea and vomiting, which were treated at the field hospital by the administration of opiates. Three weeks subsequently, the patient was transferred to Frederick, Maryland. On October 25th, fæces escaped through the lower wound, which had been for several days in a sloughing state. The artificial anus continued open until November 15th. On November 25th and December 11th, there were attacks of colic, followed by reopening of the fæcal fistula. By the end of December, the wounds appeared sound and permanently healed, and the patient was transferred to Baltimore, and subsequently was discharged from service.

Private James T. Dowdy, 28th Virginia (Rebel) Regiment, aged twenty-three years, was wounded at the battle of Gettysburg, July 3d, 1863, by a conoidal musket-ball, which entered at the tip of the ensiform cartilage, and remained in the body. He was removed to one of the Gettysburg field hospitals. On July 4th, fourteen hours after he was shot, he passed the ball at stool. There was no general peritonitis, and the wound healed promptly, and the patient was transferred to Baltimore, and thence sent to City Point, Virginia, for exchange.

Recoveries after wounds of the large intestines have been much more numerous than after wounds of the ileum or jejunum.

No case has been reported in which it was thought expedient to apply a suture to the intestines after gunshot wounds.

Gunshot wounds of the liver were usually followed by extravasation into the abdominal cavity and rapidly fatal peritonitis. Of 32 cases in which the diagnosis was unquestionable, all but 4 terminated fatally. Abstracts of two of the fortunate cases are appended:

Private Fritz Siebel, Co. D, 139th New York Vols., aged twenty-three years, was wounded at Cold Harbor,

PERFORATING GUNSHOT WOUND OF THE ABDOMEN.
CASE OF LIEUTENANT DEICHLER

GUNSHOT WOUNDS OF THE ABDOMEN.

Virginia, June 3d, 1863, by a musket-ball, which entered the right hypochondriac region, below the tenth rib, and passed out posteriorly an inch and a half to the right of the spine. He was admitted to Harewood Hospital, at Washington, on June 18th, in a very feeble state. There was a fœcal discharge from the wound, mixed with bile. The ball had passed through the colon and the liver. There was great abdominal pain, an anxious countenance, nausea, and the other symptoms of traumatic peritonitis. A cold water-dressing was applied, and opium was administered in full doses. On July 1st, the pain on pressure was circumscribed, and the general symptoms were less threatening. The discharge from the wound was unaltered. On September 1st, the wound of exit had healed, and the anterior wound discharged only a thin serum. On September 14th, the wound of entrance closed. The patient was furloughed on October 8th, 1863, and on the expiration of his furlough was returned to duty.

Corporal W. A. C. Biles, Co. K, 25th North Carolina (Rebel) Regiment, was wounded at Gettysburg, July 3d, 1863, by a conoidal musket-ball, which passed through the lower portion of the right lobe of the liver. He was treated at one of the field hospitals at Gettysburg, and his case was carefully observed by Surgeon H. Janes, U. S. Vols. There was a free discharge of bile from both the wound of entry and of exit. There was circumscribed pain and tenderness on pressure, but apparently no extra-abdominal extravasation. The wounds continued to discharge bile until August 27th. On November 1st, the patient was transferred to West's Buildings Hospital, at Baltimore, and on November 12th, 1863, he was sent to City Point, Virginia, for exchange, his wound being entirely healed.

All the cases of gunshot wounds of the spleen that have been reported, were fatal. No symptoms are mentioned that particularly distinguished these from other gunshot injuries involving the abdominal cavity, and it is quite possible that the list of recoveries may include cases in which this viscus was injured, though the diagnosis was not made out.

A case is recorded of a lacerated wound of the abdominal walls, with lesion and protrusion of the pancreas, a portion of which is reported to have been excised. It appears probable that it was rather a portion of the omentum that was removed. Several cases are reported in which it was believed that recovery took place after gunshot wounds of the kidney:

Private Groff, Co. D, 61st Pennsylvania Vols., was admitted on June 8th, 1862, to Fifth Street Hospital, in Philadelphia, for wounds received at the battle of Fair Oaks, June 1st, 1862. He had a flesh wound of the left hip, another of the right thigh, and a wound in the left lumbar region, which was considered to be a penetrating wound of the abdomen. Immediately after he was struck, blood passed freely by the urethra. When he entered the hospital, he had hæmaturia. His wounds healed, however, kindly, and he left the hospital entirely well.

Sergeant Galloway, Co. H, 8th Pennsylvania Reserves, was wounded at South Mountain, September 14th, 1862, by a musket-ball, which passed through the abdomen. He was treated at Satterlee Hospital, in Philadelphia. He had hæmaturia, and pain and tenderness in the region of the left kidney. He ultimately recovered.

It can hardly be considered that the evidence of gunshot wound of the kidney was, in these cases, unequivocal.

Gunshot wounds of the bladder, when the projectile entered above the pubes or through the pelvic bones, have proved fatal, so far as the records have been examined. There are many examples of recovery, however, from injuries of the parts of the bladder uncovered by the peritonæum.

Several examples of recovery, after protrusions of the abdominal viscera through gunshot wounds, have been reported. In two cases in which loops of small intestine issued, they were immediately returned and retained by means of adhesive strips and bandages, and the patients recovered with ventral hernia. The escape of omentum, through wounds, would not appear to be a very serious complication, for in many cases portions of protruding omentum have been excised, and the patients have, nevertheless, recovered promptly.

In relation to gunshot wounds of the great vessels of the abdomen, a few words will be said in treating of ligations.

Penetrating wounds of the abdomen, complicated with fractures of the vertebræ, uniformly proved fatal. A single extract will suffice to show the usual progress of such cases.

Corporal John E——, Co. M, 14th New York Heavy Artillery, was wounded before Petersburg, in July, 1864. He was sent to Washington, and admitted to Douglas Hospital, with peritonitis and complete paraplegia. A musket-ball had entered at the right hypochondriac region, passed downwards through the right lobe of the liver and the abdominal cavity, and fractured the second and third lumbar vertebræ. He died on August 3d, 1864.

Fig. 20.—Gunshot fracture of the second and third lumbar vertebræ. Spec. 3583, A. M. M.

At the Army Medical Museum are specimens of 18 gunshot wounds of the stomach or intestines, 10 of the liver, 8 of the spleen, 10 of the kidneys, 4 of the bladder, and 6 of the genito-urinary organs.

GUNSHOT FRACTURES OF THE PELVIS.

The records under this head include only the cases in which the abdominal cavity was not penetrated. From the beginning of the war to October 1st, 1864, 359 such cases have been reported. Recovery took place in 97, death in 77, and the result is still to be ascertained in 185. In 256 cases the ilium alone was injured, the ischium alone in 19, the pubes in 12, the sacrum in 32, and in 40 cases the lesions extended to two or more portions of the innominata.

The gravity of these cases depended upon the location and extent of the fracture. The majority of recoveries were from fracture of the ilium by musket-balls, in which the crest was grooved, or comparatively slight injury was inflicted. Yet there were many examples of perforation of the body of the ilium with ultimate recovery. The following is an abstract of such a case:

Major H. A. Barnum, 12th New York Vols., was wounded at Malvern Hill, July 1st, 1862, by a conoidal musket-ball, which entered midway between the umbilicus and the anterior superior spinous process of the left ilium, passed through the middle of the ilium, and emerged posteriorly. On July 2d, he was captured and taken to Libby Prison, a distance of eighteen miles, in an express wagon. On July 17th, he was taken to Aikens' Landing in an ambulance, a distance of seventeen miles, and exchanged. He was conveyed by water to Albany, and thence by rail to Syracuse, New York. At no time were any symptoms of peritonitis manifested. On October 1st, Major Barnum went to Albany, where Dr. March dilated the anterior wound by an incision and extracted several fragments of the ilium, and directed that a tent should be worn. Promoted to the command of the 149th New York Vols., Colonel Barnum took the field in January, 1863. He wore the tent about a month, when the anterior wound healed. About the middle of March, a large abscess formed, and evacuated itself at the site of the anterior wound. In April, Dr. March again cut down to the ilium, and introduced a tent. No loose fragments of bone were found. The Colonel resumed his duties, and commanded his regiment at Gettysburg. In January, 1864, another large abscess formed, and discharged posteriorly. The orifice was enlarged by Dr. L. A. Sayre, of New York, and a seton of oakum was passed from before backwards through the entire track of the ball. This was worn for several weeks, when Surgeon M. K. Hogan, U. S. Vols., substituted a seton of candle-wick, which was gradually reduced in size, and finally replaced by a single linen thread. A photograph of the patient was taken at the Army Medical Museum in August, 1865. The wound still discharged slightly, and the thread seton was still worn. Promoted to be a brigade commander, General Barnum has been almost continually in the field for the past two years. He participated in the campaigns of Atlanta, Georgia, and Carolina, was shot through the right forearm at Kenesaw Mountain, and received a shell wound of the side at Peach Tree Creek.

In most cases of injury of the pelvic bones, very tedious suppuration ensued, and surgery could do but little, except to facilitate the escape of pus, and to remove dead bone as it became separated. The returns corroborate the observation of Stromeyer, that there is a great liability to pyæmia in gunshot fractures of the pelvis.

GUNSHOT WOUNDS OF THE GENITO-URINARY ORGANS.

In this category are included gunshot wounds of the genitals or urinary organs that are not complicated with fractures of the pelvis, or with penetration of the abdominal cavity. To October 1st, 1864, the reports furnish 457 such wounds, of which 37 had a fatal result.

Surgeon S. W. Gross, U. S. Vols., reports the singular history of a soldier of the 16th U. S. Infantry, struck at Shiloh, on the right side of the penis, by a conoidal musket-ball, which buried itself in the corpus cavernosum, and became encysted. It gave no pain, and the patient refused to have it extracted.

The following is an interesting case of gunshot wound of the bladder:

Private Conrad L——, Co. A, 23d Indiana Vols., aged thirty-two years, was wounded at Vicksburg, Miss., June 23d, 1863, by a fragment of a hand-grenade, which entered the right nates two inches outside of the end of the coccyx, and passed into the bladder, where it lodged. Urine passed by the wound immediately after its reception. The patient was admitted into the General Hospital at Jefferson Barracks, Missouri, August 5th, 1863. His general health was much impaired. The urine passed mainly by the wound, and was largely mixed with pus and blood. The treatment directed comprised warm fomentations, mild diuretics, stimulants, and nutritious diet. On February 20th, 1864, a catheter was with much difficulty passed by the urethra, and the presence of a foreign body was ascertained. On March 19th, the general condition was improved, the wound was so far closed as to admit only a large-sized probe. Attempts to pass a catheter or to probe the wound caused chills and febrile irritation. On April 2d, 1864, the lateral operation of lithotomy was performed by Surgeon John F. Randolph, U. S. A., the patient being anæsthetized by equal parts by bulk of chloroform and ether. A rectangular fragment of shell, largely incrusted with earthy phosphates, was extracted. It was two inches in length, seven-eighths of an inch in width, and three-eighths of an inch in thickness. It weighed two ounces and five grains troy. On April 12th, the urine passed by the wound. On April 27th, the wound had healed, and the patient was soon afterwards restored to his ordinary condition of health. The incrusted fragment of shell is preserved in the collection of the Army Medical Museum (Spec. 88). It weighs 898 grains, portions of the phosphatic deposit having crumbled away.

FIG. 30.—Fragment of grenade incrusted with calculous matter, extracted from the bladder by lithotomy. Spec. 88, A. M. M.

GUNSHOT WOUNDS OF THE UPPER EXTREMITIES.

When unaccompanied by lesions of the vessels and nerves, the gunshot flesh wounds of the upper extremity are not very serious injuries. All foreign bodies having been extracted, they commonly heal, under the use of water-dressings and the lightest bandaging, in a few weeks. The 21,248 cases entered on the registers are all copied from the reports for the last quarter of 1863 and the first two quarters of 1864.

The gunshot fractures of the upper extremity are recorded in four classes: those of the scapula and clavicle, which are not, at the same time, penetrating wounds of the chest; those of the shaft of the humerus and either of its articular extremities; those of the ulna and radius; and those of the carpus and metacarpus. It is only with the second class that much progress has been made. This comprises 2408 cases of gunshot fractures of the humerus that have been examined and recorded. Recovery followed in 1253 cases, death in 436, and the result is as yet undetermined in 719 cases. In the 1689 completed cases, amputation or excision were practised in 996, and conservative treatment was adopted in 693, with a ratio of mortality of 21 per cent. in the former and 30 per cent. in the latter. But it is premature to make deductions from statistics which are daily augmenting and tending towards completion.

Gunshot lesions of the upper extremity are illustrated at the Army Medical Museum by 978 specimens, including examples of almost every variety of contusion and fracture, of the repair of fractures, of consecutive diseases of bones, and of excisions, amputations, and their secondary lesions. A few specimens are copied here.

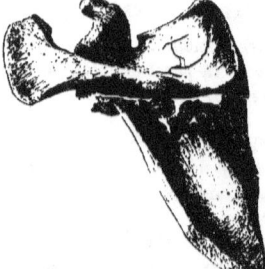

Private William F——, Co. F, 18th Massachusetts Vols., aged thirty years, was wounded at the second battle of Bull Run, August 30th, 1862, by a conoidal musket-ball, which entered to the left of the spinal column, and, passing outwards, traversed the body of the scapula and the muscles of the upper part of the arm. The patient was conveyed to Union Chapel Hospital, at Alexandria. On the 3d, and again on the 5th of September, misshapen pieces of ball and a few fragments of bone were extracted through an incision on the outer edge of the scapula. On September 19th, symptoms of purulent infection were manifested. An active treatment by stimulants, quinia, iron, and ammonia, was instituted, but unavailingly, and on September 25th, 1862, the case terminated fatally. At the autopsy, a large collection of extravasated blood was found beneath the scapula, and between the muscles of the shoulder. There was extensive serous effusion in the left pleural cavity, and numerous metastatic foci in both lungs.

FIG. 31.—Left scapula, showing a gunshot fracture, nearly parallel with the spine of the scapula, with two fragments of a conoidal musket-ball. *Spec.* 809, A. M. M.

A soldier of the 2d Division of the 12th Army Corps had his left arm shattered by an elongated musket-ball, in the attack on the stone wall on the heights at Fredericksburg, December 14th, 1862. Primary amputation at the shoulder-joint was performed, and the patient recovered. The specimen illustrates the ordinary longitudinal splitting produced by a conoidal ball in the shaft of a long bone.

Private B—— W——, Co. I, 37th New York Vols., aged twenty-two years, was wounded at Williamsburg, Virginia, May 5th, 1862, in the right elbow, by a conoidal musket-ball. A simple dressing was applied, and he was removed to Yorktown, and thence to Philadelphia, where he was admitted to Race Street Hospital. No report could be obtained of the progress of the case until March 13th, 1863, when the patient was transferred to the McClellan General Hospital, at Nicetown, with extensive necrosis of the shaft of the humerus and caries of the elbow-joint. About the joint and arm there were numerous sinuses, through which a profuse purulent discharge escaped, and, occasionally, small fragments of detached bone. Under a supporting treatment, the general condition improved. About the middle of July, it was first noticed that the patient's legs were œdematous. General anasarca ensued, and an examination of the urine showed that it was highly albuminous. The patient became rapidly worse, and on August 12th, an uncontrollable diarrhœa set in, accompanied by vomiting. The case terminated fatally, August 22d, 1863. The characteristic lesions of Bright's disease were revealed by the autopsy.

FIG. 33.—Necrosis of the shaft of the humerus, following a gunshot wound of the elbow. *Spec.* 2749, A. M. M.

FIG. 32.—Left humerus, comminuted by a conoidal musket-ball. *Spec.* 1082, A. M. M.

GUNSHOT WOUNDS OF THE LOWER EXTREMITIES.

Of these, 30,014 cases have been recorded, of which 4862 were fractures, and 25,152 were flesh wounds. The latter were transcribed from the reports from October 1st, 1863, to October 1st, 1864. It has not been practicable as yet to tabulate the flesh wounds of the lower extremities that occurred in the earlier part of the war.

For gunshot fractures of the femur, two registers have been kept. On one, all cases were entered. On the other, only those in which the histories of the cases had been carefully scrutinized, and in which the locality and extent of the injury were clearly designated in the reports. In the latter register 1823 cases had been entered on September 1st, 1865, or about one-third of the total number that have been reported.

GUNSHOT WOUNDS OF THE LOWER EXTREMITIES.

Gunshot wounds of the knee-joint, with or without fracture of the patella, or of the epiphyses of the femur or tibia, have been recorded in like manner, to the number, thus far, of 1183.

Of the 1823 cases of gunshot fracture of the femur that have been entered on the permanent records, the results have been ascertained in 1233. Of the 1183 cases of gunshot wounds of the knee-joint, the results are known in 740.

While it is deemed premature to discuss these results when it may be reasonably hoped that the completed statistics will definitely settle the important questions that are here involved, it is yet thought expedient to report them, chiefly that the magnitude of the subject may be put in evidence, and that the absolute necessity for long and patient investigation may be acknowledged.

The following table exhibits at a glance the results of 2003 cases of gunshot fracture of the femur, or of gunshot wounds of the knee-joint, out of a total of 3106 cases hitherto recorded. The fractures of the femur are separated according to regions. The left hand column gives the number of cases belonging to each region of which the ultimate results have been satisfactorily determined. The right hand column gives the total number of cases of injuries of each region that have been recorded. The intermediate columns give the comparative results of treatment by amputation, excision, or attempt at conservation of the limb, the number of recoveries and deaths and unfinished cases in each category being mentioned, and the rate of mortality calculated for the finished cases alone.

Table, exhibiting the Results of 2003 Terminated Cases of Gunshot Fracture of the Femur, or of Gunshot Wounds of the Knee-Joint, out of 3106 Cases that have been entered on the Records.

	Total Termin-ated.	Amputation.				Excision.				Conservative Measures.				Aggre-gate.
		Recovered.	Died.	Undetermined.	Mortality rate of determined cases.	Recovered.	Died.	Undetermined.	Mortality rate of determined cases.	Recovered.	Died.	Undetermined.	Mortality rate of determined cases.	
Gunshot Fractures of Femur, implicating Hip-Joint	82	0	2	0	100·	2	10	1	83·33	0	68	14	100·	97
Gunshot Fractures of upper third of Femur	387	8	24	11	75·	7	18	6	72·	93	237	100	71·81	603
Gunshot Fractures of middle third of Femur	346	42	51	47	54·83	2	13	10	86·66	106	132	148	55·46	551
Gunshot Fractures of lower third of Femur	418	131	112	117	46·09	1	1	0	50·	72	101	137	57·70	672
Gunshot Wounds of the Knee-Joint, with or without Fracture	770	121	331	266	73·23	1	9	1	90·	50	258	146	83·76	1183
	2003	302	520	441	63·26	13	51	18	79·68	321	796	544	71·26	3106

In examining the above table in detail, it is seen that the results are ascertained in 822 of the 1263 cases treated by amputation, or 65 per cent.; in 64 of the 82 cases treated by excision, or 78 per cent.; and in 1117 of the 1761 cases treated by conservative measures, or 63 per cent.

The only recorded recoveries after gunshot fracture of the femur involving the hip-joint are those in which excision was practised. In fractures of the upper third, the mortality rate is greatest for the cases treated by amputation. There were 43 of these cases, and in 19 of them the amputation was done at the hip-joint. Excision gives 7 recoveries after fractures of the upper third; 2 of these were excisions of the head and a portion of the shaft of the femur, 4 were formal excisions of the continuity, and 1 was a removal of fragments and rounding off of sharp edges of bone, which was admitted among the excisions with some hesitation. Under conservative measures 93 cases of fracture of the upper third had survived the injury a year or more, and are reported as recovered. The mortality rate of the completed cases of amputation for gunshot wounds of the knee-joint is large, and will probably be modified when the results of the numerous unfinished cases are recorded. It depends partly, however, upon the excessive mortality of intermediate amputations of knee-joint injuries. With six or eight exceptions, the 50 recoveries without amputation classified with gunshot wounds of the knee-joint were examples of fractures of the patella, in which the evidence that the joint was opened was not unequivocal.

Comparing in gross the 822 finished cases treated by amputation, with the 1117 treated by conservation, the mortality rate of the former has the advantage by 8 per cent.; an advantage that is maintained in the different regions, except in the upper third. It must be remembered that the amputations include most of the bad cases, and those in which preservation of the limb was attempted and abandoned.

But little progress has been made in the examination and registration of the fractures of the tibia and fibula. Only 1056 have been recorded, of which 696 are terminated cases, chiefly belonging to the earlier periods of the war. Of these, 169, or 24 per cent., were fatal.

A similar remark applies to the fractures of the tarsus and metatarsus. But 629 cases have as yet been recorded.

For gunshot fractures of the phalanges, it has been thought superfluous to keep a separate register, as the majority of such cases will appear on the register of amputations of the toes.

At the Army Medical Museum, the gunshot injuries of the lower extremity are illustrated by 1984 specimens, comprising examples of almost every conceivable form of contusion or fracture, illustrations of secondary lesions, and of reparative attempts in all stages, wet preparations showing the appearances of wounds of entrance and exit, the ravages of hospital gangrene, wounds or consecutive lesions of the great vessels, numerous drawings, casts, and photographs, and, among the latter, representations of over seventy patients, who had so far recovered after gunshot fracture of the femur as to be able to move about.

The specimens of fractured or diseased bones at the Museum are arranged according to the regions involved, the primary being separated from the secondary lesions, and the illustrations of operations being classified apart. Representations of a few specimens will be introduced here.

In Stromeyer's classification of the action of bullets on bone, the fifth division is that in which the ball pierces the bone and forms a canal without causing further splintering. Examples are common in the upper portion of the tibia, but very rare in the upper extremity of the femur. The following is such an instance:

ON SPECIAL WOUNDS AND INJURIES.

Captain James M. L——, Co. I, 20th Indiana Vols., was admitted into Columbia College Hospital, at Washington, June 29th, 1862, with two gunshot wounds, received a day or two previously in one of the battles before Richmond. The first wound was through the left lumbar muscles. After receiving it the officer fell, and while lying on the field he was again struck by an elongated musket-ball, which entered on the outer side of the left thigh, a little below the great trochanters, and, passing upwards and inwards, lodged. A finger could be readily passed into the perforation in the femur, but the ball could not be reached. Three formal attempts to ascertain its position and accomplish its removal were made unsuccessfully. The patient died from exhaustion on August 19th, 1862. The near proximity of the ball had not induced any disease of the hip-joint. The specimen and the facts relating to it were contributed by Assistant Surgeon W. M. Notson, U. S. A.

An illustration of a comminuted gunshot fracture in the trochanteric region is given in the section on excisions of the head of the femur. Of comminuted fractures of the shaft of the femur by the conoidal musket-ball, the following is a fair example:

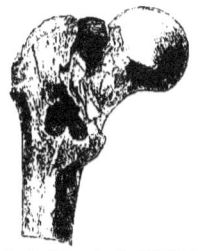

FIG. 34.—Upper extremity of left femur perforated by a conoidal ball. Spec. 365, A. M. M.

Private John Draker, Co. I, 57th Pennsylvania Vols., aged twenty-five years, was wounded while on picket duty on the Rapidan, November 27th, 1863. A conoidal musket-ball passed through the muscles of the right thigh, and, entering the middle of the left thigh at its inner side, flattened itself against the femur, and shattered the bone. The patient was transferred to Alexandria by rail, and admitted, December 4th, 1863, to the Second Division U. S. A. General Hospital. He died December 13th, 1863.

Just above the condyles, where the cancellated structure of bone predominates, musket-balls often make a clean perforation. But the wedge-like action of the elongated musket-ball almost invariably involves longitudinal splintering. The following is a good illustration:

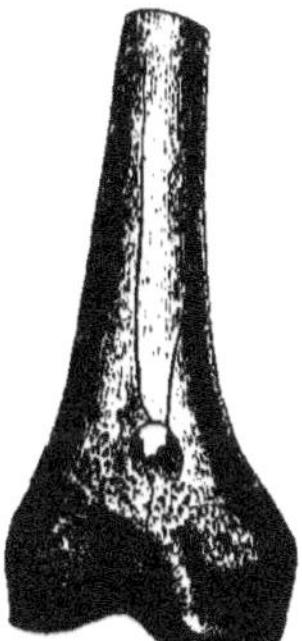

Private Samuel S. Kopp, Co. E, 10th Pennsylvania Reserves, was shot through the lower third of the right thigh, by a musket-ball, at the second battle of Bull Run, August 28th, 1862. The ball entered just above the patella, and made its exit in the popliteal space. The patient was taken, after a few days, to Alexandria. On September 20th, 1862, his thigh was amputated at the middle. He survived the operation two days.

The later writers on military surgery have duly insisted upon the different effect upon bones of the impact of round musket-balls and of the cylindro-conical projectiles. The degree of difference in the injuries inflicted has, perhaps, been exaggerated. It is unquestionably true, however, that the round ball usually produces much less longitudinal splintering than the conoidal ball, with its greater weight and immense force of propulsion and wedge-like action. In the case which furnished Specimen 3228, A. M. M., where a round ball entering the outer condyle behind, passed upwards, forwards, and inwards through the bone, it was practicable to amputate successfully much nearer the track of the ball than would have been admissible in the case quoted just before.

FIG. 35.—Fracture of the shaft of the left femur by a musket-ball. Spec. 1907, A. M. M.

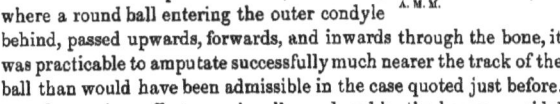

FIG. 36.—Perforation of the right femur by a musket-ball. Spec. 70, A. M. M.

One curious effect, occasionally produced by the heavy conoidal ball in striking the femur, has not been very generally noticed. The bone is fissured and comminuted, though less than is common,

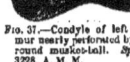

FIG. 37.—Condyle of left femur nearly perforated by a round musket-ball. Spec. 3228, A. M. M.

at the point at which the ball impinges, while at two or three inches above or below this point, according as the point of impact is below or above the middle of the shaft, a nearly transverse fracture of the shaft is produced. The accompanying figure is an example; but the Museum contains a dozen better illustrations. The best are of cases in which a ball has struck the condyles anteriorly, and the shaft is snapped across two inches above. In several of these specimens, the transverse fracture is not connected by fissures with the comminuted fracture produced by the ball. It appears that these injuries were produced by balls fired at short range.

When the femur is simply contused by a ball, a limited necrosis commonly ensues from the destruction of the periosteum, and inflammation of the medullary cavity often results, and death from pyæmic infection. The records would indicate that gunshot contusions of the long bones, a subject ably discussed* of late by Surgeon J. A. Lidell, U. S. Vols., are more dangerous accidents than comminuted gunshot fractures even. Of gunshot contusions of the femur, there are seventeen specimens at the Army Medical Museum. Several of these bones were sawn through the long axis, immediately after the death of the patient, and colored drawings were prepared, exhibiting the appearances of the inflamed or suppurating or gangrenous medulla.

FIG. 38.—Fracture of the upper third of the left femur by a conoidal musket-ball. Spec. 1148, A. M. M.

Cases in which a portion of the shaft of the femur is gouged out, or a part of its cylinder crushed without entire division of the continuity, are also very fatal. The following is an example:

Private Orson B. Norwood, Co. K, 3d Michigan Cavalry, was wounded July 15th, 1863, in a skirmish near Jackson, Tennessee. He was acting as a vidette at the time, and was stationed on a bridge. The ball, fired from below, produced a long fissure in the lower third of the inner aspect of the femur, and was itself split by the compact lamina of the bone. This patient was removed to the General Hospital, at La Grange, Tennessee, July 22d, 1863. The thigh was then erysipelatous, and amputation was deemed inadvisable. September 27th, 1863, he was removed to the Washington Hospital, at Memphis, where he died of pyæmia, October 2d, 1863. The fragment of the inner surface of the femur, though but slightly separated from the diaphysis, was found to be necrosed.

FIG. 39.—Lower end of right femur, split by a conoidal musket-ball. Spec. 1798, A. M. M.

The series at the Army Medical Museum, illustrating the reparative efforts of nature after gunshot fractures of the femur, consists of 190 specimens, and is of exceeding interest. A few cases are selected. The first shows the extent of repair ten weeks subsequent to the injury.

Private E. W. A——, Co. G, 5th Florida (Rebel) Regiment, aged eighteen years, was wounded July 3d, 1863, at the battle of Gettysburg, by a conoidal musket-ball, which shattered the upper third of the left femur. He was first treated at a field hospital, but on August 5th, 1863, was admitted to Camp Letterman General Hospital. At that date, the patient was reduced by profuse suppuration; he was greatly emaciated, and large bed-sores had formed on his back. On August 12th, a troublesome diarrhœa set in. He lingered

FIG. 40.—Left femur, exhibiting attempts at repair after a gunshot fracture of the upper third. The patient survived ten weeks. Spec. 1938, A. M. M.

---

* American Journal of Medical Sciences, vol. xlix. p. 17, et seq.

till September 15th, 1863, when he died from exhaustion. The large foliaceous masses of callus uniting the fragments were extremely delicate and brittle.

In the next case, the patient likewise survived ten weeks after a comminuted gunshot fracture of the middle third.

Corporal H. Burns, Co. H, 31st New York Vols., was struck by a conoidal ball, at the battle of Chancellorsville, May 3d, 1863. The missile fractured the shaft of the left femur, with the usual longitudinal splintering. On May 8th, the patient was admitted to Douglas Hospital, at Washington, and it was decided to attempt to save the limb. This was first suspended by Smith's anterior splint. Afterwards Hodgen's apparatus was applied, and apparently answered a better purpose; but large abscesses having formed in the thigh, and free incisions becoming requisite, a long fracture-box, filled with bran, was substituted. On June 16th, 1863, the ball and several fragments of detached bone were removed. The patient died on July 11th, 1863, from exhaustive suppuration. Several days before his death gangrenous patches appeared on the left leg. (Figure 41.)

In the next case, the patient survived more than four months.

Sergeant Sewell T. Douglas, Co. G, 1st Regiment Maine Heavy Artillery, aged twenty-eight years, was wounded at the battle of Spottsylvania, and was admitted to Emory Hospital, at Washington, May 22d, 1864. A musket-ball entering posteriorly, had fractured the lower third of the left femur, and lodged in the medullary cavity. The injured limb was placed on a double inclined plane, and moderate extension was used. Internally, stimulants and tonics were employed. In August, 1864, the patient suffered from severe diarrhœa. There was a copious ill-conditioned discharge from the wound. The patient died September 26th, 1864, from exhaustion, and, at the autopsy, a deposition of callus was found at the seat of injury, enclosing several necrosed splinters and a battered musket-ball.

Fig. 41.—Partially consolidated gunshot fracture of the middle third of the left femur. Spec. 1643, A. M. M.

In the following case the process of repair had gone on for nine months, and union was nearly complete, when the patient was carried off by an intercurrent disease.

Fig. 42.—Partially consolidated gunshot fracture of the left femur. Spec. 3207, A. M. M.

Private Christian Holzworth, Co. B, 20th Indiana Vols., was wounded at the second battle of Manassas, August 29th, 1862, by a conoidal musket-ball, which entered on the anterior aspect of the upper third of the left thigh, and lodged against the femur, which was fractured with extensive longitudinal splitting. He was conveyed to Armory Square Hospital, at Washington. No particulars of the treatment employed can be ascertained, but it is reported that in March, 1863, he was able to go about on crutches, and that he was "doing well" until the latter part of May, when an attack of cerebro-spinal meningitis supervened, and terminated fatally on May 25th, 1863. Upon examination of the injured limb, the fractured extremities of the femur were found to be united, with great angular deformity, by irregular arches of callus. A fragment of the ball was enclosed between the arches. The specimen was contributed by Assistant Surgeon Byrne, U. S. A. (Figure 43.)

The next figure represents a specimen in which consolidation is quite firm. The patient succumbed to phthisis seven months after the injury.

Private Luman M. Millius, Co. K, 6th Pennsylvania Reserves, was wounded at Antietam, September 17th, 1862, by a conoidal musket-ball, which entered a little below the great trochanter of the right thigh, shattered the upper third of the femur, and lodged beneath the skin on the inner part of the right thigh, whence it was extracted through an incision. The patient was treated in a field hospital until the middle of October, when he was transferred to the General Hospital, at Smoketown.

Fig. 43.—Partially consolidated gunshot fracture of the left femur. Spec. 1161, A. M. M.

Although a slender man, with a narrow chest and feeble organization, his condition on admission was not unpromising. During the autumn of 1862, the suppuration was copious, and fragments of necrosed bone were occasionally discharged. Under a nourishing diet, the patient's strength was supported remarkably. On January 21st, 1863, the fracture was firmly consolidated. The limb was shortened four inches. The wound on the inner side of the thigh had closed. There was a slight fistula, with trifling discharge at the wound of entrance. The patient passed several hours daily in the open air, on crutches. About this time, cough and night-sweats, and other indications of tuberculosis of the lungs, appeared, and confirmed phthisis was soon established. The patient died March 9th, 1863. (Figure 44.)

FIG. 44.—Upper half of right femur, exhibiting a consolidated gunshot fracture. *Spec.* 1042, A. M. M.

Of gunshot injuries of the knee-joint, the Museum possesses 355 specimens. A number of illustrations will be given.

The case that furnished Specimen No. 2134 (Private Baldwin, Co. K, 42d Indiana Vols.) was treated by laying open the knee-joint, by free incisions, as soon as suppuration was established. The patient was wounded September 20th, at Murfreesboro', and died December 12th, 1863. The injury to the outer condyle was very slight. The specimen was contributed by Surgeon Israel Moses, U. S. Vols.

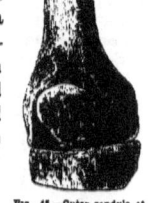

FIG. 45.—Outer condyle of right femur, grooved by a musket-ball. *Spec.* 2134, A. M. M.

Dr. Bellanger has recorded* five fatal cases of gunshot injuries of the knee-joint treated by free incisions into the articulation, and Surgeon Lidell, U. S. Vols., has published three such cases.† The records contain a score of similar examples. Yet amputations for gunshot injuries of the knee that have reached the secondary period are scarcely less disastrous.

FIG. 46.—Gunshot fracture of the internal condyle of the left knee. *Spec.* 1599, A. M. M.

The next case well illustrates the obscurity of symptoms and difficulty of diagnosis of a serious gunshot injury of an articulation so accessible for examination as the knee. The fracture of the internal condyle was not discovered until after death. The specimen was contributed by Surgeon J. A. Lidell, U. S. Vols.

Private Kisner, aged twenty-nine, Co. E, 7th Michigan Cavalry, was wounded June 19th, 1863, while on picket at Chantilly, Virginia, by an elongated carbine-ball, which entered in front at the middle of the left thigh. He was admitted to hospital, in Washington, on June 26th, and the ball was cut out from beneath the integument on the inner aspect of the knee. On the next day, there was pain and tenderness of the joint. Death took place July 18th, 1863.

In the next case a conoidal ball, fired from a great distance, has crushed the anterior part of the femur just above the condyles, and produced fissures that extend to the joint. The patient that furnished this specimen was wounded at Petersburg, March 31st, was amputated at Emory Hospital, April 7th, and died on June 24th, 1865. The specimen was contributed by Surgeon N. B. Mosely, U. S. Vols.

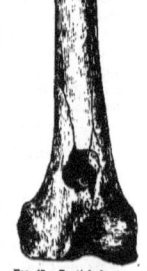

FIG. 47.—Partial fracture of the left femur by a conoidal ball, which has lodged in the cancellated structure. *Spec.* 4071, A. M. M.

The two following figures exhibit the common appearances of fractures of the bones composing the knee-joint by round musket-balls.

Private Richard Williams, 28th Pennsylvania Vols., was wounded September 16th, 1862, at the battle of South Mountain, by a musket-ball, which entered near the outer hamstring, and lodged between the condyles of the right femur. He was conveyed to Washington, D. C.,

---

* American Journal of Medical Sciences, vol. xlvi. p. 42.   † Ibid., vol. xlix. p. 295.

GUNSHOT WOUNDS OF THE LOWER EXTREMITIES.

and admitted into Mount Pleasant General Hospital, September 22d, 1862. On September 30th, his right thigh was amputated by flap incisions. At this date the limb was excessively swollen; the discharge of pus was profuse; abscesses had burrowed in the soft parts, and irritative fever existed to an alarming degree. The case terminated fatally on October 2d, 1862.

Private —— ——, a soldier of the 3d Division of the 1st Army Corps, was wounded at Gettysburg, Pennsylvania, on July 1st, 1863, by a musket-ball, which entered through the right popliteal space, fissured the internal condyle of the femur, and lodged in the head of the tibia. He underwent amputation at the lower third of the thigh on July 15th, and died July 17th, 1863. The specimen was contributed by Surgeon Quinan, in charge of the Division Hospital. (Figure 49.)

FIG. 49.—Amputated end of right femur and head of tibia, with a round musket-ball impacted in the latter. Spec. 1481, A. M. M.

FIG. 48.—Lower extremity of right femur, the outer condyle split off by a round musket-ball. Spec. 50, A. M. M.

Three patients have been photographed at the Army Medical Museum who had recovered without amputation after gunshot injuries of the knee-joint. (Photographs Nos. 63, 64, and 78.) Four or five additional cases appear upon the records. In scarcely any of these cases could it be asserted that the danger of consecutive disease of the knee-joint was passed. The "curious fact," adverted to by Surgeon I. Moses, U. S. Vols.,* "that more men had been discharged the service at that post [Louisville, Kentucky] who had received gunshot wounds of the knee-joint with recovery than when amputation of the thigh had been performed," is directly contradicted by the official reports from that post.

The following is the most carefully compiled of the abstracts of cases of recovery after gunshot wounds involving the knee. Photograph 63, A. M. M., represents the patient.

Private Peter Stuck, Co. E, 116th Pennsylvania Vols., was wounded on May 12th, 1864, at the battle of Spottsylvania, and was admitted, on May 18th, to Douglas Hospital, in Washington. The projectile, which was probably a conoidal musket-ball, had entered at the inner edge of the right patella, passed directly through the articulation, and made its exit near the centre of the popliteal space. The inner condyle was slightly grooved, but the ball passed mainly through the intercondyloid notch. There was an abundant thin discharge of mingled pus and synovia. The joint was somewhat swollen, but the inflammatory symptoms and constitutional disturbance were moderate. The patient was of a delicate organization. The treatment was limited to rest and water-dressings. On June 9th, there was swelling and pain in the joint, and a febrile reaction. Poultices were applied to the wound of exit, the anterior wound having healed. In a few days the bad symptoms abated. In the latter part of August, 1864, the patient began to walk about on crutches, the leg being flexed at an angle of 135° with the thigh. In October, the limb was bandaged to a movable angular splint, and the flexion was gradually reduced. Almost complete extension was obtained without exciting inflammation in the joint. The patient kept his bed during this period of the treatment. For the following eight months nothing of special interest transpired. There were several attacks of inflammation of the joint; but they were moderate in degree, and were readily subdued by poulticing. On such occasions abscesses sometimes formed in the thigh. For the greater part of the time the patient's appetite was fair, his bowels regular, his sleep refreshing. When inflammatory mischief was threatened, poultices, hot fomentations with flannel covered with oiled silk, and applications of tincture of iodine were employed. At other times, cold water-dressings, with charpie to absorb the discharge, were used. Ice was never applied. A photograph was taken July 9th, and the patient was discharged from service and the hospital July 14th, 1865. The posterior wound was still open, and a probe could be

FIG. 50.—Destruction of the left knee by a shell explosion. Spec. 700, A. M. M.

---

* American Journal of Medical Sciences, vol. xlvii. p. 341.

38   ON SPECIAL WOUNDS AND INJURIES.

introduced through it for three inches. There was a large deposit of new bone. The patella was firmly anchylosed to the femur. The facts of the case were forwarded by Assistant Surgeon Wm. F. Norris, U. S. A.

Two more illustrations of gunshot injuries of the knee-joint are here introduced:

The patient who furnished the first (Private B. M——. Co. A, 28th Massachusetts Vols.) was brought to Washington on December 26th, 1862, his left knee having been shattered by a shell at the battle of Fredericksburg, on December 14th. He died on December 29th. Evidently primary amputation could alone have saved this man, and this was probably impracticable on that disastrous day. (See Figure 50 on the preceding page.)

In the next case of shell wound involving the knee-joint (Private C. H. M——, Co. F, 1st Maine Heavy Artillery), primary amputation was performed on October 2d, by Surgeon Jamieson, 86th New York Vols. The patient died of exhaustive suppuration on October 27th, 1864. (Figure 51.)

FIG. 51.—Upper portion of left tibia comminuted by a fragment of the base of a shell, which is attached. Spec. 4121, A. M. M.

Of gunshot injuries of the tibia and fibula, two examples are given, one of fracture by a musket-ball, the other of comminution by solid shot:

A general officer was wounded at the assault on Port Hudson, May 27th, 1863, by a conoidal musket-ball, which passed from the inner to the outer aspect of the right leg, and shattered the upper thirds of the tibia and fibula. A staff surgeon extracted a number of detached fragments of bone, and dressed the limb, and, on June 2d, the patient was removed to New Orleans. The wounds were opened, and decomposed coagula, pus, and bone splinters in large quantities were evacuated. The constitutional symptoms were of the most aggravated character. About the middle of June, amputation was performed at the lower third of the thigh by Professor Warren Stone, with the very slightest hope of success. The patient, however, struggled through, and ultimately wore an artificial limb with comfort. The specimen and the particulars of the case were contributed by Prof. F. Bacon, of Yale College, formerly Surgeon U. S. Vols. (Figure 52.)

Major General D. E. Sickles, U. S. Vols., was wounded on the evening of the second day of the battle of Gettysburg, by a twelve-pounder solid shot, which shattered his right leg. General Sickles was on horseback at the time and unattended. He succeeded in quieting his affrighted horse and in dismounting unassisted. Aid arriving promptly, he was removed a short distance to the rear, to a sheltered ravine, and amputation was performed low down in the thigh by Surgeon Thomas Sim, U. S. Vols. The patient was then sent to the rear, and the following day was transferred to Washington. The stump healed with great rapidity. On July 16th, the patient was able to ride about in a carriage. Early in September, 1863, the stump was completely cicatrized, and the general was able again to mount his horse. The specimen was contributed to the Army Medical Museum by General Sickles, and the facts of the case by his staff surgeon, Dr. Sim. (Figure 53.)

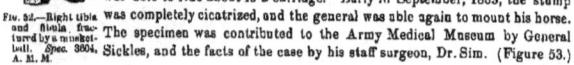

FIG. 52.—Right tibia and fibula fractured by a musket-ball. Spec. 3604, A. M. M.

FIG. 53.—Right tibia and fibula shattered by a cannon-shot. Spec. 1335, A. M. M.

GUNSHOT WOUNDS OF THE ARTERIES.

The number of cases reported under this head is extremely small. In the campaign of the Army of the Potomac from the Rapidan to the James, in May, June, and July, 1864, of a total of 36,508 gunshot wounds, only 27 belonged to this category. The cases of compound fracture complicated with injuries of the large vessels, the cases in which limbs are carried away by solid shot or shell, and the cases in which all the tissues of a limb are disorganized by contusion from a large projectile and the vitality of the arteries is destroyed, are all returned under other heads. Those only are included in which the canal of a large vessel is primarily opened, and in which this is the principal accident. Such cases are to be sought for among the dead on the battle-field rather than in the field hospitals. Surgeon J. A. Lidell, U. S. Vols., reports that on the morning of March 25th, 1865, he examined 43 bodies of soldiers killed in the combat near Fort Steadman, in the lines before Petersburg; 23 were shot in the head, 15 in the chest, and 5 in the abdomen. "The bodies of all those wounded in the abdomen were very much blanched, as if they had died of hæmorrhage, and the same remark held true in regard to all but two or three of those wounded in the chest." In the few cases of primary gunshot lesions of the arteries that came under treatment, it was usually found that only a portion of the calibre of the vessel had been carried away, and that retraction had been thus prevented. But 44 cases are entered on the records. In most of them, ligatures were placed above and below the seat of injury; but, in a few instances, the main trunk was tied at a distance, and amputation was practised when the bleeding recurred. Twenty of the 44 cases terminated fatally.

A number of drawings at the Army Medical Museum, exhibiting the course of balls directly in the track of the great vessels of the neck or of the limbs, illustrate the fact so well known to military surgeons of the great resiliency of the large arteries. The dread of primary hæmorrhage on the battle-field is confined to the inexperienced. It was so exaggerated at the beginning of the war, that it was seriously proposed by several benevolent associations that every soldier should carry a field tourniquet with his equipments.

GUNSHOT WOUNDS OF VEINS.

No cases have been reported in which the bleeding could not be controlled by pressure.

GUNSHOT WOUNDS OF NERVES.

Only those cases are recorded as yet upon the register that were reported in the last quarter of 1863 and the first quarter of 1864. Numerous and careful observations on this class of injuries have been received from the Christian Street Hospital, in Philadelphia, in which wards were especially assigned, in 1863, for the treatment of such cases.

SABRE AND BAYONET WOUNDS.

The number of sabre and bayonet wounds that have come under treatment has been comparatively small; 105 cases of the former, and 143 of the latter comprise nearly all that have been reported for the first three years of the war. Of these wounds, two-thirds were received in action, and the remainder were inflicted by sentinels or patrols. There are 11 deaths from sword wounds recorded, and 6 from bayonet wounds. At the Army Medical Museum there are 9 specimens of sabre cuts of the cranium,* a specimen of punctured fracture of the skull by a bayonet, and a preparation exhibiting a bayonet thrust through the stomach.† From General Sheridan's

---

* Specimens 235, 970, 971, 974, 1672, 2623, 3307, 3684, 4206.   † Specimen 2258, A. M. M.

campaign in the Shenandoah Valley, 25 sabre wounds are reported; and from the battle of Jonesborough, in Georgia, 30 bayonet wounds. After the first battle of Bull Run, several of the wounded left upon the field were bayoneted by the insurgents.* A patient, brought afterwards to Georgetown, received no less than fourteen stabs. A similar instance occurred after the battle of Fair Oaks.† Later in the war such atrocities were very infrequent. A few abstracts are subjoined of cases of sword and bayonet wounds:

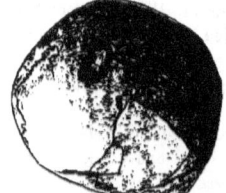

Private R—— H——, Co. C, 7th Colored Regiment, U. S. Artillery, was wounded at Fort Pillow, Tennessee, April 12th, 1864, by three sabre cuts on the left side of the head, one of the wounds penetrating the skull. The symptoms are not recorded, but it is stated that the patient died on April 21st, 1864, and that the post-mortem examination revealed a large extravasation of blood upon the brain, and a splinter an inch and a half long from the inner table driven through the dura mater.

FIG. 54.—Three sabre cuts on the left parietal. *Spec.* 3307, A. M. M.

Private J. T. B——, Co. F, 7th Michigan Cavalry, was captured on July 3d, 1863, at Gettysburg, his horse being shot under him. He was hurried to the rear with other prisoners. In the subsequent retreat he was unable to keep up with the column, and all efforts to goad him on being unavailing, a confederate lieutenant, in command of the provost guard, cut him down, and left him for dead by the roadside. He was brought in by a scouting party, and admitted to the Cavalry Corps Hospital. On the 25th of July, he was sufficiently rational to give the above account to Surgeon Rulison, 9th New York Cavalry. He was in a very depressed state at this time. His pulse was weak, and beat from 40 to 45 per minute. He was indisposed to mental exertion; but when aroused and interested was quite rational. He lingered until August 15th, 1863, the tendency to stupor becoming greater and greater towards the close. The autopsy revealed a sabre cut six inches long, which had raised an osseous flap, adherent at its base, from the left parietal, and cloven the right parietal, with great splintering of the vitreous plate. The sabre had penetrated the dura mater on the left side, and on the right side the meninges were injured by the depressed inner table. The posterior lobes of both hemispheres of the brain were extensively disorganized. The specimen, with the above history, was contributed by Surgeon W. H. Rulison, 9th New York Cavalry, since killed in battle.

FIG. 55.—Section of the posterior portion of a cranium, showing a sabre cut of both parietals parallel to the lambdoidal suture. *Spec.* 1672, A. M. M.

FIG. 56.—Portion of a sphenoid bone transfixed by a sword. *Spec.* 1612, A. M. M.

Private John H——, aged twenty-five, of the guard of Lovell General Hospital, Portsmouth Grove, Rhode Island, was confined on February 28th, 1863, in a strong box, as a punishment for bringing liquor into camp. When released, he rushed upon the sergeant of the guard and struck him, whereupon the sergeant drew his sword and put himself *en garde*. In this position the prisoner made a second assault, but the ground being uneven he slipped, and fell heavily upon the point of the sword, and to the ground. When raised, his face was bleeding, and he was insensible. He was examined by the medical officer of the day, who found a slight cut on the ala of the nose, and ascribed the insensibility to intoxication, and ordered him to the fall on the head. The prisoner was removed to the guard-house and there spent the night. In the morning, he was still unconscious and breathed stertorously, and had a slow pulse and dilated pupils. He was removed to a ward in the hospital, and the remedies commonly employed in cases of apoplexy were prescribed. There was no return of consciousness, and the case terminated fatally on March 2d, thirty-one hours after the injury. At the autopsy, it was found that the sword had entered at the right nostril, pierced the right superior turbinated bone and the body of the sphenoid, and caused a transverse fracture at the base of the posterior clinoid process. There was much extravasated blood in the cranial cavity, especially on the surface of the right hemisphere.

---

* Surgeon Joseph R. Smith's Report.
† Report of Assistant Surgeon H. E. Brown, 70th New York Vols.

TETANUS.

Private Thomas B——, Co. B, 90th Ohio Vols., was admitted into Hospital No. 1, Nashville, Tennessee, on November 27th, 1863, with a bayonet wound behind the left parietal protuberance, inflicted by a sentinel, whom the patient, being intoxicated, had refused to obey. For several days after admission he was somnolent and obstinately constipated. Under the use of powerful purgatives this condition was removed, and the wound nearly cicatrized. But, on December 8th, the patient complained of headache, and a probe passed through the small orifice of the wound revealed the presence of denuded and detached bone. A crucial incision was made and the fragments of dead bone were removed. On December 11th, there was more headache, and a tendency to stupor; the pulse was at 48; there was intolerance of light and sound; the scalp was tumid; the wound gaping, and filled with fungous granulations. The incisions in the scalp were extended, an ice-bladder was applied to the head, and purgatives and purgative enemata were employed. A day or two subsequently cerebral hernia took place; then extended suppuration in the left hemisphere; then delirium and coma, and death on December 23d, 1863. The description and specimen were contributed by Assistant Surgeon C. J. Kipp, U. S. Vols.

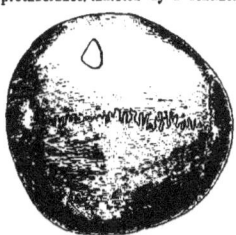

FIG. 57.—Skull-cap, exhibiting a fracture of the left parietal bone by a bayonet. Spec. 2179, A. M. M.

SIMPLE FRACTURES AND MISCELLANEOUS WOUNDS.

The number of cases reported is quite large, and the record is still very incomplete. For the first two years of the war, the monthly reports give of simple fractures alone 2864 cases with 92 deaths.

The Army Medical Museum possesses comparatively few illustrations of this class of injuries, and it is to be desired that this department of the collection may be augmented.

Specimen No. 6 presents a good example of a united simple fracture of the femur through the trochanters. It was taken from a man of forty, who died of pneumonia two years after recovery from the local injury.

The number of incised and fractured wounds received in broils and altercations is quite numerous. The following is an interesting example of this class of cases:

Private George S——, Co. B, 15th New York Engineers, was stabbed in the back by a dirk, April 20th, 1863, at Falmouth, Virginia, in an altercation with a comrade. The blade passed between the transverse processes of the fourth and fifth vertebræ, and severed the spinal cord. The man fell instantly, completely paraplegic. He was admitted to Armory Square Hospital, at Washington, April 22d. On April 27th, he began to pass his fæces and urine involuntarily, and bed-sores appeared on the portions of the lower part of the body exposed to pressure. He sank gradually, and died from exhaustion on May 27th, 1863. The specimen was contributed by Assistant Surgeon C. C. Byrne, U. S. A.

FIG. 59.—Fourth, fifth, and a portion of the sixth dorsal vertebræ, sawn asunder to exhibit a dirk which traversed the spinal canal. Spec. 1160, A. M. M.

FIG. 58.—Firmly consolidated simple fracture of the left femur. Spec. No. 6, A. M. M.

TETANUS.

The 363 cases of traumatic tetanus recorded in the register for that subject are all that have been reported during the war. The proportion to the total number of wounds is not large. In the Schleswick Holstein war, Stromeyer had 6 cases among 2000 wounded. In Napoleon's campaign in Egypt, in the Peninsular campaign, and in the revolt in India, the ratio appears to have been larger than this. Among 12,094 wounded, the British in the Crimea had 19 cases only.

The histories of the 363 reported cases of tetanus are generally satisfactory in their details of symptoms, progress, and treatment: 336 cases terminated fatally. Of the 27 recoveries reported, the disease was of a chronic form in 23. In the 4 remaining cases, the symptoms were very grave. In 2, recovery took place under the use of opiates and stimulants; in 2, after amputation of the wounded part.

The great majority of the cases were treated by the free use of opium, conjoined with stimulants and concentrated nourishment. Chloroform inhalations were very generally employed during the paroxysms of spasmodic contraction. Subcutaneous injections of the salts of morphia and atropia were frequently used. Cathartics, quinia, camphor, cannabis indica, bromide of potassium, strychnia, belladonna, and aconite are mentioned among the remedies employed. Cups, blisters, turpentine stupes, and ice were among the applications made to the spine; and fomentations with opium or tobacco were, in some cases, applied to the wound. Amputation, the division of nerves, and the extirpation of neuromata in stumps were the surgical measures sometimes employed. The results have not modified the conclusion of Romberg, that "wherever tetanus puts on the acute form, no curative proceeding will avail, while in the milder and more tardy form, the most various remedies have been followed by cure." The value of nicotine, of the Calabar bean, and of curare* as curative agents in tetanus was not tested.

Autopsies were made in many cases; but with almost negative results. There were no microscopic examinations to corroborate or disprove the assertions of Rokitansky and Demme,[†] that tetanus has a constant anatomical lesion, consisting in a proliferation of the connective tissue of the white medullary substance of the medulla oblongata, of the inferior peduncles of the cerebellum, of the crura cerebri, and of the spinal cord, producing a viscous mass, abounding in nuclei, and never progressing to the formation of fibres. It is frequently mentioned, however, that great congestion of the brain and spinal cord was observed, a condition on which the lesions of the connective tissue above described are believed to depend.

The records abound with illustrations of the influence of sudden vicissitudes of temperature in producing this fatal affection, and of the effect which unextracted balls and other foreign bodies and matter confined under fasciæ appear to exercise upon its development. It seems probable also that the disease occurred in a larger proportion of cases among the troops serving in the more Southern States; but this and other generalizations must be deferred until the records are more minutely examined.

SECONDARY HÆMORRHAGE.

On this important subject the records are still very incomplete. There are 1450 special reports relating to it yet to be examined, which will furnish a large number of cases to be transcribed upon the register. The cases have been reported in three

---

* According to H. Demme, of 22 cases of traumatic tetanus treated by the latter agent, 8 recovered. See Schweiz. Zeitschrift für Heilkunde, ii. 356.
† Schmidt's Jahrbucher, vol. cxii.

classes: bleeding proceeding from a stump, from a gunshot wound, or from an artery previously ligated in its continuity. Cases of the latter series have not been placed on the registers of secondary hæmorrhage, but the repetition of the bleeding has been noted in the history of the case in the volume of the registers of surgical operations devoted to ligations.*

Of the two other classes, 1037 cases have been examined and recorded on the registers of secondary hæmorrhage. Of these, 387 were cases of secondary bleeding from a stump, and 650 were cases of secondary hæmorrhage from gunshot wounds. Of the first class, 233, or 60 per cent., ended fatally; of the second, the termination was fatal in 330 cases, or 51 per cent.

In the 1037 recorded cases, the femoral artery was ligated 93 times for bleeding from stumps, and 45 times for bleeding from wounds; the subclavian was tied 5 times for bleeding after amputation at the shoulder-joint, and 6 times for hæmorrhage from gunshot wounds of the axilla. The common carotid was ligated 15 times for hæmorrhage from the deep branches of the internal carotid. Amputation was practised 78 times for secondary bleeding from gunshot wounds, and reamputation was performed 14 times when other means of arresting hæmorrhage from stumps had failed.

The 387 cases of secondary hæmorrhage from stumps were chiefly examples of arterial bleeding. In 95 cases, the hæmorrhage was, perhaps, mainly venous, and was checked by elevating the stump, or applying cold water, ice, pressure, or the solution of the persulphate of iron. When the hæmorrhage was arterial, the most common practice was to tie the main vessel, at the second bleeding, as near as was prudent to the end of the stump. In a few cases, the artery was successfully tied on the face of the stump. The results of tying the vessel above, according to Anel's method, were very unfortunate.

In reviewing the 650 recorded cases of secondary hæmorrhage from gunshot wounds, it appears that, during the earlier part of the war, there were many surgeons who were not sufficiently impressed by the precepts of Bell and Guthrie, and who frequently treated secondary hæmorrhage from gunshot wounds by tying the main trunk at a distance from the wound, even when the bleeding occurred at a comparatively early period. Later in the war, however, it was the universal practice to endeavor to secure both ends of the bleeding vessel at the seat of injury, and some brilliant examples are recorded in which this was accomplished in wounds of the posterior tibial or popliteal, when limbs had become infiltrated and swollen, and the difficulties of the operations were immense.

PYÆMIA.

On this subject 281 reports have been examined, and the individual cases detailed in them have been transcribed upon the registers: 251 special reports on the subject remain to be examined. The histories of 754 cases are recorded in the register, the post-mortem observations accompanying a large proportion of the fatal cases. These number 719, or 95·35 per cent. Pyæmia supervened in 377 cases of gunshot injury in which no operation had been performed, and after 295 cases of amputation, of which

* See page 85 of this Report.

155 were cases of amputation in the continuity of the femur. The purulent infection was subsequent to excision of the shafts of long bones in 27 cases, and to excisions of joints in 28 cases.

These figures by no means represent the frequency with which pyæmic poisoning has occurred. It has been one of the great sources of mortality after amputations, and its victims are to be counted by thousands. The small number of cases on the register are taken from special reports. Several valuable papers have been contributed on the pathology of this affection, and a number of statistical reports on its treatment. The conclusions of the latter are adverse to the therapeutical utility of the sulphites and hyposulphites in this disease.

A series of colored drawings, illustrating the embolic phenomena attendant on pyæmia, the metastatic dépôts, etc., have been prepared at the Army Medical Museum.

SURGICAL OPERATIONS.

All surgical operations are recorded on the registers of the office, according to the form which will be presented on a subsequent page, in treating of excisions of the head of the femur. The name and military description of the patient are given, the nature and date of his injury, an account of the operation, a notice of the local lesions which made it necessary, and of the constitutional condition of the patient at the period it was performed. A summary of the progress and after-treatment follows, and the result, if ascertained, the name of the operator, and the post-mortem appearances, when known, if the case terminated fatally. If the case furnished a pathological preparation to the Army Medical Museum, a reference is made to the number of the specimen on the catalogue.

While this plan involves much labor, it effectually precludes the duplication of cases, and ensures, probably, the highest attainable degree of statistical accuracy. The name and military designation of the patient being known in all cases, the ultimate results of operations can be traced, hereafter, and errors may be corrected.

Operations have been reported in this form from all general hospitals since October, 1863. But nearly half of the sixteen thousand operations now recorded were taken from special reports and field returns belonging to an earlier period of the war, and it was necessary that these should first be transcribed on the proper forms, a task that has been accomplished by clerks who were students of medicine, their work being revised by a medical officer.

AMPUTATIONS.

The histories of 13,397 amputations for gunshot injury have been examined and recorded, and the final results have been ascertained in 9705 cases. The following table exhibits the number belonging to each region, and includes both primary and secondary cases. It shows the regular increase in the rate of mortality as the trunk is approached.

Amputations of the Superior Extremities.	Recovered.	Died.	Total.	Per cent. of Mortality.
Fingers and Parts of the Hand	1778	29	1807	1·60
Wrist	34	2	36	5·55
Elbow	19	0	19	
Forearm	500	99	599	16·52
Arm	1535	414	1949	21·24
Shoulder-Joint	144	93	237	39·24
Total of Upper Extremity	4010	637	4647	13·70
Amputations of the Inferior Extremities.				
Toes	784	6	790	·75
Partial Amputations of the Foot	108	11	119	9·24
Ankle-Joint	58	9	67	13·43
Leg	1737	611	2348	26·02
Knee-Joint	52	64	116	55·17
Thigh	568	1029	1597	64·43
Hip-Joint	3	18	21	85·71
Total of Lower Extremity	3310	1748	5058	34·55
Aggregate	7320	2385	9705	24·57

AMPUTATIONS OF THE FINGERS AND PORTIONS OF THE HAND.—The cases that have been transcribed on the records form but a small proportion of the total number included in the reports. In the 1807 terminated cases, the mortality has been comparatively large. The causes of death in the 29 fatal cases is stated to have been: in 4, pyæmia; in 4, erysipelas; in 2, gangrene; in 1, tetanus; in 18, different intercurrent diseases, as typhoid and malarial fevers, pleurisy, etc.

AMPUTATIONS AT THE WRIST.—The disarticulation at the wrist has been performed in preference to the amputation of the forearm, when the hand was totally disorganized. When practised by the circular method it is a good operation. The results of the cases examined are satisfactory, the mortality being ten per cent. less than in amputation of the forearm.

AMPUTATIONS OF THE FOREARM.—Except in those cases in which the wrist or lower extremity of the radius have been shattered by large projectiles, this amputation has commonly been practised secondarily. It has been impracticable to examine all the cases that have been reported. Of the terminated cases that have been transcribed upon the records, 99 died and 500 recovered. Of the latter, 397 have been supplied with artificial limbs. In the forearm, the amputation by the double flap method has been generally preferred.

AMPUTATIONS AT THE ELBOW.—The returns corroborate the conclusions of Dupuytren, Malgaigne, and Legouest, who combat the disfavor into which this operation has fallen. It was done infrequently in the late war, but 19 cases having been reported. But in all of these the ultimate results have been ascertained, and were favorable in every instance. The success of Salleron and other French surgeons with this operation in the Crimea is well known. Whenever, then, it is impracticable to amputate the forearm, disarticulation at the elbow should be preferred to amputation of the arm. The oval method answers the purpose best in this locality.

AMPUTATIONS OF THE ARM.—Of 2774 cases of amputation of the arm that have been entered on the registers, the results are ascertained in 1949 cases: 1535 recovered, and 1014 of these patients have been furnished with artificial arms.

AMPUTATIONS AT THE SHOULDER-JOINT.—It is creditable to the surgery of the war that the number of cases of amputation at the shoulder-joint reported is less than the number of cases of excisions of the head of the humerus, and that the latter operation appears to have been adopted in nearly all the cases in which it was admissible. The reported cases of amputation at the shoulder-joint, for the entire period, number 458; of excisions of the head of the humerus, there were 575. Of the 237 terminated cases of amputation, 93 died, a ratio of mortality of 39·2, which is 6·7 per cent. greater than the mortality in excisions. The amputations of the upper extremity for gunshot injuries are illustrated at the Army Medical Museum by 89 examples of diseases of stumps, and by a large number of plaster casts and photographs, exhibiting the successful results of operations.

AMPUTATIONS OF THE TOES.—Of 784 cases that have been examined, 6 were fatal. Tetanus supervened in one case, and phlegmonous erysipelas invaded the leg in another. In the four remaining cases, the fatal termination was due to causes foreign to the operation.

PARTIAL AMPUTATIONS OF THE FOOT.—Of the 160 recorded cases, 119 were terminated, with a mortality of 9·24 per cent. The tarso-metatarsal operation of Hey or Lisfranc was performed 25 times; the medio-tarsal operation of Chopart 45 times. The remaining cases were ablations of toes with one or more of the metatarsals. There are several casts of stumps, made by Chopart's method, at the Army Medical Museum, which exhibit the drawing up of the heel which so frequently occurs after this operation.

AMPUTATIONS AT THE ANKLE-JOINT.—The record is far from complete. In the terminated cases, Syme's method was employed in 25 cases, Roux's method in 2 cases, and Pirogoff's in 9 cases. Several casts and photographs of well-rounded stumps, obtained by the latter procedure, are deposited in the Army Medical Museum. But the operation appears to be regarded with but little favor. Baron von Horronitz, Surgeon-in-Chief of the Russian Marine, in his recent visit to this office, mentioned that Pirogoff had himself abandoned it, finding the segment of the os calcis likely to become necrosed. An abstract of a favorable case, with an illustration, is subjoined:

AMPUTATIONS. 47

Lieutenant W. C. W——, Co. I, 5th Michigan Cavalry, was wounded April 1st, 1865, at the battle of Five Forks, by a conoidal musket-ball, which passed through his left ankle-joint He was immediately carried to the hospital at City Point, and amputation at the ankle was performed on the same day by Surgeon St. Clair, 5th Michigan Cavalry. The articulating surfaces of the tibia and calcaneum were removed, and the cut surfaces were brought into apposition. On April 16th, 1865, the patient was transferred to Armory Square Hospital, at Washington. On admission, he was in a feeble condition. An erysipelatous blush extended above the knee on the injured side; an abscess had formed in the lower part of the flap had been taken place. With the employment of stimulants and nutritious diet with emollient applications to the limb, there was a gradual improvement, until April 28th, 1865, when symptoms of pyæmic infection supervened. Rapidly recurring chills, an icteroid coloration of the skin and conjunctiva, anorexia, and a frequent feeble pulse, suggested the gravest prognosis. Energetic treatment was adopted. An ounce of brandy was given every two hours, and quinia, sesquichloride of iron, and beef tea were freely administered. On May 6th, the grave symptoms began to subside, and, by the end of the month, the patient was fairly convalescent. On June 26th, he was pronounced well. The os calcis had firmly united to the tibia, and there was a good solid stump. A cast in plaster was taken from it (Spec. 2298, A. M. M.), and a few days subsequently a photograph, which is numbered 75 in the Photographic Series of the Army Medical Museum.

FIG. 60.—Stump after a Pirogoff amputation.

AMPUTATIONS OF THE LEG.—Of the 3802 amputations of the leg that have been recorded, the results have been ascertained in 2348. The ratio of mortality was 26·02, which will doubtless be augmented by further examination of the returns. The operation just above the malleoli, sometimes called Lenoir's operation, has not been very largely practised, but it has given some excellent results, and its mortality rate is surprisingly small. The majority of the cases were amputations at the middle of the leg and at the place of election. The circular method has been most commonly employed. Larrey's operation through the head of the tibia has been done but little, though an examination of the specimens at the Army Medical Museum leads to the conviction that this procedure might have been substituted, in some instances, for disarticulation at the knee-joint, or amputations at the lower third of the thigh. Of the 1737 patients that recovered after amputation of the leg, 1057 have been furnished with artificial limbs.

AMPUTATIONS AT THE KNEE-JOINT.—This operation has found numerous advocates during the war, and has been frequently performed. The returns to October, 1864, give 132 cases, of which 52 recovered and 64 died. In 6 cases, amputation of the thigh was subsequently performed, with 3 recoveries and 3 deaths. In 10 cases, the result is undetermined. These figures are encouraging, and if we look at the primary operations alone, the result is still more gratifying. Of 49 cases of primary amputation at the knee-joint, 31 recovered and 16 died; while 2 underwent reamputation, of whom 1 recovered, and 1, a tuberculous subject, died. This gives a percentage of mortality in primary amputations at the knee-joint of 34·9. The mortality in primary amputation at the lower third of the thigh is much larger than this: indeed, it has been already indisputably proved by the Crimean statistics, and by M. Malgaigne, that the mortality in amputation augments in exact proportion as the incisions approach the trunk.

At the Army Medical Museum there is a photograph, accompanying Specimen 2778, of the fine, well-rounded stump of Private Nevelling, Co. A, 71st Pennsylvania

Vols., who was wounded at White Oak Swamp, and amputated, at Philadelphia, by Acting Assistant Surgeon T. G. Morton. The objection to amputations at the knee-joint, that the resulting stump is ill adapted to the use of an artificial limb, is set at rest by the results obtained by Hudson and other manufacturers, who distinctly declare that the stumps from the operation at the knee-joint give a base of support far better than any possibly to be gained in thigh-stumps.

It is well known that M. Legouest emphatically pronounces the disarticulation at the knee "une mauvaise opération, plus grave que l'amputation de la cuisse dans la continuité, et qui doit etre rejetée de la pratique," basing this assertion on the Crimean returns; but it is probable that the more extended experience of the late war will lead surgeons to share the convictions of Macleod, Baudens, and Malgaigne, that this operation is altogether preferable to the amputation at the lower third of the thigh.

AMPUTATIONS OF THE THIGH.—In 1597 terminated cases, 568 recovered and 1029 died, or 64·43 per cent., which is within a fraction of the mortality after amputations of the thigh in the English army in the Crimea during the latter part of the campaign. In the French army in the Crimea, the whole number of amputations of the thigh for gunshot injuries was 1666, of which 1531, or 91·89 per cent., terminated fatally.

Of these 1597 amputations, the date of operation is ascertained with precision in 1061. Of these, 423 were primary and 638 were intermediate or secondary. The ratio of mortality was 54·13 in the former, and 74·76 in the latter.

In the 568 recoveries after amputation of the thigh above mentioned, the patients have been supplied with artificial limbs in 254 cases, and reports are on file of 439 other cases of recovery after this operation in which artificial limbs have been provided. These cases are not entered on the registers, because the returns exhibiting the deaths for the corresponding periods have not yet been reached.

AMPUTATIONS AT THE HIP-JOINT.—At the commencement of the war, the uniform fatality of amputation at the hip-joint in the Crimean war was impressed upon the minds of surgeons, and many believed that the operation should be discarded altogether. Still, it has been occasionally performed, and several lives have unquestionably been saved by it. A noted case is that of Kelly, whose appearance, after recovery, is represented in the plate opposite. The following is an abstract of the case:

Private James E. Kelly, Co. B, 56th Pennsylvania Vols., aged twenty-eight years, was wounded at about 9 o'clock of the morning of April 29th, 1863, in a skirmish of the First Division, First Corps, on the Rappahannock, nearly opposite the "Pratt House," below Fredericksburg. A conoidal musket-ball, fired from a distance of about three hundred yards, shattered his left femur. A consultation of the senior surgeons of brigades decided that exarticulation of the femur was expedient, and the operation was performed, at four in the afternoon, at the "Fitzhugh House," by Surgeon Edward Shippen, U. S. Vols., Surgeon-in-Chief of the First Division. The single flap method was adopted, and the amputation was accomplished with slight loss of blood. The patient was at first placed in a hospital tent, and was transferred, May 22d, to the Corps Hospital, progressing favorably. By May 28th, all the ligatures had been removed. On June 15th, 1863, the patient was captured by the enemy, and was removed to the Libby Prison, in Richmond. Up to this date there had been no bad symptoms. On July 14th, Kelly was exchanged, and was sent to the Annapolis U. S. A. General Hospital. On his admission, he was much exhausted by profuse diarrhœa. The internal portion of the wound had united, but the external portion was gangrenous. Applications of bromine were made to the sloughing surface without amelioration. A chlorinated soda lotion was substituted, and in the latter part of July, there was a healthy granulating surface. On December 23d, 1863, the wound had entirely healed, and Kelly visited Washington and obtained an honorable discharge from service, and a pension. Kelly then went to his home, near Black Lick P. O., Indiana County, Pennsylvania. A letter dated January 12th, 1865, received from him at this office, and represented him as in excellent health and spirits at that time. A year after the operation, a photograph of the stump was obtained. The accompanying plate is copied from it.

SHIPPEN'S SUCCESSFUL AMPUTATION AT THE HIP JOINT.

A successful primary case, operated upon at Memphis, by Dr. Fenner, is reported by a student of Dr. F. H. Hamilton, late Medical Inspector U. S. A., who saw the subject of it after his complete recovery.

A successful secondary case, reported by Assistant Surgeon C. Wagner, U. S. A., was a reamputation of a diseased stump. Necrosis of the femur was induced by osteomyelitis, and the disarticulation was effected at a period when the traumatic phenomena had entirely disappeared. The particulars of this case are subjoined:

Fig. 61.—Appearance of stump three months after secondary amputation at hip joint.

Private Eben. E. Smith, Co. A, 11th Maine Vols., aged nineteen years, was wounded at the engagement at Deep Bottom, near Drury's Bluff, Virginia, on August 16th, 1864, by a musket-ball, which fractured the head of the right tibia. He was admitted at the U. S. General Hospital, at Beverly, New Jersey, on August 22d, 1864. On admission, the injured knee-joint was swollen and painful, and there was irritative fever of a moderate grade. On September 12th, secondary hæmorrhage occurred, and the thigh was amputated by circular incisions at the lower third, by Acting Assistant Surgeon T. M. Morton, U. S. A., the patient being under chloroform. The case progressed favorably until October 17th, when secondary hæmorrhage recurred, and was arrested by ligating the femoral artery in Scarpa's triangle. The stump remained swollen and painful, and furnished a profuse fœtid suppuration. Osteomyelitis supervened; the end of the femur protruded, and was removed by the chain-saw. Necrosis finally extended as high as the trochanters, and numerous abscesses formed. On January 19th, 1865, amputation at the hip-joint was performed, under chloroform, by Acting Assistant Surgeon J. H. Packard, U. S. A., the antero-posterior flap operation being adopted. On January 27th, there was hæmorrhage from the stump, and the external iliac artery was tied. The ligature separated on February 17th, and two days afterwards there was profuse bleeding from the divided artery, which was controlled by pressure for fourteen days. After this the patient rapidly improved. In April he was reported well, and Hospital Steward Baumgras, one of the artists of the Army Medical Museum, was sent to Beverly, and made the drawing from which the engraving was taken. It is numbered 67 in the Surgical Series of Drawings of the Surgeon General's Office. On April 12th, 1865. Smith was transferred to White Hall Hospital, near Bristol, Pennsylvania. Assistant Surgeon W. H. Forwood, U. S. A., reports that, on May 27th, 1865, he was discharged from service quite well and strong, the wounds being entirely healed. The necrosed lower portion of the femur is Specimen 3709; the upper portion is Specimen 81, A. M. M.

Another successful secondary disarticulation of the femur is reported, which was also a case of reamputation, necessitated by disease of the femur. The first amputation was performed at the lower third of the thigh on account of a bayonet wound of the knee-joint. The case is consequently excluded from the tabular statement of amputations for gunshot injury. The patient is represented in Photograph 113, A. M. M.

Private Lewis Francis, Co. I, 14th New York Vols., aged forty-three years, was admitted to Ladies' Home U. S. A. General Hospital, New York City, on October 28th, 1863. He had been wounded by a bayonet in the right knee, at the battle of Bull Run, July 21st, 1861, and was taken prisoner, and suffered amputation of the thigh in Richmond, Virginia, May 28th, 1862. The femur becoming diseased subsequently, its protruding extremity had been sawn off. What remained of the femur was necrosed, when the patient arrived in New York, and, on May 21st, 1864, the flaps were laid open, and the necrosed femur was removed by Surgeon Alexander B. Mott, U. S. Vols. No untoward symptoms followed, and the patient recovered, and was discharged from the service, August 12th, 1864.

A memorandum is subjoined of all amputations at the hip-joint for gunshot injury that have been reported. Nine were primary, and twelve were secondary operations. This is followed by a table exhibiting the results of this operation in previous wars.

SURGICAL OPERATIONS.

AMPUTATIONS AT

No.	Name of Operator.	Name and Rank of Patient.	Nature and Date of Injury.
1	David P. Smith, Surgeon U. S. Vols.	Private on Hospital Steamer Crescent City.	Comminution of the upper half of the femur by canister, April 6th, 1862.
2	Prof. Geo. E. Blackman, Act. Asst. Surgeon U. S. A.	Private on Hospital Transport.	Gunshot fracture of upper extremity of femur, April 6th, 1862.
3	E. S. Fenner, Surgeon P. A. C. S.	A private of the Confederate Army.	Gunshot fracture of the left femur, March, 1862.
4	Edward Shippen, Surgeon U. S. Vols.	Private James E. Kelly, aged 28, Co. B, 56th Penn. Vols.	Conoidal ball comminuted upper extremity of left femur, April 29th, 1862.
5	B. Howard, Asst. Surgeon U.S.A.	Private J. Martin, aged 20, Co. I, 146th N. Y. Vols.	Conoidal ball fractured the upper part of left femur, July 13th, 1863.
6	Unknown.	Private William Waters, Co. K, 123d N. Y. Vols.	Gunshot fracture of left femur, May 15th, 1864.
7	Prof. J. M. Carnochan, Act. Asst. Surgeon U. S. A.	Private of 9th Corps, aged 28.	Left femur shattered by a shell, May 18th, 1864.
8	Edward Shippen, Surgeon U. S. Vols.	Private J. M. Brown, Co. K, 63d Indiana Vols.	Fracture of upper third of right femur by a conoidal musket-ball, June 16th, 1864.
9	Edward Shippen, Surgeon U. S. Vols.	Private of 23d Corps.	Conoidal ball shattered head and neck of femur, and involved the hip-joint.
10	Peter Pineo, Medical Inspector U. S. A.	Private P. Johnson, Co. C, 2d Delaware Vols.	Fracture of the upper third of the right femur, and wound of the femoral artery, by a conoidal musket-ball, Dec. 14th, 1862.
11	Alexander Ingram, Asst. Surgeon U. S. A.	Private Charles Lockey, aged 19, Co. E, 7th Wisconsin Vols.	Upper third of right femur fractured by a musket-ball, May 12th, 1864.
12	H. C. Roberts, Asst. Surgeon U. S. Vols.	Private Levi Eckley, aged 33, Co. I, 67th Ohio Vols.	Gunshot fracture of left thigh, May 20th, 1864.
13	Albert C. Gorgas, Surgeon U. S. Navy.	Seaman George Cook, aged 21.	Rifle-ball passed through both testicles, and entered left thigh, comminuting the femur and passing out, Feb. 1st, 1864.
14	Edwin Bently, Surgeon U. S. Vols.	Private Michael O'Neil, aged 19, Co. E, 58th Mass. Vols.	Gunshot comminuted fracture of right femur, by a conoidal musket-ball, June 8d, 1864.
15	J. C. McKee, Asst. Surgeon U. S. A.	Private Daniel H. Bowman, aged 24, Co. C, 110th Penn. Vols.	Gunshot comminuted fracture of upper third of right femur, July 27th, 1864.
16	F. Hassenburg, Act. Asst. Surgeon U. S. A.	Private Lewis Larry, aged 23, Co. A, 1st New Orleans Vols.	Amputation of thigh on account of gunshot fracture. Subsequent necrosis of femur. First injury July 17th, 1864.
17	Dr. Gurdon Buck, New York City.	Lieutenant Charles H. Hawkins, Co. C, 4th N. Y. Cavalry.	Amputation of right thigh, on account of gunshot fracture of femur received June 8th, 1862.
18	Edwin Bently, Surgeon U. S. Vols.	Sergeant Lewis Carroll, aged 38, Co. A, 1st Delaware Vols.	Gunshot fracture of right femur just below lesser trochanter, by a musket-ball, Oct. 22d, 1864.
19	J. H. Packard, Act. Asst. Surgeon U. S. A.	Private Eben. E. Smith, aged 19, Co. A, 11th Maine Vols.	Amputation of right thigh on account of gunshot fracture. Subsequent necrosis of femur. First injury Aug. 16th, 1864.
20	C. Wagner, Asst. Surgeon U.S.A.	Private John Williams, aged 44, Co. F, 13th Ohio Cavalry.	Gunshot fracture of left femur, Sept. 30th, 1864.
21	E. Griswold, Surgeon U. S. Vols.	Private Geo. M. Spencer, aged 17, Co. B, 2d N. Y. Mounted Rifles.	Gunshot fracture of right femur, March 31st, 1865.

AMPUTATIONS.

THE HIP-JOINT.

Date of Operation.	Result.	Authority.	Remarks.
April 8, 1862.	Died in five days.	Smith's Report, Surgical Records, A, No. 11. J. H. Brinton's Report.	Was transferred to a hospital at St. Louis.
April 8, 1862.	Died in twenty minutes.	Surgeon J. H. Brinton's Report.	A patient wounded at Shiloh.
March, 1862.	Recovered.	Report from Memphis U. S. A. General Hospital.	Operation performed twenty-four hours after reception of wound.
April 29, 1863.	Recovered.	Shippen's Report. Vanderkieft's Report. Letters from Kelly.	Was quite well in the summer of 1865. Spec. 1148, A. M. M. Drawings 31 and 72, Surg. Series, S.G.O.
July 14, 1863.	Died in forty-eight hours.	Report of Surgeon Flandrin, N. Y. Vols. History of Specimen 1379, Army Med. Museum.	See Specimen 1379, Army Medical Museum.
May 15, 1864.	Died May 15th, 1864.	Report of Army of Cumberland, Book ix. p. 355, S. G. O.	
May 18, 1864.	Died in ten hours.	Letter of Prof. Carnochan of Nov. 7th, 1864.	Done at 9th Corps Hospital, at battle of Spottsylvania.
June 16, 1864.	Died in one hour.	Special Report of Surgeon Shippen, U. S. Vols.	A primary operation.
1864.	Died in less than one hour.	Special Report of Surgeon Shippen, U. S. Vols.	A primary operation.
Dec. 27, 1862.	Died in a few hours.	Letter from Medical Inspector Pineo.	See Specimen 710, Army Medical Museum, and Photographic Series A. M. M., No. 14.
May 21, 1864.	Died in twenty-four hours.	Quarterly Report of Surgical Operations from Judiciary Square Hospital.	
May 24, 1864.	Died in four days.	Quarterly Report of Chesapeake Hospital.	
1864.	Died in less than two hours.	Report from U. S. Naval Hospital, Norfolk, Va.	See Specimen 2773, Army Medical Museum.
August 10, 1864.	Died in nineteen days.	Quarterly Report from Third Division General Hospital, Alexandria, Va.	Ligation of external iliac artery. See Spec. 3098, Army Med. Museum.
Sept. 15, 1864.	Died in one day.	Quarterly Report from Lincoln General Hospital, Washington, D. C.	
Sept. 21, 1864.	Died in nine days.	Quarterly Report from University General Hospital, New Orleans, La.	Reamputation.
Sept. 21, 1864.	Died in one day.	Report from St. Luke's Civil Hospital, New York City, and letter from Professor Buck.	Reamputation.
Nov. 11, 1864.	Died in eight days.	Report from Alexandria Hospital.	See Specimen 1020, Army Medical Museum.
January 9, 1865.	Recovered.	Quarterly Report from U. S. A. General Hospital, Beverly, New Jersey.	Reamputation. See Specimen 81, Army Medical Museum, and Photographic Series A. M. M., No. 29.
Feb. 17, 1865.	Died in one day.	Quarterly Report from U. S. A. General Hospital, Beverly, N. J.	See Specimen 84, Army Medical Museum.
April 12, 1865.	Died before removal to the ward.	Quarterly Report from Judiciary Square General Hospital, Washington, D. C.	An excision of the head of the femur was first practised.

SURGICAL OPERATIONS.

Table, showing the Mortality of Amputations at the Hip-Joint for Gunshot Injury, including Primary, Intermediate, and Secondary Cases.

	Recovered.	Died.	Total.
Larrey's primary cases...	......	6	6
Larrey's intermediate cases...	1	......	1
Guthrie's Ciudad Rodrigo case (intermediate)...	......	1	1
Guthrie's Waterloo case (primary)...	1	......	1
S. Cooper's case..	......	1	1
Blandin's cases (in 1794)..	......	3	3
Hutin (Mém. de Méd. Mil., t. xliv.)..	......	2	2
Brownrigg (Elvas, 1811)...	......	1	1
Wedemeyer (Bull. de Férusac, t. iii. p. 161)..	......	2	2
Letulle (Siége d'Anvers)...	......	1	1
Clot Bey (Logonest's table)..	......	1	1
Jublot (Legouest's table)...	......	3	3
Guyon (Algeria, 1840)..	......	1	1
Sédillot (Annales de la Chir, t. ii. p. 279)..	......	5	5
Richet (Journées de Juin, 1848)..	......	1	1
Robert (Idem)..	......	1	1
Gnersant (Idem)..	......	1	1
Vidal (Idem)..	......	1	1
Baudens (Traité des Plaies d'Armes à Feu)...	1	......	1
Schleswick Holstein cases...	......	6	6
Langenbeck's case (Schleswick Holstein)..	1	......	1
Two operations in the English Army in the Crimea by the Director General..........	......	2	2
A soldier of the 33d English Regiment..	......	1	1
Two other cases prior to April, 1855, in the English Army in the Crimea...............	......	2	2
Seven enlisted men and two officers (Med. and Surg. Hist. of Brit. Army in the Crimea)	......	9	9
Twelve primary cases in the French Army in the Crimea........................	......	12	12
Mounier's case at Dolma Batchi..	......	3	3
Legouest's case (really recovered, and died of cholera)............................	......	1	1
Four other secondary cases in the French Crimean hospitals..................	......	4	4
Bertherand's case after the engagement at Novara (Campagne d'Italie de 1859, p. 37).	......	1	1
Jules Roux's cases at Toulon (all secondary)..	4	2	6
Primary cases in the late war..	2	7	9
Secondary cases in the late war..	1	11	12
	11	92	103

There seem to be but three conditions under which early amputation at the hip-joint is admissible in military surgery, viz., when nearly the entire thigh is carried away by a large projectile, when the totality of the femur is destroyed by osteomyelitis, and, possibly, when, with comminution of the upper extremity of the femur, the femoral vessels are wounded.

The experience of M. Jules Roux, in the Italian war, seems to prove conclusively that secondary amputations at the hip-joint are less dangerous than primary ones.

As to the method of operating, it may be observed that the anterior single flap procedure has of late been generally preferred.*

Amputations of the lower extremity are illustrated at the Army Medical Museum by numerous casts, drawings, and photographs, by 9 specimens of shattered femurs removed by amputation at the hip-joint, and by 211 specimens of the diseases of the

---

* Since this report was put in print, two additional cases of amputation at the hip-joint have been reported. In the case of Private F. Kelb, Co. H, 7th New York Vols., whose right femur was fractured at Fredericksburg, by a musket-ball, in December, 1862, Dr. R. F. Weir amputated at the hip-joint, at St. Luke's Hospital, New York, on June 7th, 1865, on account of necrosis of the entire femur. The stump nearly healed; but the patient died October 4th, 1865, of pulmonary tuberculosis. On October 12th, 1865, Surgeon E. Bently, U. S. Vols., amputated at the hip-joint, in the case of Private Lemon, 6th Maryland Vols., on account of necrosis of the left femur, resulting from a gunshot fracture of the upper third, received at the battle of the Wilderness, May 5th, 1864. The patient was in a satisfactory condition on November 24th, 1865. (Specimen 4386, A. M. M.)

AMPUTATIONS. 53

bone after amputation. Wood-cuts of a few of the latter are subjoined. In regard to Specimen 4225, the following particulars are recorded:

Private Daniel S. Crawford, Co. A, 47th Pennsylvania Vols., aged twenty-seven, was wounded at Cedar Creek, October 19th, 1864, his right leg being fractured at the middle third. Amputation at the middle of the leg was performed the same day. On October 26th, he was transferred to the National Hospital, at Baltimore, and thence to the Jarvis Hospital, where it was found that the amputated extremities of the tibia and fibula were necrosed. On March 25th, 1865, lateral flaps were reflected and five inches of the diseased bones were resected by Acting Assistant Surgeon W. G. Small, U. S. A. After this the stump

FIG. 62.—Necrosis of right tibia and fibula after amputation of the leg. *Spec.* 4225, A. M. M.

healed promptly, and the patient was discharged from service May 31st, 1865. (See Surg. Rec. S. G. O., Amputations, vol. vi. part ii. p. 141.)

Specimen 2778 presents a remarkable example of the exaggeration of the natural process by which the amputated ends of bones are rounded off. The redundant osseous formation presents the histological characters of ordinary callus. In the case which furnished this specimen, a successful secondary amputation was performed through the knee-joint.

Cases of myelitis after amputation of the thigh have furnished the Museum with a large number of sequestra comprehending the entire circumference of the bone. The accompanying example is remarkable

FIG. 63.—Hyperostosis of the extremities of the right tibia and fibula after amputation. *Spec.* 2778, A. M. M.

for the unusual length of the sequestrum, and from the fact that the patient recovered after its removal. It was contributed, with the following narrative, by Assistant Surgeon W. Thomson, U. S. A.:

Corporal H. H. Ellis, Co. I, 16th New York Vols., was wounded at Chancellorsville, May 3d, 1863, and admitted into Douglas Hospital, at Washington, May 8th, 1863. A conoidal ball had comminuted the left patella (Spec. 1852, A. M. M.), and the knee-joint was involved. On the 13th of May, the thigh was amputated at the lower third by the circular method. This patient's health was much impaired by chronic diarrhœa, and after the operation, his condition was unpromising. Secondary hæmorrhage occurred on May 20th, and recurred on the 21st, when the femoral artery was tied in Scarpa's triangle. For many weeks this man clung to life by the slenderest thread. The thigh stump was greatly

9⅞ inches.

FIG. 64.—Cylindrical sequestrum from the left femur after amputation at the lower third of the thigh. *Spec.* 1853, A. M. M.

swollen and very tender on pressure. The line of incision, however, was not unhealthy in appearance, and the discharge was moderate. From the inner angle of the stump the necrosed extremity of the femur protruded. August 9th, 1863, the sequestrum was found to be loose, and was removed. After its extraction there was considerable hæmorrhage; nevertheless, convalescence now proceeded rapidly. A formation of new bone, replacing the original femur, could be readily felt. The stump was not shorter than at first. It soon closed entirely, was firm, and in every respect satisfactory. The man was discharged from the hospital, and from the service of the United States, October 26th, 1863. In December, 1864, he reported himself in good health.

The next specimen illustrates the numerous class of cases in which pyæmia accompanies osteomyelitis, and proves fatal before the dead bone is sufficiently detached to be extracted. The involucrum is thin and eroded. The specimen, with the following facts relating to it, was forwarded by Surgeon E. Bently, U. S. Vols.:

FIG. 65.—Necrosis of the amputated end of the left femur. *Spec.* 3343 A. M. M.

Private Andrew H——, Co. B, 6th New Jersey Vols., was wounded May 6th, 1864, at the battle of the Wilderness, by a musket-ball, which entered the left knee-joint, at the upper outer margin of the patella. He was admitted to the 3d Division General Hospital, at Alexandria, Virginia, on May 26th. On July 9th, a large abscess near the elbow was laid open. Others formed along the thigh, and were likewise opened. On July 16th, the thigh was amputated in the lower part of the middle third. The case terminated fatally on July 26th. The autopsy revealed numerous metastatic foci in the lungs; the liver was fatty; the spleen much enlarged. There were bed-sores on the back, and the body was much emaciated.

EXCISIONS.

The number of excisions after gunshot injuries that have been transcribed from the reports is given on page 6 of this report, and indicates that this branch of conservative surgery was largely practised in the late war. It is proposed here to review very briefly the records of the individual excisions.

EXCISIONS OF THE WRIST.—The 35 cases included in this category were all examples of partial excision. In 27, the ends of the radius or ulna, or of both, were removed, and, in some instances, shattered fragments of the upper row of carpal bones. In 8, the greater part of the carpus was excised. Death took place once from pyæmia, and twice from exhaustion from protracted suppuration and irritative fever: 26 cases are reported as recovered. In 2 cases, amputation of the forearm became necessary. The reports are unsatisfactory in relation to the amount of mobility left in the hand, and the cases are now under investigation with reference to this point.

As the literature of this subject is meagre, a few illustrative cases are appended:

Private Joseph Hoover, Co. A, 62d Pennsylvania Vols., aged twenty-six years, was wounded at Spottsylvania, May 12th, 1864, by a musket-ball, which passed through both wrists. He entered Judiciary Square Hospital, at Washington, on May 26th. His right forearm had been amputated on the field. On May 30th, Assistant Surgeon A. Ingram, U. S. A., removed nearly all the left carpus, the styloid process of the ulna, and the carpal end of the first metacarpal bone, and made free incisions over the ulna and the dorsum of the hand for the evacuation of pus. The patient recovered, and was discharged from service. The condition of the hand is not reported.

Surgeon H. Culbertson, U. S. Vols., removed the cuneiform and pisiform, and a portion of the os magnum, and extracted fragments of the unciform and semilunare in the case of Private Neal, Co. D, 3d Wisconsin, who was shot through the carpus, at Dallas, Georgia. The patient recovered with some use of his hand, and entered the Veteran Reserve Corps, April 1st, 1865.

Assistant Surgeon C. Bacon, U. S. A., excised the lower portion of the right radius, the trapezoid, scaphoid, os magnum, and the second, third, and fourth metacarpals, in the case of Private Bard, Co. I, 1st Pennsylvania Vols., who was wounded at Antietam. The result is stated to have been favorable.

Photograph 59 of the Army Medical Museum represents the forearm and hand of Major C. W. Hobbs, 7th New York Heavy Artillery, who was wounded at Cold Harbor, Virginia, June 3d, 1863, by three musket-balls. One inflicted a flesh wound of the left thigh, passing across the popliteal space, close to the hamstring tendons. A second fractured the third and fourth metacarpal bones of the left hand, and made its exit near the wrist. The third entered the left hand between the distal extremities of the first and second metacarpals, comminuting the second and third metacarpals, the unciform and cuneiform bones, and the lower extremity of the ulna, and made its exit on the outer side of the forearm. Primary excision was performed by Surgeon J. E. Pomfret, 7th New York Heavy Artillery. Two inches of the distal extremity of the ulna were removed, with the fractured bones of the carpus and metacarpus, and three outer fingers. The case progressed without any untoward complication, and recovery was complete in two months. The remaining portion of the radio-carpal articulation was not anchylosed, and the movements of the thumb and forefinger were unimpaired.

Professor Joseph Lister's recent paper,[*] in which are narrated the successes obtained by his method of excising the entire wrist-joint for caries, encourages the hope that the same operation may be hereafter successfully adopted in cases of gunshot wounds of the wrist.

---

* Lancet, American edition, July, 1865, p. 306.

EXCISIONS OF THE ELBOW.—The returns for three-fourths of the entire period give 315 cases of excision of the elbow, and the results are ascertained in 286 cases. In 16 cases, amputation of the arm became necessary: 62 cases terminated fatally, or 21·67 per cent., which is a mortality a fraction greater than that resulting from amputations of the arm. This result is altogether opposed to the Schleswick Holstein and Crimean experience, and will doubtless be modified when the statistics are completed. It may be ascribed partly to the fact that the returns for the earlier part of the war include quite a large proportion of partial excisions, which are far more hazardous than complete removal of the articular surfaces.

The Army Medical Museum possesses 98 specimens of the injured epiphyses removed in excisions of the elbow, and a goodly number of photographs of patients in whom the operation has been performed.

The happy results of this well established operation are so fully known, that it is unnecessary to give more than a single illustrative case:

Private William D. Riley, Co. D, 86th New York Vols., aged twenty-one years, was accidentally wounded at Brandy Station, Virginia, November 26th, 1863, by a musket-ball, which shattered the inner condyle of the right humerus and the olecranon process of the ulna. He was admitted to Mansion House Hospital, at Alexandria, the same day, having bled quite largely on the way. On December 19th, 1863, Surgeon Charles Page, U. S. A., excised the elbow-joint, employing the H-shaped incision. Two and a half inches of the lower extremity of the humerus, an inch of the upper extremity of the ulna, and a small portion of the head of the radius were removed. The case progressed most favorably, and in May, 1864, Riley went to his home, on furlough, with a useful arm. He was subsequently discharged from service. In 1865, he re-enlisted in Co. K, 5th Regiment, First Army Corps, with the approval of Lieutenant Colonel Dougherty, Medical Director of the Corps. "The man went through the manual before me," Surgeon Dougherty writes, "and stated his readiness to do all the duties of a soldier. He wished it recorded that he was competent and prepared, in order that, during the term of his service, he might be held to full duty. The degree of motion was, perhaps, one-third of the normal amount." A photograph of the patient (No. 54, A. M. M.) was taken in June, 1865, at the Army Medical Museum.

EXCISIONS OF THE SHOULDER-JOINT.—Nearly all of the cases that have been reported during the war have been recorded. The results are given in the following table:

Table, exhibiting the Results of Cases of Excisions of the Shoulder-Joint for Gunshot Injuries.

	Primary Operations.	Secondary Operations.
Died	50	115
Recovered	160	183
Results undetermined	42	25
	252	323
Aggregate	575	

The percentage of mortality is 23·3 in primary cases, 38·59 in secondary cases, or a mean ratio of 32·48. The ratio in amputations at the shoulder-joint is 39·24, a percentage of 6·76 in favor of excision. Of 36 cases of gunshot fracture of the head of the humerus, selected as favorable cases for the expectant plan and treated without excision or amputation, 16 died, or 44·4 per cent., a ratio in favor of excision of 11·96 per cent. But it is superfluous to offer further proofs in behalf of this admirable operation.

Esmarch* makes the curious observation, that resection of the left shoulder gives less favorable results than the operation on the right side. This statement is not confirmed by the returns. Of 442 terminated cases in which mention is made of the side injured, the right shoulder was involved in 200 and the left in 242. The operation resulted fatally in 72 of the former, or 36 per cent., and in 71 of the latter, or 29·3 per cent. The greater frequency of injuries requiring the operation on the left side is doubtless due to the exposed position of the left shoulder in firing.

Generally the operation has been done in cases in which the head of the bone was alone implicated, and consisted simply in a decapitation of the humerus. Partial excisions have been seldom practised. The method commonly preferred was that by a single vertical incision, though some operators raised a V-shaped flap, and all endeavored to include the wound made by the ball in the incisions. It is frequently mentioned that the long tendon of the biceps was preserved. In 29 cases, portions of the clavicle, or of the coracoid and acromion processes and neck of the scapula, were excised, as well as the head of the humerus. Only 4 of these cases terminated fatally, and the average result in the recovered cases was as satisfactory as the ordinary result in decapitation of the humerus.

FIG. 56.—Ball impacted in the head of the humerus. A typical case for excision. Spec. 1200, A. M. M.

Where the shaft of the humerus has been extensively shattered, our surgeons have not been deterred by the prohibition of Guthrie, but have frequently removed the head with even five and six inches of the diaphysis. It is true, as Stromeyer has clearly shown, that in gunshot fracture of the surgical neck of the humerus, with extensive longitudinal splitting, the fissures rarely implicated the epiphysis; yet no good purpose seems to be answered by leaving the head of the bone in these cases, and excellent results are obtained after excision of the head with very considerable portions of the shaft. The following case is an example:

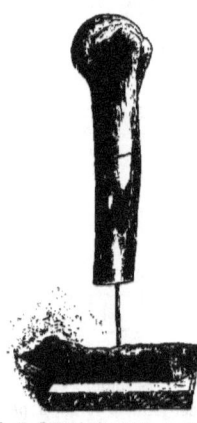

Private John F. Readon, Co. C, 6th New York Cavalry, aged twenty-two years, was wounded at Culpepper, Virginia, October 11th, 1863, and entered Armory Square U. S. General Hospital, at Washington, on the following day. It was found that his right

FIG. 57.—Excised head and shaft of right humerus, with the fragment of shell that caused the fracture. Spec. 1738, A. M. M.

FIG. 58.—Appearance of the patient who furnished the foregoing specimen, two years subsequent to the operation. Photographed on wood.

humerus had been fractured by a fragment of shell, which was removed from its lodgement under the deltoid muscle, and proved to be four inches long and one inch broad, and to weigh nine ounces. The head and upper third of the shaft of the humerus were then excised through a straight incision, by Surgeon D. W. Bliss, U. S. Vols. The patient recovered

---

* Statham's edition of Esmarch, American edition, 1862, p. 57.

without a bad symptom, and with a remarkably useful limb. He visited the Army Medical Museum nearly two years after the operation, and a photograph was then taken of his arm. The motions of the forearm and hand were unimpaired. The arm could be moved forwards and backwards with considerable freedom. The hand could be readily raised to the mouth, and placed in the position represented in the wood-cut.

In the remarkable case of Private Cleghorn, 1st New Jersey Cavalry, after an excision of the head and upper third of the humerus, the remainder of the bone became necrosed, and was excised, together with the articular ends of the radius and ulna, and yet a limb was preserved, which, with the aid of ingenious apparatus, is very useful. (Photograph 112, A. M. M.)

Numerous patients have been photographed at the Army Medical Museum, in whom, after excision, a very satisfactory degree of motion at the shoulder-joint existed. Photograph No. 103, A. M. M., represents the case of Lieutenant Jacobs, who retains to a remarkable degree the power of abducting the arm, which is usually very limited. The control over the movements of the arm is much augmented by the contrivance furnished by the makers of surgical apparatus, in which elastic bands supply the diminished power of the deltoid and biceps.

Sixty-one excised heads of humeri have been contributed to the Museum.

EXCISIONS OF THE ANKLE-JOINT.—Of 22 recorded cases, 8 were excisions of the tibio-tarsal articulation, and the remainder were nearly all ablations of portions of the tarsal bones. Of 18 terminated cases, 12 recovered and 6 died.

Five of the fatal cases are reported by Surgeon R. B. Bontecou, U. S. Vols., the operations being described as "excisions of the ankle-joint" in four cases, and in one as "excision of the lower end of the tibia and head of astragalus." They were all secondary operations, performed on account of perforation of the ankle, with comminution, by musket-balls. They seem to have been formal resections, and not mere gougings of necrosed bone. The results are sufficiently discouraging.

The sixth fatal case is reported by Surgeon J. A. Lidell, U. S. Vols. It was a secondary excision of portions of the calcaneum and astragalus.

Surgeon Whitehill, U. S. Vols., reports a complete excision of the calcaneum and astragalus in the case of Private Roberts, 7th Wisconsin Battery, with the prospect, two months after the operation, of a useful limb.

Assistant Surgeon Billings, U. S. A., removed the external malleolus, the entire astragalus, and a portion of the scaphoid, in the case of Private Ludwig Ettinger, 58th New York Vols., and eight months afterwards the patient could walk with the aid of a cane.

In the case of a negro boy of nineteen, with a ball lodged in the astragalus, Dr. Billings extracted the ball and fragments of the astragalus, and the patient recovered without anchylosis, and was able to walk with no perceptible limp two months after the operation.

Surgeon J. A. Lidell, U. S. Vols., extracted the shattered fragments of the cuboid and external cuneiform in the case of Private Ganlert, Co. K, 6th New York Cavalry, with satisfactory results.

It appears, then, that the judicious use of the gouge and bone forceps is admissible in gunshot wounds of the ankle-joint; but that the formal excisions are rarely successful.

SURGICAL OPERATIONS.

EXCISIONS OF THE KNEE-JOINT.—Prior to the present war, there were but seven recorded examples of excision of the knee for gunshot injury. These were, the elder Textor's case* (in 1847); the Schleswick Holstein case† (1851), in which Fahle operated by Stromeyer's direction; Mr. Lakin's case‡ (1855), in the Crimea; the Alumbaugh case§ (1857), in the Indian mutiny; the case of a man in the London hospitals wounded by bird shot|| (1861); a similar case at Birmingham¶ (1861); and lastly, Verneuil's case.**

Verneuil's case and the Birmingham case were successful. The patients were lads of seventeen and nineteen.

Modern surgeons have bravely striven to escape the deplorable necessity which has led to the establishment of the imperative rule of amputation in every gunshot fracture involving the knee-joint, and such eminent authorities as Legouest and Macleod have advised that excision should be substituted for amputation in cases in which the injury to the epiphyses is inconsiderable, the patient young and robust, and the requisite hygienic and surgical resources for careful after-treatment attainable. Unhappily, in an active campaign in the field, these circumstances are rarely met in conjunction.

During the late war, complete excision of the knee-joint has been performed eleven times. An abstract of each case is here furnished:

Private Alexander Rider, Co. I, 76th Pennsylvania Vols., aged twenty-five, was admitted into Hospital No. 1, Beaufort, South Carolina, October 24th, 1862. He was wounded at Pocotaligo, South Carolina, October 22d, 1862, by a rough lead canister ball, which entered over the front of the external condyle of the right femur, passed through the articulation, and lodged in the popliteal space. October 24th, 1862, Surgeon Reed B. Bontecou, U. S. Vols., removed the ball by an incision, and sawed off the lower portion of the condyles of the femur, and excised a very thin slice from the head of the tibia. An H-shaped incision was employed. The transverse cut was accurately brought

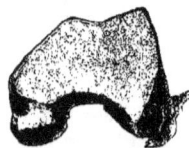

FIG. 69.—Condyle of right femur, excised on account of gunshot fracture of the external condyle. Spec. 2030, A. M. M.

together by lead-wire sutures. The azygos artery was tied. The circulation and appearance of the limb were good, but there was some swelling of the knee-joint, which was painful on pressure or when moved. At the date of operation the patient was in good health. An ice-bag and lint wet in a solution of morphia were applied to the joint. October 25th, 1862, sulph. magnes. ʒi. The ice dressing was continued till November 2d. About this time there was a troublesome diarrhœa, which was checked by pills of opium and nitrate of silver. Diet, milk porridge. October 27th, the limb was placed in a trough, stuffed with hay, which afforded much relief. Before this the pain had been excessive. November 8th, no evidence of inflammation about the knee. Transverse incision healed without suppuration. November 18th, has steadily improved. December 1st, the bones had apparently united, and the incisions had healed except at a point on either side of the joint, from which a few drops of pus escaped on pressure. December 20th, starch bandage. December 26th, febrile disturbance. An erythematous blush over skin of lower extremity. Bandage removed. December 28th, febrile symptoms gone. The man was this day sent to the North on the steamer "Star of the South." He was seen by Dr. Bontecou in July, 1863, at "Fort Wood" Hospital, New York Harbor. He was not then able to walk, but subsequently did so with the aid of a cane. He was discharged from service August, 1863. In the summer of 1865, he was again heard from by Dr. Bontecou, and was still in good health.

Corporal Charles Derrell, Co. F, 74th Indiana Vols., aged twenty-seven, was admitted, November 25th, 1863, into Branch No. 6, Field Hospital, Chattanooga, Tennessee, with fracture of the right knee-joint, by a round musket-

---

* Fuch's Dissertat. 1854; and O. Heyfelder's Traité des Résections, par E. Bœckel. Paris, 1863, p. 106.
† Friedrich Esmarch, Die Resectionen nach Schusswunden, Kiel, 1851; and Statham's Esmarch, p. 113.
‡ Macleod, Notes on the Surgery of the Crimea, p. 349.
§ Edinburgh Medical and Surgical Journal, October, 1860.
|| The Lancet, April 20th, 1861.   ¶ Medical Times and Gazette, May, 1861.
** Gazette Hebdomadaire, Nov. 1862; Soc. de Chirurgie de Paris, Séance de 10 Juin, 1863; and Legouest, Traité de Chirurgie d'Armée, p. 750.

ball, received on date of admission, at Mission Ridge. Missile had entered on inner aspect of the joint, fractured the inner condyle of the femur, and passed obliquely downwards and outwards, lodging in the head of the tibia. November 26th, Surgeon James Heller, 38th Ohio Vols., operated. An anterior semicircular incision, including the wound of entrance, being made, and the patella removed, seven-eighths of an inch was sawn from both tibia and femur. Two arteries required torsion, none ligature. The patient was in robust health at the time of the operation. About December 25th, symptoms of exhaustion were manifest. A supporting treatment was adopted, without avail. Death, January 18th, 1864.

Private Gardiner Lewis, Co. B, 19th Indiana Vols., aged twenty-two, was wounded at the battle of Gettysburg, July 1st, 1863, by a round musket-ball, which lodged in the internal condyle of the right femur. On November 27th, 1863, he was admitted into Jarvis U. S. A. General Hospital, Baltimore, Maryland, the knee being disorganized and discharging a fœtid pus. On December 1st, Acting Assistant Surgeon F. Hinkle, U. S. A., excised the articular ends of the tibia and femur, sawing off an inch of the condyle of the femur, and three-fourths of an inch of the head of the tibia. An H-shaped incision was employed. At the time of the operation the patient was feverish, anxious, without appetite, and sleepless from intense pain. He did well until several days after the operation, when he had a chill. Chills recurred each alternate day, and other symptoms of purulent infection were manifested. On December 23d, the case terminated fatally. The autopsy revealed metastatic foci in the lungs, and six ounces of pus in the left pleural cavity. The incisions were healed, and the ends of the bones were found in apposition, but no union had occurred. The excised portions of the femur and tibia are preserved in the Army Medical Museum. (Spec. No. 1956.)

FIG. 70.—Excised knee-joint. A round ball in the inner condyle of right femur. Spec. 1956, A. M. M.

Private Jacob Miller, Co. A, 3d Pennsylvania Cavalry, aged thirty-eight, was admitted December 5th, 1863, into the 3d Division U. S. A. General Hospital, Alexandria, Virginia, with a compound comminuted fracture of the right patella, involving the knee-joint. The injury was received in action, November 27th, 1863, at Mine Run, Virginia. On December 7th, 1863, Surgeon Edwin Bently, U. S. Vols., excised half an inch of the articulating extremities of the femur and tibia, and removed the patella. The parts were considerably swollen at the time of operation, and the patient was prostrated. Profuse suppuration ensued. A stimulating and supporting treatment was adopted; but the case resulted fatally, from pyæmia, on December 18th, 1863.

Corporal Jesse Sims, Co. B, 4th Ohio Vols., aged twenty-three, was admitted, December 5th, 1863, into the 3d Division U. S. A. General Hospital, at Alexandria, Virginia, with gunshot fracture opening the right knee-joint, received on the 27th of November, 1863, at Mine Run, Virginia. On December 8th, an excision of an inch and a half of the tibia and fibula, and an inch of the femur, was made by Surgeon Edwin Bently, U. S. Vols. The parts were much swollen and the patient greatly prostrated and anxious. Simple dressings were applied. Pyæmia was soon developed, and death occurred on the 13th. A post-mortem examination showed no attempt at repair. The wound was sloughing. Metastatic abscesses were formed along the inside of the thigh, and one at the base of the lower lobe of the right lung. (Spec. 1909, A. M. M.)

Private Thomas Clark, Co. D, 2d New Hampshire Cavalry, was wounded in a skirmish near Alexandria, Louisiana, on May 4th, 1864, by a musket-ball, which entered the popliteal space, and, passing behind the artery, emerged two inches above the joint on its outer side, having fractured the external condyle. The patient was admitted to the General Hospital, at Alexandria, Louisiana, on the day that he was wounded. Immediate amputation was advised, but the patient objected so strenuously, that excision was substituted. Assistant Surgeon John Homans, Jr., U. S. A., removed two inches of the condyles of the femur, and half an inch from the head of the tibia, through a straight incision across the joint, the patient being under the influence of chloroform. The limb was put in a fracture-box, the wound being closed by sutures. No great depression followed the operation immediately. The patient took a full anodyne, and rested well. Next morning, his leg was very cold, and no pulsation could be discerned in any of the arteries below the knee. The patient was placed on a transport steamer and sent to New Orleans, where he died a week after the operation. The report adds that no necroscopic examination was made, and no satisfactory explanation could be given of the arrest of the circulation in the limb; but it seems highly probable that the explanation is to be found in the proximity of the track of the ball to the popliteal artery, and the formation of an occluding clot in that vessel.

Sergeant Henry J. Moore, Co. F, 7th Maine Vols., aged twenty-four, was admitted, May 24th, 1864, into the 3d Division U. S. A. General Hospital, at Alexandria, Virginia, with a wound of the left knee-joint, from a conoidal ball, received May 12th, 1864, in the battle of Spottsylvania, Virginia. An excision had been made by an unknown operator, by a straight incision across the anterior aspect of the joint. On admission, the limb was in a fracture-box, the wound partially closed by sutures, and discharging but very little. The patient was prostrated by the fatigue of transportation to the hospital, and he died of exhaustion on the 26th of May, 1864.

Corporal George W. Hays, Co. K, 2d Michigan Vols., aged nineteen, was wounded on June 17th, 1864, before the intrenched lines at Petersburg, Virginia, by a musket-ball, which shattered the left knee, and fractured the right patella and opened the right knee-joint. Primary amputation at the lower third of the left thigh was performed at the field hospital, and the patient was transferred to Washington, where he was admitted to Harewood Hospital, on June 20th. On admission, the stump was in a satisfactory condition; the right knee-joint, however, was disorganized. The ball, after fracturing the patella, had passed through the articulation, grooving the head of the tibia. On June 24th, the patient was etherized, and Surgeon Bontecou, U. S. Vols., excised two-thirds of the condyles of the femur, the articular surface of the tibia, and the shattered patella. The limb was dressed with the bandage of Scultetus, and supported by bran bags. The case terminated fatally on July 2d, 1864. The specimen is No. 3046, Army Medical Museum.

Private D. F. R——, Co. I, 49th Georgia (Rebel) Regiment, was wounded and taken prisoner at Petersburg, Virginia, on April 2d, 1865. A conoidal musket-ball struck his right knee, and fractured the patella and the external condyle of the femur. He was admitted at the General Hospital, at Fort Monroe, on April 13th. The joint was intensely inflamed, and there was great suffering. On April 18th, the patient was placed under the influence of chloroform, and Surgeon D. G. Rush, 101st Pennsylvania Vols., excised the knee-joint, removing an inch from the femur, half an inch from the tibia, and the entire patella. The patient rallied well after the operation; but the wound began to suppurate freely, and the case terminated fatally on April 26th, 1865. At the autopsy, it was found that there was no attempt at reparation.

FIG. 71.—Excised knee-joint. Spec. 4212, A. M. M.

Of the tenth case it is only known that a complete excision of the knee-joint for gunshot injury was performed at Fairfax Seminary Hospital, in the autumn of 1862, and that the case terminated fatally, but not until the H-shaped incision had nearly healed. The pathological preparation from the case was forwarded to the Army Medical Museum by Acting Assistant Surgeon Bannister, and is numbered Specimen 600, but it is unaccompanied by a history.

The success claimed in the next case is so extraordinary as to suggest some doubts of its authenticity. It appears on the quarterly report of the General Hospital at Kansas City, Missouri, for the last quarter of 1863.

Private Samuel Miller, Co. L, 1st Missouri State Militia, was admitted into the General Hospital, at Kansas City, Missouri, April 1st, 1863. He was wounded near Independence, Missouri, on December 28th, 1862, the ball having fractured the outer condyle of the right femur, passed obliquely through the patella, and lodged in the head of the tibia. On April 7th, 1863, Acting Assistant Surgeon Joshua Thorne, U. S. A., performed an excision of the outer condyle of the femur, with part of the shaft, removing by an oblique section two and a half inches from the femur, together with the patella and articulating surface of the tibia. No anæsthetic was used. The wound was full of shattered bone, and an extraordinary amount of pus came out of the joint. There was severe pain and extensive inflammation in the leg. The patient was much emaciated from copious diarrhœa. Skin dark and dry, very like parchment. At the time of the operation he was nearly insensible, pulse 120 and feeble. He was greatly prostrated after the operation, but on the next day he revived. Nutritious diet, with porter, was given him, and he continued to improve. Complete bony anchylosis resulted, with the leg bent about ten degrees. On December 8th, 1863, Miller was discharged from service. He was able to walk almost as well as ever.

Seven partial excisions of the knee-joint for gunshot injury have been reported. Three of these were excisions of the patella. The operators were Surgeon Bontecou, U. S. Vols., Surgeon Mosely, U. S. Vols., and Acting Assistant Surgeon Coale, U. S. A. The patients survived the operations fifteen, eighteen, and twelve days, respectively.

Surgeon John A. Lidell, U. S. Vols., laid open the knee-joint, and removed the fragments of a patella, shattered by a musket-ball. His patient lived ten days. Acting Assistant Surgeon Theo. Siebold, U. S. A., made a free incision into a knee-joint disorganized by inflammation following a gunshot fracture, extracted fragments of the head of the tibia and of the patella, removed the semilunar cartilages, painted the synovial membrane with tincture of iodine, and scraped the articular cartilages from the end of the condyles. His patient survived twelve days. In two cases the head of the fibula was excised, and portions of the head of the tibia. Both recovered. In these cases, reported by Surgeon Judson, U. S. Vols., and Dr. Bournonville, it does not clearly appear that the articulation was opened.

EXCISIONS OF THE HEAD OF THE FEMUR.—In 1861, our information in regard to excisions of the head of the femur for gunshot injury was summed up by Dr. Hodges in his excellent monograph,* and in 1863, by M. Legouest† and M. Bœckel.‡

Dr. Hodges quotes the observations of Oppenheim, Seutin, Schwartz, and Baum, and the six cases given in the Surgical History of the British Army in the Crimea, and with more detail by Macleod. Legouest adds Textor's case, and Bœckel ascribes a case to Guthrie, which is apocryphal. Dr. Esmarch refers to another case operated on by Dr. Ross, and described in the *Deutsches Klinik* for 1850, No. 41.

Statistical Table of Excisions of the Head of the Femur for Gunshot Injury prior to the late war.

No.	Surgeon.	Date of operation.	Result.	Remarks.	Authority.
1	Oppenheim.	May 5th, 1820.	Died in 17 days. The fatal event was attributed to true typhus.	Performed for a gunshot fracture of the head of the femur and rim of the acetabulum.	Hamburg. Zeitschrift, vol. I. p. 137.
2	Seutin.	1832.	Died in 9 days.	Gunshot fracture of the neck of the femur.	Histoire Chirurgicale du Siége d'Anvers, par H. Larrey, Mém. de Méd. Mil. t. 34.
3	Textor.	1847.	Died in 9 days.	Gunshot fracture of the trochanters, followed by caries.	Heyfelder's table. Traité des Résections, p. 68.
4	Schwartz.	May 13th, 1849.	Died on May 20th, 1849.	Gunshot fracture through the trochanters of the left femur, received April 23d, 1849.	Esmarch, Am. ed., p. 103.
5	Ross.	1850.	Fatal.	Caries of the head of the femur, resulting from gunshot injury.	Deutsches Klinik, No. 41.
6	Baum.	1854.	Died in 22 hours.	Gunshot fracture of the head of the femur.	Lohmeyer, Ueber Schusswunden, p. 109.
7	Macleod.	July 6th, 1855.	Died in 1 week, with symptoms of cholera.	Fracture of the trochanter and neck of the left femur by a musket-ball, on June 18th, 1855.	Macleod's Notes on the Surgery of the Crimean War, p. 338.
8	Blenkins.	1855.	Died in the 5th week.	Fracture by shell of the upper part of right femur.	Ibid., p. 341.
9	Crerar.	August, 1855.	Died in a fortnight.	Fracture of the femur high up by shell.	Guthrie's Commentaries, 5th ed., p. 622.
10	O'Leary.	August, 1855.	Recovered.	Fracture of the great trochanter by a shell.	Med. and Surg. History of the British Army in the Crimea, vol. ii. p. 378.
11	Hyde.	1855.	Died in 5 days.	Upper extremity of femur comminuted by a grape-shot.	Macleod's Notes, p. 344.
12	Combe.	1855.	Died in a fortnight.	Gunshot fracture of the neck of the femur.	Ibid., p. 344.

There were then on record, previous to the late war, twelve cases of this operation, with one success. This was the case reported by Surgeon O'Leary of the 68th British Infantry, who excised the head and several inches of the shaft of the femur for Private Thomas Mackenena, the great trochanter being shattered by a fragment of shell. Experience having demonstrated the uniform fatality of gunshot fractures of the head or neck of the femur when abandoned to the resources of nature, and the excessive mortality of amputations at the hip-joint for gunshot injury, the highest authorities in military surgery were then unanimous in advising, under suitable conditions, excision of the head of the femur, until, as Baron Hippolyte Larrey expressed it, the experiments of the future proved more discouraging than the experience of the past.§

How far this advice has been acted upon in the late war, may be seen from the following table, which exhibits also the form in which all surgical operations are recorded on the registers of this office.

---

* The Excisions of Joints. Boston, 1861, pp. 204.   † Op. cit.
‡ Traité des Résections, par le Docteur O. Heyfelder, traduit de l'Allemand, avec additions et notes, par le Docteur Eug. Bœckel. Paris: Baillière, 1863, pp. 310.
§ Bulletin de l'Académie de Médecine, Nov. 12th, 1861.

TABULAR STATEMENT OF THE OPERATIONS OF EXCISIONS OF THE HEAD THE SURGEON

Hospital and Hospital Number.	Name, Rank, Company, Regiment. Age. Date of Admission to Hospital.	Description and Date of Wound or Injury. On what Occasion received.	Date of Operation.	Operation.	Condition of Injured Parts at Time of Operation.
1. E Street Infirmary, Washington, D. C.	Timothy Greely, Private Co. C, 5th Excelsior (74th N. Y. Vols.). Age, —. Admitted October 5, 1861.	Round ball from smooth-bore musket entered near fold of nates, passed through femur, between trochanters, opened hip-joint and made its exit anteriorly.	October, 1861.	Excision of the head, neck, and trochanters of the femur.	A stream of blood, and another of synovia (clear and pellucid), issued from wound of exit. External wound small.
2. Nashville, Tenn.	———, Private. An infantry soldier of Gen. Buell's Army. Admitted March 18, 1862.	Fracture of upper extremity of femur by a musket-ball. In a skirmish near Nashville, just before the occupation of the city by Gen. Buell.	March, 1862, a few days after the injury.	Excision of the head, neck, and trochanter of the femur.	The fracture was limited to the neck and trochanteric region.
3. Cliffburne U. S. A. General Hospital, Washington, D. C.	T. C. Christopher, Private Co. D, 18th S. C. (Confederate). Age, 21. Admitted May 17, 1862. A robust and muscular man, but melancholy and despondent.	Wounded May 5, 1862, by a minié-ball, which entered two inches below and behind the trochanter major of the left side, and, passing forward, upward, and inward, remained in the body.	May 20, 1862.	A curvilinear incision four inches long was made behind the trochanter major, and parallel to the axis of the limb; through this the shattered fragments of the head and neck were removed; the ball was then found in the obturator foramen, and removed; the hæmorrhage was slight. Chloroform (pure) used.	Tissues about joint swollen, and limb shortened and everted; sanious pus discharging from wound; neck of femur comminuted and head split into two pieces; acetabulum uninjured; the trochanter major was intact, and was left so by the operation.
4. National U. S. A. General Hospital, Baltimore, Md.	John W. Nelling, Private Co. K, 1st Massachusetts Vols. Age, 25. Admitted July 25, 1864.	A musket-ball entered the right groin and implicated the hip-joint. The patient was taken prisoner, and confined at Richmond for three months. White Oak Swamp, June 30, 1862.	August 21, 1862.	Excision of the head and neck of the right femur, through a straight incision carried down to the bone; the head was found stricken off from the neck of the epiphysis, and only retained in the acetabulum by the ligamentum teres. Chloroform.	Ball entered right groin, passed horisonially backwards, and escaped posteriorly.
5. Field Hospital, Gainesville, Va.	———, Private, Gen. R. King's Division. Admitted August 28, 1862.	Ball entered over great trochanter of left femur, shattered the trochanter and produced a long fissure, running down the shaft to two inches below the lesser trochanter; the missile then entered the pelvis. Gainesville, Va., August 28, 1862.	August 28, 1862.	Excision of the head, neck, trochanters, and two inches of the shaft of the left femur; the extreme length from the tip of the trochanter to the point at which the shaft was sawn, was four and three-fourths inches.	Head and neck of the femur were sound; the great trochanter was split off in five fragments; from its base a very oblique fracture ran downwards and inwards, and produced a complete solution of continuity of the shaft about two inches below the lesser trochanter.

EXCISIONS.

OF THE FEMUR FOR GUNSHOT INJURY THAT HAVE BEEN REPORTED TO GENERAL'S OFFICE.

Constitutional State of Patient at Time of Operation.	Progress, Treatment, etc.	Result. Cause of Death.	REMARKS.
Pulse but slightly depressed; patient congratulates himself on slight extent of his injury, as he supposes.	Sank gradually.	Survived the operation but a few days.	Operator, John W. S. Gouley, Asst. Surgeon U.S.A. Case taken from Sanitary Report of Surgeon John T. Calhoun, 5th Excelsior, December 31st, 1861. (See paper No. 71.)
Satisfactory. Surgeon Goldsmith thought the case peculiarly well adapted for the operation of excision.	Failed gradually, and died within one week.	Died March, 1862.	Operator, A. H. Thurston, Surgeon U. S. Vols. Case reported verbally by Surgeon M. Goldsmith, U. S. Vols.
Very fair; pulse 100; rather weak. He had complained of severe pain in the hip and knees. He reacted well from the chloroform, and expressed himself as feeling much better.	Simple water-dressing was applied to the wound. The foot was fastened by strips of adhesive plaster to a strip of wood at the foot of the bed, which being elevated, the weight of the body made extension. Brandy, egg-nog, beef essence, etc., given freely.	Died May 24th, 1862, at 7 P.M., of exhaustion. The autopsy revealed a clot of blood, about three ounces in weight, between the peritonæum and iliacus internus of the left side, probably from the rupture of a small arterial branch.	Operator, J. S. Billings, Asst. Surgeon U.S.A. This may be called a typical case of a gunshot injury requiring exsection of the hip-joint. Everything appeared favorable, the patient being young, strong, and healthy, and the injury seemingly uncomplicated. Army Medical Museum, Specimen No. 19. Special Report of Dr. Billings.
Feeble.	Patient rallied well from operation. Very little blood was lost. Limb sustained by anterior splint. Progressed favorably until the afternoon of August 25th, when a sudden and extremely profuse gush of dark blood took place from the anterior bullet wound and posterior incision, which caused death in a few minutes.	Died August 25th, 1862.	Operator, Robert Bartholow, Asst. Surgeon U. S. A. Parts much softened and semi-gangrenous; end of excised neck denuded of periosteum and necrosed; femoral vein melted down, and was not, at the point of injury, distinguishable from surrounding tissues; a quantity of dark fluid blood found anteriorly under the integuments. Army Medical Museum, Specimen No. 400.
The symptoms were grave, and the prognosis unfavorable.	Internal hæmorrhage from some vessel in the pelvic cavity.	The man fell into the hands of the enemy. In all probability he survived but a few hours.	Operator, Peter Pineo, Brigade Surgeon U. S. V. Army Medical Museum, Specimen No. 71. The specimen has been photographed, and a wood-cut taken from it. Photographic Series, No. 13. Letter from Lt. Col. Pineo.

SURGICAL OPERATIONS.

TABULAR STATEMENT OF THE OPERATIONS OF

Hospital and Hospital Number.	Name, Rank, Company, Regiment. Age. Date of Admission to Hospital.	Description and Date of Wound or Injury. On what Occasion received.	Date of Operation.	Operation.	Condition of Injured Parts at Time of Operation.
6. Cliffburne U. S. A. General Hospital, Washington, D. C.	——, Private, Army of Virginia. Admitted September 2, 1862.	Minié-ball entered the left hip directly over the trochanter major, and embedded itself in the neck of the bone. Second Bull Run, August 29, 1862.	Sept. 4, 1862.	Straight incision was made over trochanter major, and all fragments removed; the head of the femur was then removed, and the shaft of the femur cut off with a chain-saw at the level of trochanter minor.	Trochanter major and neck of femur split and comminuted; head of bone not injured; no joint opened; tissues about joint but slightly swollen, and discharging healthy pus.
7. Warehouse Hospital, Georgetown, D. C.	F. Machlin, Private Co. ——, 11th Pennsylvania Vols. Age, ——. Admitted September 8, 1862.	Musket-ball entered the right buttock and emerged an inch and a half below and within the anterior superior spinous process of the right ilium, comminuting the neck of the femur.	Sept. 20, 1862.	Excision of head and neck of right femur; a straight incision five inches long from a point two inches behind and one inch below the anterior-superior spinous process to the trochanteric region; removal of neck at junction with trochanter, with chain-saw; exarticulation of head; one small vessel tied.	Neck of femur in fragments; head in situ, and not fractured; shaft uninjured; foot everted; limb shortened; acetabulum uninjured.
8. College Hospital, Georgetown, D. C.	Charles E. Marston, Private Co. F, 1st Massachusetts Vols. Age, 19. Admitted September 6, 1862.	A large bullet wound one inch anterior to and on a level with the right trochanter major; no exit; comminution of the head and neck of the femur. Second Bull Run, August 30, 1862.	Sept. 27, 1862.	Excision of head and neck of the right femur; a slightly curved incision, five inches long, on the outside of the thigh, the shot-hole in the middle of the incision; rough end of femur removed by small saw; one small vessel tied; conoidal ball removed.	Limb half as large again as its fellow; neck broken into at least forty small fragments; trochanter uninjured; head shattered.
9. No. 3 U. S. A. General Hospital, Frederick, Md.	Cornelius Callaghan, Private Co. ——, Pennsylvania Vols. Age, ——. Admitted September 19, 1862.	A shell wound of the outer upper portion of left thigh, with fracture of trochanter major.	Sept. 29, 1862.	An examination under chloroform, recommended by Medical Inspector Coolidge and Surgeon Milhau, U. S. A., revealed a fracture through the trochanter and fissure extending within the capsule; the incision was extended three inches below the trochanter major, and a chain-saw was passed around the shaft of the femur, which was divided just below the seat of fracture; the head of the bone was then disarticulated; no vessels required ligature.	The trochanter was entirely separated and detached by muscular action.

EXCISIONS OF THE HEAD OF THE FEMUR—Continued.

Constitutional State of Patient at Time of Operation.	Progress, Treatment, etc.	Result. Cause of Death.	REMARKS.
This man had suffered greatly from the journey from the field, and had diarrhœa of a malarial type.	He reacted well after the operation. Was placed on a fracture bed, and extension made on the leg by means of a weight. Diarrhœa increased in severity.	Died September 24th, 1862, of exhaustion caused by colliquative diarrhœa.	Operator, J. S. Billings, Asst. Surgeon U. S. A. No autopsy. "The man died from malarial complications, and not, in my opinion, from the wound or operation." Special report of Dr. Billings.
Most unfavorable. By careful nursing, and the use of stimulants, beef essence, etc., condition so far improved that the operation was regarded as justifiable.	Wound syringed; rallied after operation; in six hours pulse 136; free from pain; gradually sank.	Died September 21st, 1862.	Operator, B. A. Clements, Asst. Surgeon U. S. A. No autopsy. Surgical Series, Army Medical Museum, vol. i. page 41, Specimen No. 320.
Pulse 112; a delicate boy; pale; tongue dryish; general condition bad, but not so bad as in Machlin's case.	Sand-bags to keep limb in position. Pulse quick and feeble.	Died September 30th, 1862, 8 P. M.	Operator, B. A. Clements, Asst. Surgeon U S. A., assisted by staff of hospital and Asst. Surgeon Alden, U. S. A. Autopsy showed that lower half of the acetabulum was fractured. Surgical Series, Army Medical Museum, vol. i. p. 43, Specimen No. 328.
Comparatively favorable.	September 30th. Patient comfortable; pulse 120; takes full diet; sleeps at night. Oct. 1st. Thigh swollen; profuse sweating. Oct. 2d. Diarrhœa and fever; at night, vomiting and hiccough.	Died October 4th, 1862.	Operator, J. H. Bill, Asst. Surgeon U. S. A. No facilities for autopsy, and none made. Symptoms, those of pyæmia. Army Medical Museum, Specimen No. 840.

SURGICAL OPERATIONS.

TABULAR STATEMENT OF THE OPERATIONS OF

Hospital and Hospital Number.	Name, Rank, Company, Regiment, Age, Date of Admission to Hospital.	Description and Date of Wound or Injury. On what Occasion received.	Date of Operation.	Operation.	Condition of Injured Parts at Time of Operation.
10. Fairfax Seminary U. S. A. General Hospital, Va.	Joseph Brown, Private Co. 1, 3d Michigan Vols. Age, 38. Admitted September 11, 1862.	A musket-ball passed through the trochanter of the left femur at the second battle of Bull Run. After lying exposed on the battle-field for three days, the patient was taken to Centreville, and thence to Fairfax Seminary Hospital. On two occasions fragments of bone were removed from the wound.	March 21, 1863.	A large exploratory incision was made from three inches above to five inches below the trochanter; the femur was divided squarely by powerful bone-cutting forceps, six inches below the trochanter; the neck of the femur was so much diseased that the head of the bone was then removed.	Early in March the limb began to swell immoderately, and the discharge from the wound became scanty and fœtid; much callus had been thrown out. A drawing of the case represents much burrowing of pus amid the muscles of the thigh.
11. Frederick General Hospital, Md. No. 5.	Edward Hunt, Private Co. D, 71st Pennsylvania Vols. Age, 24. Admitted January 20, 1863.	Missile entered two inches above trochanter major, and grazed the neck of femur; passed out at the nates.	Feb. 23, 1863.	Excision of the head of the femur, the neck being divided by the lion-jawed cutting forceps; very little blood lost. Chloroform.	Profuse suppuration, estimated at a quart in twenty-four hours; abscesses about the hip and upper part of thigh.
12. Field.	James Tallman, Sergeant Co. H, 16th Wisconsin Vols.	Comminuted fracture of left femur by a conoidal musket-ball. After Jackson, Miss., May 14, 1863.	May 16, 1863.	Excision of the head and portion of the shaft of the left femur.	Head of femur comminuted, and shaft shattered three inches below the surgical neck.
13.	Private. Confederate.	Gunshot fracture of the upper extremity of the femur.	1863.	Excision of the head of the femur. Chloroform. Secondary operation.	
14. "Stewart" Confederate Hospital, Richmond, Va.	——— Jarratt, Lieutenant, 15th North Carolina Confederate States Army.	Comminuted gunshot fracture of the upper extremity of the left femur by a conoidal musket-ball.	January 9, 1864.	Excision of the head, trochanters, and several inches of the shaft of the left femur. Chloroform.	
15. Judiciary Square U. S. A. General Hospital, Washington, D. C. 7019.	Charles Cleavor, Private Co. C, 2d U. S. Infantry. Age, ——. Admitted May 18, 1864.	Compound comminuted fracture of femur involving the joint and four inches of shaft by minié-ball. Spotsylvania, Va., May 12, 1864.	May 19, 1864.	Excision of head of bone and four and a quarter inches of shaft; incision curved, and six inches in length.	Extensive laceration of soft parts; pus, of an ill-conditioned character, burrowing in every direction.

EXCISIONS OF THE HEAD OF THE FEMUR—*Continued.*

Constitutional State of Patient at Time of Operation.	Progress, Treatment, etc.	Result. Cause of Death.	REMARKS.
Loss of appetite; pulse small and frequent.	Rallied with difficulty from the shock of the operation. In forty-eight hours an erysipelatous blush pervaded the whole thigh, and typhoid symptoms were manifested. A catheter was passed into the wound, and maintained there as a drainage tube. The wound was frequently washed out through this tube. March 26th. A rigor, apparently caused by hæmorrhage to the extent of six ounces. After the first few days the limb was supported by the anterior splint of Professor Smith, and subsequently by a kind of hammock. Brandy, beef tea, and eggs were given in large quantities.	April 30th, 1863. Nearly well. May 31st, 1863. Entirely well. August 22d, 1863. Successful result.	Operator, David P. Smith, Surgeon U. S. Vols. A letter from this man, dated Coopersville, March 21st, 1864, in which he speaks of himself as being in good health. He walks about and attends to home business, splits and saws a little wood, but complains of some pain in the leg and stiffness in the knee. On the whole, he says, "there is a constant improvement, and he is exceedingly thankful for the service done him by his surgeon." Another letter, dated September 26th, 1865, states that he continues in good health. Army Medical Museum, Specimen No. 1192. Surgical Series of Drawings, S. G. O., No. 73, represents the appearance of the patient in August, 1863.
Emaciated, and has night-sweats.	Recovered well from chloroform, but never fairly reacted from the shock of the operation.	Died February 25th, 1863.	Operator, H. A. Dubois, Asst. Surgeon U.S.A. Specimen 3907, Army Medical Museum.
....	Patient removed to a comfortable hospital in Jackson the same day. Gradually sank.	Died May 19th, 1863.	Operator, Henry S. Hewit, Surgeon U. S. V. History compiled from his verbal report.
....	....	Died.	Operator, a Confederate Surgeon. See Confederate States Medical and Surgical Journal, vol. i. No. 10, p. 155, October, 1864.
Satisfactory.	Very favorable. It was stated by Dr. Latimer that the patient could ultimately walk without crutches, with the aid of a cane and a high-heeled boot.	The patient so far recovered, at the end of six weeks from the date of operation, as to be able to be removed to his home in North Carolina. He was last heard from in September, 1864, when all sinuses had healed, and considerable weight could be borne on the injured limb.	Operator, J. B. Reed, Surgeon Confederate States Army. The facts in this case were obtained by Surgeon Otis, U. S. Vols., from Dr. Latimer, Asst. Surgeon C. S. A., who conducted the after-treatment in Lieut Jarratt's case. Army Medical Museum, Photographic Series No. 41.
Not good.	Charpie soaked with permanganate of potash, applied to wound; tonics and stimulants internally.	Died May 23d, 1864, of pyæmia.	Operator, J. H. Thompson, Act. Asst. Surgeon U. S. A.

SURGICAL OPERATIONS.

TABULAR STATEMENT OF THE OPERATIONS OF

Hospital and Hospital Number.	Name, Rank, Company, Regiment. Age. Date of Admission to Hospital.	Description and Date of Wound or Injury. On what Occasion received.	Date of Operation.	Operation.	Condition of Injured Parts at Time of Operation.
16. Judiciary Square U. S. A. General Hospital, Washington, D. C. 6974.	Alexander Ewing, Private Co. A, 140th Pennsylvania Vols. Age, 30. Admitted May 18, 1864.	Compound comminuted fracture of upper part of left femur, implicating hip-joint. Wilderness, Va., May 13, 1864.	May 19, 1864.	Excision of head of bone below trochanter; an incision of about five inches was made over great trochanter, taking in the wound of entrance.	There was much inflammation and swelling of soft parts.
17. Stanton U. S. A. General Hospital, Washington, D. C. 1085. "Ward" Hospital, Newark, N. J.	Hugh Wright, Private Co. G, 8th New Jersey Vols. Age, 28. Admitted May 25, 1864.	A minié-ball entered the right thigh one inch to the inner side of the femoral artery and about two inches below Poupart's ligament, and passed backward and downward, shattering the neck and trochanter of the femur. The ball lodged behind the bone. Wilderness, Va., May 5, 1864.	May 27, 1864.	Resection of head, neck, and both trochanters of femur; made an incision six inches in length over the trochanter major down to the bone; extracted the fractured splinters, and removed the head and neck of the femur; found the ball, a minié, lying behind the neck of femur. Sulphuric ether.	An abscess had formed about the seat of fracture; the bone was much comminuted, and many of the fractured splinters were detached; the ball had not been extracted.
18. Mt. Pleasant U. S. A. General Hospital, Washington, D. C. 9897.	John Phelan, Captain Co. A, 73d N. Y. Vols. Age, 22. Admitted May 16, 1864.	Gunshot wound of left thigh, with compound comminuted fracture of neck and upper end of femur. Spottsylvania C. H., Va., May 14, 1864.	June 3, 1864.	Excision of head, neck, and upper end of femur by T incision of five inches over the trochanter, extending down the line of femur.	All motion of the limb accompanied by severe pain.
19. Jarvis U. S. A. General Hospital, Baltimore, Md.	Jason M. Joslyn, Private Co. I, 7th New York Heavy Artillery. Age, 20. Admitted November 28, 1864.	Gunshot fracture of head of right femur by a piece of shell, which entered over the great trochanter, fracturing it and the neck of the femur. Cold Harbor, Va., June 3, 1864.	June 5, 1864.	Excision of the head and two inches of shaft of right femur, through an incision eight inches in length on outer side. The report from Dale Hospital states that the head and six inches of the shaft were removed.	Parts very much swollen.
20. Field Hospital, Ream's Station, Va.	Confederate Private.	Compound comminuted fracture of the neck of the right femur by a conoidal ball. Ream's Station, Va., 1864.	June, 1864.	Removal of the head, neck, and greater portion of the trochanter major of the right femur.	....

EXCISIONS. 69

EXCISIONS OF THE HEAD OF THE FEMUR—*Continued.*

Constitutional State of Patient at Time of Operation.	Progress, Treatment, etc.	Result. Cause of Death.	REMARKS.
Not favorable.	Patient lived but five days; the wound assumed no healthy action; stimulants and ice to wound; but he gradually sank.	Died May 24th, 1864, from exhaustion from surgical fever.	Operator, J. H. Thompson, Act. Asst. Surgeon U. S. A. The fracture extended into the joint, separating the trochanter from neck and splintering the shaft of bone.
Fair.	He exhibited a great deal of shock, and reacted slowly. May 28th. Pulse frequent and feeble; exhibits a good deal of nervous agitation; has some fever; tongue dry and furred in centre. June 1st. Condition much improved; wound looks well; character of the suppuration good. June 30th. Is doing well.	November 16th, 1864. Recovered. Discharged from service October 6th, 1864, by reason of expiration of term, but unable to travel. Transferred to General Hospital at Newark, N. J., April 15th, 1865. He was in tolerably good health. The limb disposed to abscesses upon any unusual exertion. Left hospital May 6th, 1865.	Operator, George A. Mursick, Asst. Surgeon U. S. Vols. Army Medical Museum, Specimen No. 3875.
Constitution naturally good; very much reduced at time of operation; discharge of pus very free; appetite poor; tongue coated; bowels moved frequently; skin moist; pulse 90 to 100.	Simple dressings of cold water and lint; discharge of pus moderate and healthy; wound looking well; no pain; nourishing diet; tonics and stimulants given freely.	Died June 21st, 1864, of asthenia, consequent from gunshot wound.	Operator, M. C. Mulford, Act. Asst. Surgeon U. S. A. Army Medical Museum, Specimen No. 2618.
Good.	Simple dressings; did well. At date of transfer the parts had entirely healed; the limb was six inches shorter than the other, and could be swung forward and backward, but could not be exercised in lateral or rotary motion.	Furloughed Dec. 21st, 1864; readmitted and transferred, February 28th, 1865, to Worcester, Mass. March 31st, 1865. Patient is in perfect health; parts healed and free from tenderness; limb movable in every direction, and perfectly under control of the muscles; while standing erect on the left foot, and placing the right on a line with the long axis of the leg, he can touch the floor with his toes; more than two inches of the shaft is apparently gone; upper end of femur enlarged, apparently by new osseous growth, to almost twice its normal diameter; has a good false joint, and leg can be made useful hereafter when strengthened by artificial appliances.	Operator, Confederate Surgeon. Transferred from Dale U. S. A. General Hospital to DeCamp U. S. A. General Hospital, August 28th, 1865. Asst. Surgeon Warren Webster's Report proves conclusively that the head of the bone was not removed in this case. The patient is figured in Photographs 106 and 107, A. M. M.
....	Smith's anterior splint was applied after operation.	....	Report of Asst. Surgeon J. S. Billings, U. S. A., Acting Medical Inspector A. of P.

SURGICAL OPERATIONS.

TABULAR STATEMENT OF THE OPERATIONS OF

Hospital and Hospital Number.	Name, Rank, Company, Regiment. Age. Date of Admission to Hospital.	Description and Date of Wound or Injury. On what Occasion received.	Date of Operation.	Operation.	Condition of Injured Parts at Time of Operation.
21. Harewood U. S. A. General Hospital, Washington, D. C. 14,050.	Henry Woodworth, Private Co. A, 4th Vermont Volunteers. Age, 18. Admitted May 25, 1864.	Gunshot wound of left thigh, ball passing transversely below the trochanter major, fracturing upper portion of femur and lodging beneath sartorius muscle. Spottsylvania C. H., Va., May 12, 1864.	July 1, 1864.	Excision of head of left femur. Sulphuric ether.	....
22. Douglas, Washington, D. C.	Peter Boyle, Private Co. D, 59th Massachusetts Vols. Age, 60. Admitted August 3, 1864.	Gunshot wound of left hip, fracturing trochanter. Petersburg, Va., July 30, 1864.	August 5, 1864.	Excision of the head of the left femur. Ether.	The ball had comminuted the neck of the femur; fleshy parts healthy.
23. Field Hospital, 5th Corps.	A. McDonald, Private Co. F, 149th Pennsylvania Vols. Admitted August 20, 1864.	Gunshot fracture of the upper extremity of the femur by a conoidal musket-ball, which lodged in the head of the bone. Weldon Railroad, Va., August 20, 1864.	August 20, 1864.	Excision of the head and neck of the femur, the bone being sawn through the great trochanter; a V-shaped incision was employed. Chloroform.	Acetabulum uninjured; ball impacted in head of the femur.
24. Field Hospital, 5th Corps.	Charles Beard, Private 12th Mississippi Regiment, C. S. A.	Gunshot fracture of upper extremity of femur by a conoidal musket-ball.	August 20, 1864.	Excision of head, neck, and trochanters of the femur; the bone was sawn at the level of the trochanter minor; ball removed. Chloroform.	The ball entered in front, badly shattered the neck of the femur, and lodged in the acetabulum, the lower margin of which was broken off, but no communication existed with the interior of the pelvis.
25. U. S. A. General Hospital, Beverly, N. J.	John Zabcrowski, Private Co. H, 7th Connecticut Vols. Age, 33. Admitted August 22, 1864.	Gunshot wound of right thigh, fracturing head of femur; minié-ball entered just below the trochanter major, passing upward and inward, fracturing the neck and injuring the head of the bone. Deep Bottom, Va., August 16, 1864.	Sept. 27, 1864.	Resection of the head and a portion of the trochanter major of the right femur, by an incision four and a half inches in length. Chloroform used. Patient reacted slowly.	Parts in a sloughing condition; great suppurative discharge from wound.

EXCISIONS OF THE HEAD OF THE FEMUR—Continued.

Constitutional State of Patient at Time of Operation.	Progress, Treatment, etc.	Result. Cause of Death.	REMARKS.
Poor; anæmic; countenance pale; pulse small.	Unfavorable; treatment supporting. Patient did not improve after operation, but rapidly sank.	Died July 2d, 1864; exhaustion.	Operator, Reed B. Bontecou, Surgeon U. S. Vols. Army Medical Museum, Specimen No. 3049.
Patient very old; 60 years; condition poor.	Reacted well after operation, but at night there was sweating with vomiting. Aug. 6th, 1864. Ate a good breakfast, but still cool sweating skin; pulse 128.	Died August 9th, 1864.	Operator, Wm. Thomson, Asst. Surgeon U. S. A. Army Medical Museum, Specimen No. 8593,
Satisfactory.	No bad symptoms followed the operation for two days, and on August 23d the patient was sent to the base hospital at City Point.	Died in less than four days after the operation.	Report of Asst. Surgeon J. S. Billings, Acting Medical Inspector A. of P. Operator, Surgeon Reams, 149th Pennsylvania Vols. Consult also letter of Asst. Surgeon Chas. K. Winne, U.S.A., of Sept. 20th, 1865.
Satisfactory.	Limb dressed in Smith's anterior splint. Aug. 21st. A marked rigor occurred a short time after the operation was completed. On the following day there was retention of the urine and great irritability of the stomach.	Died August 25th, 1864, on the fifth day after the operation.	Report of Asst. Surgeon J. S. Billings, U. S. A., Acting Medical Inspector A. of P. Consult also letter of Asst. Surgeon Chas. K. Winne, U. S. A., of Sept. 20th, 1865. Operator, Surgeon White, Indiana Vols. At the autopsy the wound was found filled with offensive sanious pus, and the sawn surface of the femur was black. The acetabulum was intensely injected.
Patient feeble; pulse 140; appetite wanting; greatly reduced in strength and flesh.	Patient rapidly sinking; stimulants.	Died September 28th, 1864, from exhaustion.	Operator, C. Wagner, Asst. Surgeon U. S. A. Post-mortem revealed nothing worthy of note except slight necrosis of the acetabulum. Army Medical Museum, Specimen No. 3716.

SURGICAL OPERATIONS.

TABULAR STATEMENT OF THE OPERATIONS OF

Hospital and Hospital Number.	Name, Rank, Company, Regiment. Age. Date of Admission to Hospital.	Description and Date of Wound or Injury. On what Occasion received.	Date of Operation.	Operation.	Condition of Injured Parts at Time of Operation.
26. St. Louis U. S. A. General Hospital, New Orleans, La. 5766.	Hugh Train, Private Co. G, 31st Massachusetts Vols. Age, 22. Admitted February 18, 1865.	Conoidal ball entered anterior surface of middle third of left thigh, ranging upwards, and making exit above left gluteus, fracturing neck of femur. Accidentally, February 1, 1865.	March 24, 1865.	Made an incision four inches in length over the great trochanter; dissected soft parts from bone; divided bone with chain-saw just below trochanter, and removed head of bone without difficulty, teres ligament being softened.	Whole thigh dissected with pus; ulcers in groin; knee drawn over to right and across; shortening, with inversion; pus very unhealthy.
27. Mt. Pleasant U. S. A. General Hospital, Washington, D. C. 17,236.	H. C. Scnct, Private Co. F, 122d New York Vols. Age, 27. Admitted April 2, 1865.	Ball entered midway and on a line with anterior-superior spinous process of left ilium and trochanter major, and lodged in the head of the femur. Petersburg, Va., March 27, 1865.	April 4, 1865.	Excision of head of left femur at anatomical neck, and extraction of ball; a T incision was made over trochanter major four by six inches. Ether and chloroform.	Limb looked very healthy, but on examination it was found that the ball had fractured the head of the femur into three pieces and lodged in it.
28. Armory Square U. S. A. General Hospital, Washington, D. C.	D. N. Patterson, Lieutenant Co. E, 45th Virginia (Rebel) Regiment. Admitted April 2, 1865.	Conoidal musket-ball entered behind left trochanter major, comminuted the head, neck, and trochanter of femur, and fractured the acetabulum. Boydton Plank Road, near Petersburg, Va., March 27, 1865.	April 3, 1865.	Excision of head, neck, and trochanters of left femur; about two inches were removed, and the ball extracted. Chloroform.	The misshapen and battered ball was buried in the obturator muscles. Back of the acetabulum a splinter of the os pubis was forced inwards into the pelvic cavity.
29. Douglas General Hospital, Washington, D. C. 6829.	Henry Phillips, Private Co. I, 146th New York Vols. Age, 34. Admitted April 6, 1865.	Gunshot wound over left trochanter, ball lodging in neck of femur. Southside Rail Road, Va., April 1, 1865.	April 8, 1865.	Excision of head, neck, and trochanter of left femur. Ether.	Bone not completely fractured; hip-joint opened.
30. Judiciary Square General Hospital, Washington, D. C. 9260.	George M. Spencer, Private Co. B, 2d New York Mounted Rifles. Age, 17. Admitted April 4, 1865.	Gunshot fracture of right femur; ball entered at great trochanter and caused extensive longitudinal splintering of the shaft, which was found subsequently to extend quite to its lower third. Dinwiddie C. H., March 31, 1865.	April 12, 1865.	Excision of head, neck, and trochanters of right femur. Chloroform.	The femur extensively shattered; copious suppuration from wound.

EXCISIONS OF THE HEAD OF THE FEMUR—Continued.

Constitutional State of Patient at Time of Operation.	Progress, Treatment, etc.	Result. Cause of Death.	REMARKS.
General health bad; night-sweats; tongue clean and moist; appetite good; bowels inclined to be costive.	Wound filled with lint; porter, chicken broth, eggs, stimulants, everything to enable him to sustain the drain upon his system. Felt easier for a few days after the operation.	Died March 30th, 1865. He became very much emaciated.	Operator, A. McMahon, Surgeon U. S. Vols. When admitted, patient stated positively that the surgeon of his regiment had given him chloroform, and examined his wound, and that the bone was not touched. There was no evidence of fracture on admission. He had walked upon the limb. The ball had injured the neck of the bone, and the subsequent caries had caused its destruction.
Patient feverish and fretful, with furred tongue.	Singultus came on immediately after operation, but was arrested; antispasmodics. April 5th, Great tympanitis. April 7th. Well-marked signs of peritonitis; a chill occurred, and lasted half an hour.	Died April 8th, 1865; acute peritonitis.	Operator, H. Allen, Asst. Surgeon U. S. A. Autopsy: Lungs healthy; liver greatly hypertrophied; lower fifth of ilium greatly inflamed and injected; tissues surrounding left hip-joint in a sloughing condition, and infiltrated with fœtid pus, which had burrowed several inches under gluteal muscles; also two inches below lesser trochanter; acetabulum denuded and a slight fracture of upper and posterior border; upper two inches of femur denuded of periosteum. Army Medical Museum, Specimen No. 526.
Very satisfactory.	Did well for two or three days, when hæmorrhage occurred. Hæmorrhage was probably from iliac vein, injured by a sharp splinter of bone.	Died April 7th, 1865.	Operator, D. W. Bliss, Surgeon U. S. Vols. Army Medical Museum, Specimen No. 4048.
Patient was somewhat exhausted, and had considerable fever; pulse and respiration nearly normal.	April 13th. Wound appears healthy; suppurates well; patient perspires freely; pulse 120. April 15th. Pulse 118. April 17th. Pulse 120; respiration 32; slight pleurisy of right side; Diarrhœa set in. April 18th. Respiration 26; pulse 130; much weaker. April 20th. Chill.	Died April 21st, 1865; exhaustion.	Operator, Wm. F. Norris, Asst. Surgeon U. S. A. Autopsy. No evidences of pyæmia found, though strongly suspected before death. Army Medical Museum, Specimen No. 3235.
Irritative fever.	It was ascertained that longitudinal splintering of the femur extended far down the shaft, and amputation at the hip-joint was performed.	Died April 12th, 1865.	Operator, E. Griswold, Surgeon U. S. Vols.

TABULAR STATEMENT OF THE OPERATIONS OF

Hospital and Hospital Number.	Name, Rank, Company, Regiment. Age. Date of Admission to Hospital.	Description and Date of Wound or Injury. On what Occasion received.	Date of Operation.	Operation.	Condition of Injured Parts at Time of Operation.
31. St. Louis U. S. A. General Hospital, New Orleans, La. 7643. Marine General Hospital, New Orleans, La.	T. E. Foulke, Private Co. D, 2d Alabama (C. S. A.). Age, 17. Admitted April 15, 1865. Admitted May 26, 1865.	Conoidal ball entered posteriorly at middle third of left thigh; extracted above anterior superior spinous process of left ilium, fracturing upper third of femur, involving trochanter and neck. Fort Blakely, Ala., April 9, 1865.	April 27, 1865.	Excision of two inches of shaft of left femur, including trochanters, neck, and head. Chloroform.	Great comminution; parts surrounding hip-joint filled with unhealthy pus.
32. St. Louis U. S. A. General Hospital, New Orleans, La. 7641.	G. W. Brantley, Private Co. C, 2d Alabama (C. S. A.). Age, 18. Admitted April 15, 1865.	Conoidal ball entered left groin, passing through, fracturing neck of left femur, emerged posteriorly from left gluteus; also gunshot fracture of external condyle of right humerus. Fort Blakely, Ala., April 9, 1865.	April 28, 1865.	Excision of head, neck, and trochanter of left femur; no ligations. Chloroform.	Thigh, groin, and surrounding parts infiltrated by unhealthy pus.

A case is reported by Acting Assistant Surgeon Siebold, U. S. A., in which only a portion of the head of the femur was removed, a ball being at the same time extracted from the acetabulum. The patient, Private Robb, 188th New York Vols., was treated at Point Lookout Hospital, and died four months after the operation.

Many other cases occurred in which the operation was admissible, so far as the local lesions were concerned. But the requisites for after-treatment were not attainable in the field hospitals, and when the patients reached the base hospitals, their condition forbade operative interference.

The annexed engraving of a specimen (No. 125), taken from a patient who died in the Patent Office Hospital, in Washington, in September, 1862, illustrates such cases.

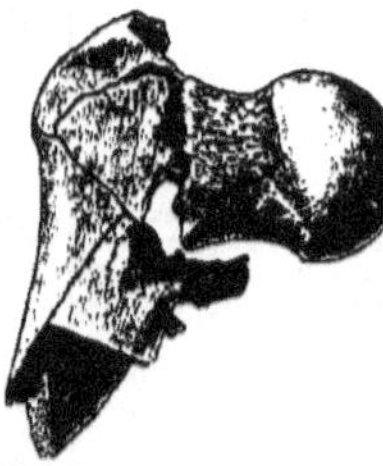

Fig. 72.—Conoidal ball embedded in the head of femur. Spec. 125, A. M. M.

Fig. 73.—Head of femur excised for gunshot injury. Spec. 3375, A. M. M.

At the Army Medical Museum there are preserved 16 excised heads of femurs, including the specimens from two of the successful cases.

Specimen 3375 exhibits the extensive comminution of the trochanters in Dr. Mursick's successful case. The black object below the neck represents the battered shapeless ball.

EXCISIONS OF THE HEAD OF THE FEMUR—Concluded.

Constitutional State of Patient at Time of Operation.	Progress, Treatment, etc.	Result. Cause of Death.	REMARKS.
Very much exhausted from profuse suppuration.	Nourishing diet; two bottles of porter daily, eggs, beef tea, and everything he desired.	Transferred to Marine Hospital, New Orleans, La., May 26th, 1865; doing well. Died June 5th, 1865; exhaustion.	Operator, A. McMahon, Surgeon U. S. Vols. This case was unfavorable for any operation; but as death evidently would otherwise result, the only hope for him was in operation.
Very much exhausted.	Did not rally well; stimulants very freely administered.	Died May 2d, 1865; capillary hæmorrhage.	Operator, A. McMahon, Surgeon U. S. Vols. No operation performed on elbow-joint, as condition of patient would not admit it.

Fig. 74.—Excised head of femur, with callus formation below the trochanters. Spec. 1192, A. M. M.

Fig. 75.—Excised head of femur. Spec. 71, A. M. M.

The specimen in Surgeon D. P. Smith's successful case indicates that nature had attempted something in the way of reparation. (Specimen 1192.)

A drawing has been made of the appearance of the limb of the patient who furnished this specimen.* (Surgical Series of Drawings No. 73, A. M. M.)

In Medical Inspector Pineo's case (Specimen 71, A. M. M.), the ball, after shattering the trochanters and neck of the femur, unhappily entered the pelvic cavity.

---

* The following letter, which is quoted in his own language, has lately been received from Mr. Brown:

BVT. LT. COL. GEORGE A. OTIS,   COOPERSVILLE, MICHIGAN, September 26th, 1865.
    Surgeon U. S. Vols.

SIR:—
    Yours of the 21st inst. has just come to hand, and I take pleasure in informing you that my general health is good; my leg is improving slowly; the knee remains quite stiff yet, but I think it is better than it was one year ago. I have some control over the movements of the thigh. When standing, can move the leg backwards and forwards, about two and a half feet, and sideways enough to bring the foot across in front of the other foot. Can bear considerable of my weight upon it, but not enough to do away with the use of one crutch yet. Cannot perceive that there is any difference in the length of the limb since I was discharged, as I use the stirrup on the crutch the same as then. There has been no breaking out of abscesses, nor any soreness of any kind since March, 1864, nor since my discharge, to amount to anything.   *   *   *   *

                                    Respectfully yours,
        (Signed)   JOSEPH BROWN,
                                         Late of Co. I, 3d Michigan Vols.

EXCISIONS IN THE CONTINUITY OF THE LONG BONES OF THE EXTREMITIES.—The great surgeons who have done most towards substituting excision for amputation in gunshot injuries of the joints have almost unanimously condemned excisions of the continuity of the long bones in the treatment of gunshot fractures. The surgical histories of the Crimean war, of the Schleswick Holstein campaigns, and of the Indian mutiny, record a few successes in resections of the shafts of the humerus, the tibia, and the bones of the forearm; but this class of operations could scarcely be considered as admitted among the established and approved procedures of surgery. The late war has furnished ample materials for arriving at definite conclusions on this subject, and for determining how far these measures can claim to be included in that true conservatism which has for its first object the saving of life, and refuses to jeopardize lives in order to save limbs.

These materials are yet to be thoroughly analyzed. So far as examined, their evidence is, on the whole, unfavorable to excisions in the continuity.

A synopsis of the results at present attained is presented in the following table:

Table, giving the Number of Cases of Excisions for Gunshot Injuries in the Continuity of the Bones of the Extremities, from the Commencement of the War to July, 1864, and the Results as far as ascertained.

	Died.	Recovered.	Amputations ultimately required.	Result not yet determined.	Total.	Percentage of Mortality in finished cases.
Excisions in the continuity of the Humerus	42	133	7	79	261	24·00
Excisions in the continuity of the Radius	11	93	8	67	174	10·57
Excisions in the continuity of the Ulna	16	100	3	51	170	13·79
Excisions in the continuity of both Radius and Ulna	5	24	1	10	40	17·24
Excisions of the Metacarpal Bones	2	30	...	18	50	6·25
Excisions in the continuity of the Femur	32	6	...	24	62	84·21
Excisions in the continuity of the Tibia	11	48	5	20	84	18·64
Excisions in the continuity of the Fibula	15	60	3	15	93	20·00
Excisions in the continuity of both Tibia and Fibula	1	4	1	2	8	25·00
Excisions of the Metatarsal Bones	5	26	...	2	33	19·23
Totals	140	524	28	288	975	26·71

After excisions of portions of the shaft of the humerus for gunshot fractures, a number of patients have certainly obtained very useful limbs. But the mortality after the operation is 3 per cent. greater than after amputation of the arm. The 52 preparations at the Army Medical Museum, illustrating this resection, indicate the frequency with which it is followed by secondary amputation or a fatal result.

Excision in the continuity of both bones of the forearm has a larger mortality ratio than amputation of the forearm.

The specimens at the Museum and the records afford emphatic arguments against formal excisions of the shaft of the femur. With one exception, the few cases that recovered were those in which, after the removal of detached fragments, the least amount of operative interference had been practised.

The mortality rate after excisions of the tibia and fibula is less than after amputation, as the statistics stand; but the number of cases in which the result is still pending is unusually large.

There have been a few cases in which portions of the lower jaw, the body of the clavicle, the ribs, or the ilium, have been removed by the gouge or the chain-saw after gunshot injuries. The results are given in the following tables:

Table, exhibiting Results of Cases of Excisions of the Bones of the Face, after Gunshot Fractures.

Number of deaths..	3
Number of recoveries..	23
Number of cases in which results, as yet, have not been obtained..	11
Total number of cases...	37

Table, exhibiting Results of Cases of Excisions of the Bones of the Trunk, after Gunshot Fractures.

Number of deaths..	7
Number of recoveries..	15
Number of cases in which results, as yet, have not been obtained..	5
Total number of cases...	27

One of the registers of excisions is devoted to the cases of trephining after gunshot injuries of the cranium. The results of this operation have already been alluded to, and are here recapitulated in a tabular form.

Table, exhibiting Results of Cases of Gunshot Fractures of the Skull, in which Trephining was performed.

Number of deaths..	60
Number of recoveries..	47
Number of cases in which, as yet, results have not been obtained..	14
Total number of cases...	121

Table, exhibiting Results of Cases of Gunshot Fractures of the Skull, in which Fragments of Bone were extracted.

Number of deaths..	61
Number of recoveries..	53
Number of cases in which, as yet, results have not been obtained..	19
Total number of cases...	133

LIGATIONS.

The following table exhibits the number of cases of ligation of the larger arteries, from the beginning of the war to March, 1864:

	Number of cases recovered.	Number of cases died.	Total.	Ratio of Mortality.
Common Carotid	12	37	49	75·71
External Carotid	...	2	2	100·
Subclavian	7	28	35	80·
Axillary	3	21	24	87·50
Brachial	53	11	64	17·18
Radial	12	2	14	14·28
Ulnar	9	2	11	18·18
Common Iliac	...	3	3	100·
Internal Iliac	...	2	2	100·
External Iliac	2	14	16	87·50
Femoral	25	83	108	76·85
Profunda	1	6	7	85·71
Popliteal	4	12	16	75·
Anterior Tibial	11	5	16	31·25
Posterior Tibial	13	6	19	31·57
Peroneal	...	2	2	100·
All others	11	4	15	26·66
Aggregate	163	240	403	....

Of the three cases of ligation of the common iliac, one was performed by Surgeon McKee, U. S. A., on account of secondary hæmorrhage from a branch of the left internal iliac. The hæmorrhage resulted from a gunshot wound of the pelvis, and occurred on the fifteenth and again on the twenty-third day. On the second bleeding, the internal iliac was tied; but the hæmorrhage was not controlled, and the main trunk was secured. The patient survived two days, and the bleeding did not recur. The appearance of the parts is represented in vol. i. p. 5 of Photographs of Surgical Cases, S. G. O., and the preparation is preserved as Specimen No. 3464, A. M. M. The second operation was performed by Acting Assistant Surgeon Isham, U. S. A., for a false consecutive aneurism of the anterior trunk of the right internal iliac, resulting from a bayonet stab through the ischiatic notch. Seven months after the wound was inflicted the rupture of the sac appeared imminent, and the operation was imperative. The patient survived four days. An occluding clot, extending to the bifurcation of the aorta, was found above the ligature. There was no peritonitis. The third operation was done at the Ward Hospital, Newark, New Jersey, for an aneurismal varix, following a stab with a penknife in the left thigh, which opened a communication between the femoral artery and vein. The patient died of peritonitis in five days. The injected vessels constitute Specimen No. 3597, A. M. M., and are represented in Photograph No. 74, A. M. M.

Two cases are recorded of deligation of the internal iliac for secondary hæmorrhage after gunshot wounds. Both terminated fatally.

Of the ligations of the external iliac, 2 recovered. One of them was the case of Private Smith, already related (p. 49), in which amputation at the hip-joint had been previously performed. The second was the case of Sergeant Ziders, Co. I, 53d Pennsylvania Vols., who received a severe flesh wound of the right thigh at Gettysburg, July 3d,

1863, with injury to the femoral artery. There was secondary bleeding, for which the femoral was tied in the wound. Bleeding recurred, and on October 8th, 1863, the external iliac was tied by Acting Assistant Surgeon Adinell M. Hewson, U. S. A. The patient recovered, and was discharged from service May 14th, 1864, the movements of his right leg being impaired by contraction of the muscles.

Of ligations of the subclavian, 35 cases are recorded. In all, the vessel was secured outside of the scaleni. In 16 cases, the operation was on the right, and in 14 on the left side; in 5 cases, the particular vessel is not mentioned. The operation was performed in 13 cases for secondary hæmorrhage after amputation of the shoulder-joint, with 4 recoveries. In 2 cases, it was done for primary, and in 15 for secondary bleeding after gunshot wounds, with injury of the axillary artery, with 2 recoveries. In 2 cases, the operation was performed for axillary aneurism. In 2 cases, with one recovery, it was required by secondary bleeding after excisions of the humerus, and in 1 case it was necessitated by a secondary hæmorrhage after a gunshot wound with injury of the subclavian.

The ligations included in the category of "all others" were of the temporal artery in 3 cases, the occipital in 2, the facial in 2, and intercostal in 2; the internal mammary, the thoracica longa, the gluteal, the superior profunda of the arm, the posterior circumflex branch of the axillary, the right dorsalis pedis, each in 1 case.

The two ligations of intercostals were performed by Assistant Surgeon B. Howard, U. S. A., and Assistant Surgeon W. H. Gardner, U. S. A., according to the plan proposed by the former, of enclosing the rib in the ligature. Dr. Howard's patient died the day after the operation was performed. The other patient recovered.

The new hæmostatic process* recommended by Professor Simpson was adopted in a few cases, with favorable results.

OTHER SURGICAL OPERATIONS.

Four additional registers of operations are kept. In one is recorded the histories of 290 cases of gunshot fractures, in which the primary sequestra of Dupuytren, or detached fragments of bone, have been extracted. Another register contains the histories of 436 cases, in which balls or other foreign bodies have been extracted. Extraneous matters extracted from gunshot wounds have been of great variety, and comprise bits of clothing and accoutrements, fragments of watches, coins, shoe-nails, teeth, etc. A collection of over 400 such bodies is preserved at the Army Medical Museum.

The register of operations for surgical diseases contains the histories of 443 cases, many of which are of great interest. For example, 15 cases of tracheotomy or laryngotomy are recorded, with six recoveries. The operation was done once, with success, in a case of croupal diphtheritis.

Finally, in the "register of operations not included in other categories," 23 cases are recorded of the treatment of wounds of the larger joints by free incisions, or of operations for ununited gunshot fractures.

---

* Acupressure, a New Method of Arresting Surgical Hæmorrhage and of Accelerating the Healing of Wounds. By James Y. Simpson, M.D., F.R.S.E. Edinburgh, 1864. Octavo, pp. xiv., 580.

ON THE MEDICAL STAFF AND THE MATERIA CHIRURGICA.

THE MEDICAL STAFF.

AFTER its organization was fairly completed, the medical staff that served in the late war was composed of a surgeon general, one assistant surgeon general, a medical inspector general, 16 medical inspectors, 170 surgeons and assistant surgeons of the regular army, 362 volunteer staff surgeons and assistant surgeons, 3000 regimental surgeons and assistant surgeons of volunteers, 2500 acting assistant surgeons or physicians serving under contract, and 6 medical storekeepers.

The medical service in the field was organized upon the basis of an independent hospital and ambulance establishment for each division of three brigades. The *personnel* of the division hospital consisted of a surgeon in charge, with an assistant surgeon as executive officer and another assistant surgeon as recorder, an operating staff of three surgeons, aided by three assistant surgeons, and the requisite number of nurses and attendants. The division ambulance train was commanded by a first lieutenant, assisted by a second lieutenant from each brigade. The enlisted men detailed for ambulance duty were a sergeant from each regiment, three privates for each ambulance, and one private for each wagon. The ambulance train consisted of from one to three ambulances for each regiment, squadron, or battery, a medicine wagon for each brigade, and two or more supply wagons. The hospital and ambulance train were under the control of the surgeon in chief of division. The division hospitals were usually located just out of range of artillery fire. Sometimes three or more of the division hospitals were consolidated under the orders of a corps medical director, who was assisted by his inspector, quartermaster, commissary, and chief ambulance officer. The medical officers not employed at the field hospitals accompanied their regiments, and established temporary depots as near as practicable to the line of battle. How faithfully this perilous duty was performed may be inferred from the fact that, during the war, thirty-six medical officers were either killed, or died from wounds received in battle. As soon as practicable, after every engagement, the wounded were transferred from the division or corps hospitals to the base or general hospitals, which at one time were 205 in number. These were under the charge and command of officers of the regular or volunteer staff, who were assisted by acting assistant surgeons, and by officers of the second battalion of the Veteran Reserve Corps.

The organization of the medical staff in the field and in permanent hospitals is very fully discussed, in papers on file in the office, by Colonel Charles S. Tripler, Dr. Jonathan Letterman, and Colonel T. A. McParlin, successively medical directors of the Army of the Potomac; by Colonel G. E. Cooper, medical director of the Army of the Cumberland; by Lieutenant Colonel J. J. Milhau, medical director of the 5th Army Corps; by Surgeon L. W. Read, U. S. Vols., surgeon in chief of the 3d Division 5th Army Corps; by Surgeon T. M. Flandreau, 146th New York Vols., surgeon in chief of brigade, and in the reports of the medical inspectors of military departments.

ON MEANS OF TRANSPORTATION OF THE WOUNDED.

The wounded who were unable to walk were removed beyond the immediate range of musketry on hand-litters. The details for bearers were usually made from the musicians of regiments.

Models of the different patterns of litters that were used are preserved at the Army Medical Museum. In the early part of the war, most of the regiments were supplied with stretchers of the old regulation pattern. It was found that the yoke

Fig. 76.—Regulation hand-litter.

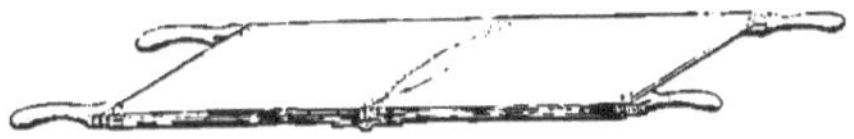

pieces were frequently lost, and that when the canvas stretcher became damp, the litter was put together with difficulty. A light and convenient pattern, known as the "Halstead litter," was subsequently largely used. Brigadier General Satterlee issued 12,867 of these litters from the purveying depot of New York alone. They were too fragile for the hard usage to which they were subjected.

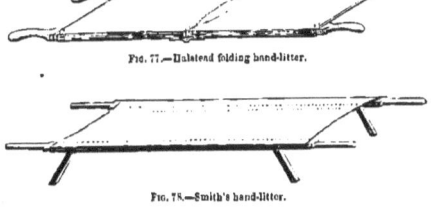

Fig. 77.—Halstead folding hand-litter.

Fig. 78.—Smith's hand-litter.

Another pattern, folding up lengthwise, in which the poles were separated by folding iron braces, was very generally used during the last two years of the war. Colonel C. McDougall issued 5548 of these from the purveying depot in Philadelphia.

Fig. 79.—Hand-litter-carriage. Scale ½ inch to the foot.

A form of litter on wheels, that had been advantageously employed by the Prussians in the war with the Danes,* was introduced too late to test its utility practically.

---

* Gurlt, Militär-Chirurgische Fragmente, Berlin, 1865; Neudörfer, Handbuch der Kriegs-Chirurgie, Leipzig, 1864; and Neudörfer, Aus dem feld-ärztlichen Berichter über die Verwundeten in Schleswig, Berlin, 1864.

A few cacolets were issued; but they were not regarded with favor by many surgeons. They were adapted only for men wounded in the upper extremities, and such patients were more comfortably transported in ambulances or baggage wagons.

FIG. 80.—Cacolet.

FIG. 81.—Wounded men transported by cacolets.

The horse-litters were also but little used. Altogether, seven or eight hundred of them were supplied to the troops; but they were soon laid aside.

FIG. 82.—Transportation of the wounded by the horse-litter.

MEANS OF TRANSPORTATION OF THE WOUNDED.

At the beginning of the war, the one-horse ambulances, designed by Surgeon General Finley and Surgeon Coolidge, and the four-horse ambulances, designed by Surgeon Tripler, were chiefly employed.

The former were intended to transport two wounded men in a recumbent position. The latter accommodated eight men, lying down. The beds in all of these ambulances were movable, and could be used as hand-litters.

The one-horse ambulances were too frail for the rough roads on which they were

Fig. 83.—The "Coolidge" ambulance.

Fig. 84.—Side view of the "Tripler" ambulance.

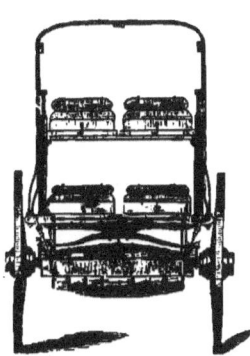

Fig. 85.—Rear view of the "Tripler" ambulance.

Fig. 86.—Side elevation of the Wheeling or Rosecrans ambulance.

employed, and soon fell into disrepute. The four-horse ambulance rendered good service, but it was very heavy. What is commonly known as the "Wheeling" ambulance, from having been first constructed at Wheeling, Virginia, from a design of General Rosecrans, soon came into very general use. It is drawn by two horses, and carries ten or twelve persons sitting, or two or three sitting and two lying down. It combines lightness and strength.

Towards the close of the war, a still better ambulance was constructed from designs furnished by Brevet Major General D. H. Rucker, of the Quartermaster's Department. It has been recommended as the regulation ambulance for the U. S. Army. Its plan is exhibited and sufficiently explained in the accompanying plate.

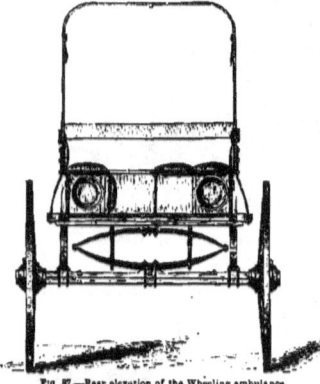

FIG. 87.—Rear elevation of the Wheeling ambulance.

Throughout the war, the system of rapidly removing the wounded to permanent hospitals, remote from the scene of hostilities, was uniformly adopted. To accomplish this, trains of hospital railway cars were constructed, and steamers were fitted up as hospital transports, or were built expressly for this service. The hospital cars were furnished with movable berths or litters, and in each train one car was provided with facilities for cooking, and with a dispensary.

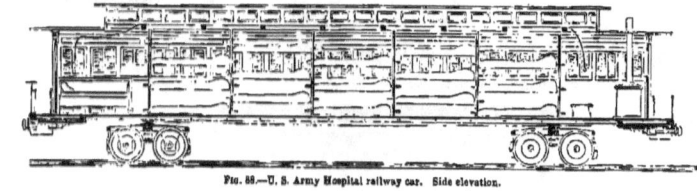

FIG. 88.—U. S. Army Hospital railway car. Side elevation.

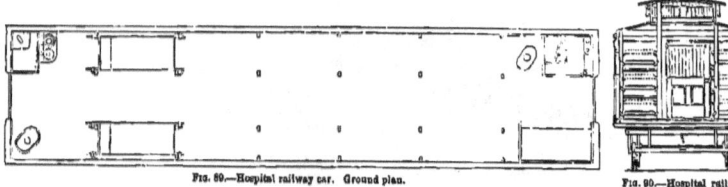

FIG. 89.—Hospital railway car. Ground plan.   FIG. 90.—Hospital railway car. Rear elevation.

During the siege operations in front of Petersburg, the sick and wounded were conveyed by rail from the hospitals near the trenches to the central avenue of the great base hospital at City Point, and unloaded at the doors of the wards.

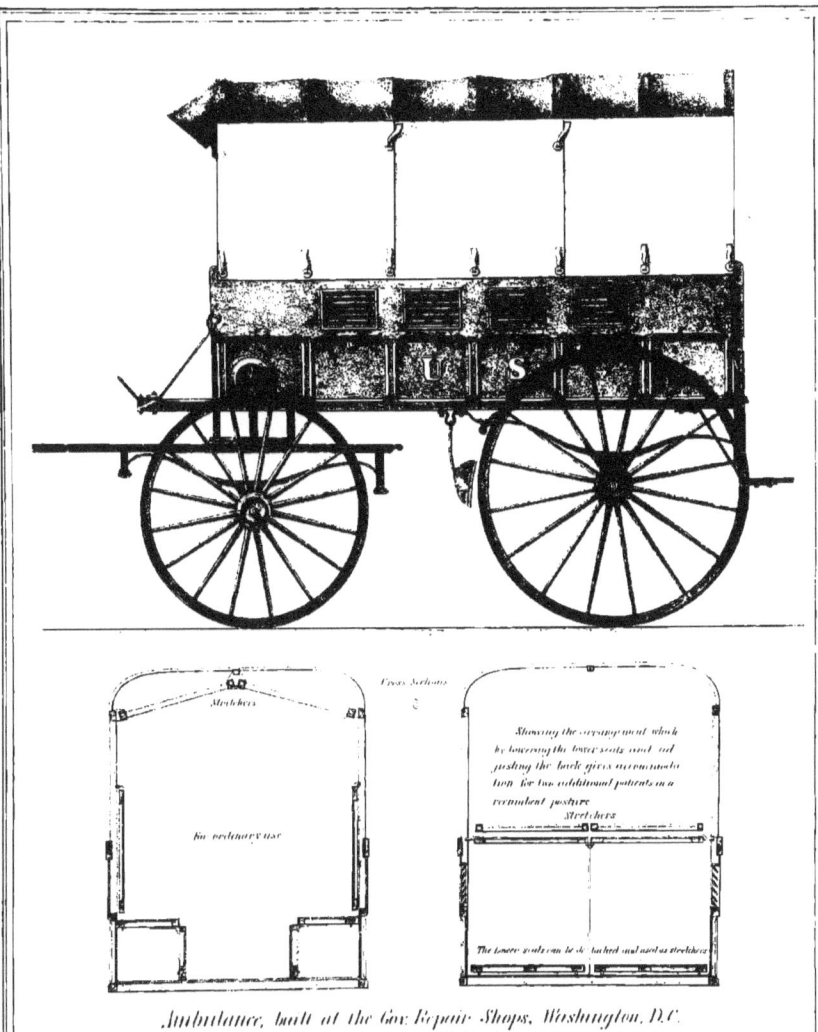

Ambulance, built at the Gov. Repair Shops, Washington, D.C.
under the direction of Brevet Major General, D.H. Rucker,
Quartermaster, U.S. Army.

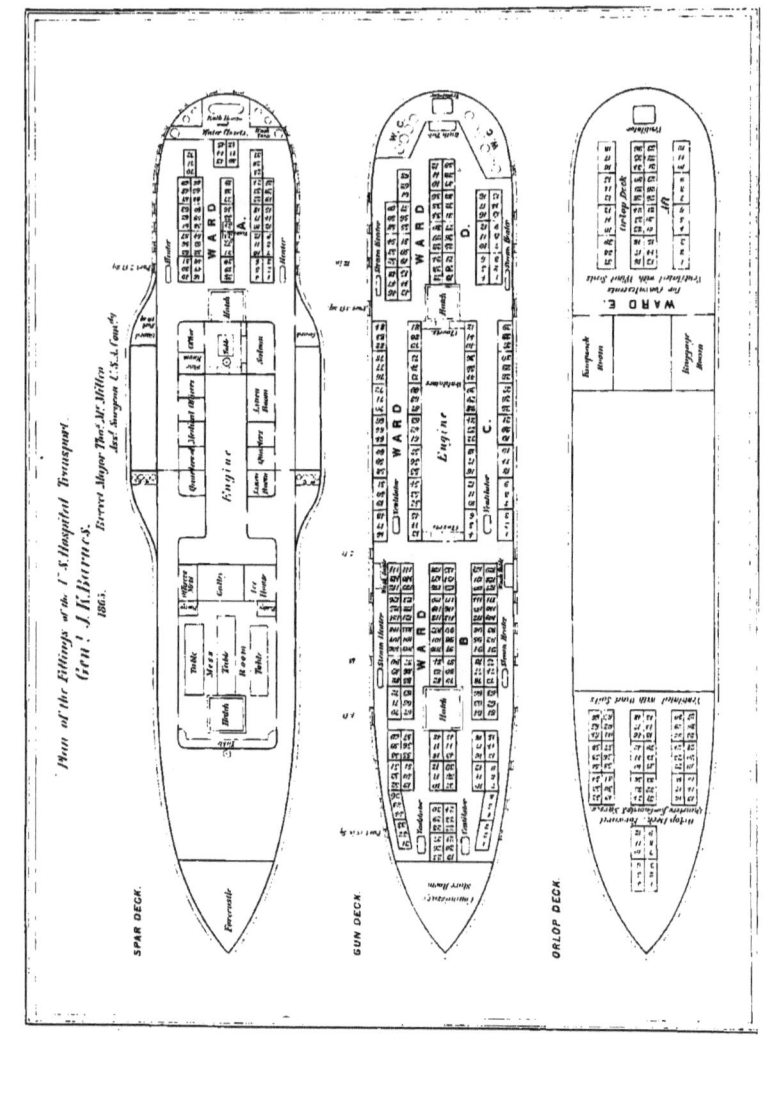

Plans and descriptions of the hospital railway trains on the lines between Washington and New York, Chattanooga and Nashville, Marietta and Louisville, are filed in this office.

When the bases of military operations were contiguous to the sea-board or to the great water-courses, the sick and wounded were removed in hospital steamers. The hospital transports on the Atlantic and on the Mississippi and its tributaries formed a large fleet. Ordinary passenger steamers were of necessity employed at first; but ultimately vessels were specially constructed for hospital purposes. The internal arrangement of one of the best of the ocean hospital transports is figured in the accompanying plate. It is a steamer of 1400 tons, 228 feet in length, provided with 477 beds. It was fitted up at New York, under the supervision of Surgeon A. H. Hoff, U. S. Vols.

EQUIPMENT, DRESSINGS, ETC.

At the beginning of the war, each regimental surgeon was provided with the instruments, medicines, and dressings enumerated in the Standard Supply Table.* In action, he was accompanied by a hospital orderly, who carried a knapsack containing a limited supply of anæsthetics, stimulants, anodynes, styptics, and materials for primary dressings. The medicine chest and bulky hospital supplies were transported in wagons of the supply train, and were often inaccessible when most urgently required.

To obviate this inconvenience, panniers were provided containing the most necessary medicines, dressings, and surgical appliances.† They were designed to be carried on the backs of pack animals, but they were too heavy to be conveyed in this manner, as were the knapsacks to be borne by men.

FIG. 91.—Hospital knapsack of wicker-work, covered with enamelled cloth.

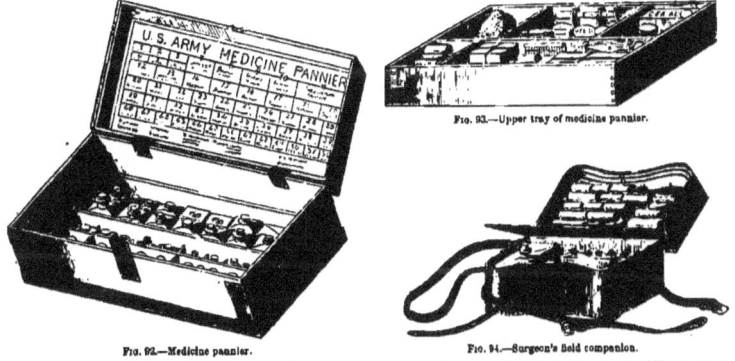
FIG. 92.—Medicine pannier. FIG. 93.—Upper tray of medicine pannier. FIG. 94.—Surgeon's field companion.

* Revised Regulations for the Army of the United States, 1861, p. 304.
† The contents of the hospital knapsacks, panniers, medicine chests, instrument cases, etc. are enumerated in Circular No. 12, S. G. O., 1862.

As the organization of the medical staff was perfected, the cumbrous regimental supplies were curtailed. The hospital orderly carried only a light haversack, or "field companion," containing indispensable drugs and dressings.

But while the regimental hospital supplies were restricted, the brigade supplies were augmented. Each brigade was provided with a "medicine wagon," which was furnished not only with drugs, but with an ample provision of stores, dressings, furniture, and appliances, an amputating table, and a limited supply of bedding. The contents of the wagons were continually replenished from the stores of the medical purveyor of the army. The medicine wagons constructed by Autenrieth and Perot were those chiefly employed in the war. A preferable model, recommended by the Medical Department, was adopted during the last year of the war, and was built at the Government workshops. It has been impracticable to prepare an illustration of it in season for this report.

FIG. 95.—Autenrieth medicine wagon.

Models of a variety of hospital knapsacks, panniers, and wagons are preserved at the Army Medical Museum, with the reports of boards on their respective merits or disadvantages.

CONCLUDING OBSERVATIONS.

In the preparation of a Surgical History of the Rebellion, there are many subjects that would claim attention, which have been scarcely adverted to in the preceding hasty review of the surgical statistics of the office and their illustrations. Among these are the influence of the state of health of the troops upon the result of wounds, the use of anæsthetics, erysipelas, gangrene, the nature of the missiles employed, and the modifications in the character of gunshot injuries produced by modern projectiles.

The complications of injuries by constitutional diseases, scorbutic, malarial, or typhoid, or by a general state of cachexia, in which pathological conditions were combined in unaccustomed synthesis, were elements that unquestionably exerted a vast influence upon the results of the surgical practice of the war. For it cannot be doubted that the frequency of osteomyelitis after amputations, the proneness to suppurative inflammation in wounds of the head and splanchnic cavities, the tendency to the sloughing of flaps, the delay in the union of fractures or the healing of wounds, and the great prevalence of pyæmia, observed at certain periods and localities, were intimately connected with the morbid causes above mentioned, which had led, in many cases, to such an impairment of the general vitality of the men as greatly to diminish their ability to resist the effects of severe injuries. In these relations, therefore, such pathological conditions should not be overlooked in the surgical annals of the war.

CONCLUDING OBSERVATIONS.   87

ANÆSTHETICS.—There have been consulted, in regard to the employment of anæsthetics, the reports of 23,260 surgical operations performed on the field or in general hospitals. Chloroform was used in 60 per cent. of these operations, ether in 30 per cent., and in 10 per cent. of the cases a mixture of the two was administered. At the general hospitals, the greater safety of ether as an anæsthetic was commonly conceded. It was often employed, and no fatal accident from its use has been reported. In the field operations, chloroform was almost exclusively used. The returns indicate that it was administered in not less than eighty thousand cases. In seven instances, fatal results have been ascribed with apparent fairness to its use. Detailed reports of these unfortunate cases are on file. The following synopsis is derived from them:

CASE I.—A soldier of a North Carolina regiment, a robust, healthy man, after the battle of Hanover Court House, May 29th, 1862, underwent amputation of the thigh. The operation was performed in the open air. He inhaled chloroform very freely. He expired just as the operation was completed. He had lost but little blood. No autopsy was held.—*Report of Surgeon Edwin Bently, U. S. Vols.*

CASE II.—D. Zebriske, Co. I, 12th Alabama Regiment, a prisoner after the battle of Antietam, had a gunshot flesh wound of the hip. A slight incision for the extraction of the ball was made October 19th, 1862, at Hospital No. 5, Frederick, Maryland. Chloroform was carefully administered. The patient expired suddenly. The autopsy threw no light on the cause of death.—*Report of Surgeon H. S. Hewit, U. S. Vols.*

CASE III.—Corporal Ballou, Co. E, 14th Pennsylvania Cavalry, was placed under the influence of chloroform, to undergo amputation of the right index and middle fingers, at Beverly, West Virginia, October 12th, 1862. He died in the midst of the operation. Slight calcareous deposits were found post-mortem about the valves of the heart.—*Report of Surgeon William B. Wynne, 14th Pennsylvania Cavalry.*

CASE IV.—Private Thomas Hamilton, Co. A, 1st Maryland Vols., aged thirty-one years, took chloroform September 3d, 1864, at Patterson Park Hospital, Baltimore, to undergo an operation for necrosis of the carpal bones. The anæsthetic was given with a large admixture of air. Sudden death ensued. The autopsy revealed fibrinous coagula in the auricles. The thoracic viscera were perfectly normal in appearance.—*Report signed by Acting Assistant Surgeons Fay, Cherbonnier, Kemster, and McLetchen.*

CASE V.—Colonel McGilvray, Chief of Artillery of the 10th Army Corps, inhaled two drachms of chloroform, September 4th, 1864, for an excision of a phalanx of the left index finger. He expired suddenly before the operation was commenced. There were no pathological appearances found to indicate the cause of death.—*Report of Surgeon A. B. Clark, U. S. Vols.*

CASE VI.—Private Robert Gormley, Co. I, 7th New York Artillery, died suddenly at McClellan General Hospital, November 29th, 1864, having taken chloroform to submit to an incision in the calf of the right leg for the removal of a ball. There was no autopsy.—*Report signed by Acting Assistant Surgeons Ely and Uhler.*

CASE VII.—Private John Johnson, Co. B, 2d Pennsylvania Heavy Artillery, a patient in Mower General Hospital, near Philadelphia, expired suddenly on May 13th, 1865, while inhaling chloroform preparatory to undergoing a surgical operation.—*Report of Surgeon J. Hopkinson, U. S. Vols.*

ERYSIPELAS.—In the ill-ventilated barracks and private edifices which were sometimes of necessity occupied as hospitals during the earlier period of the war, erysipelas was a frequent visitant. Elaborate reports on its prevalence in the hospitals of Louisville, Nashville, Memphis, and Madison have been transmitted by Surgeon Goldsmith, U. S. Vols., Surgeon Weeks, U. S. Vols., and Surgeon Culbertson, U. S. Vols.

GANGRENE.—The various forms of sloughing, phagedena, and traumatic gangrene, described in systematic authors, were among the complications of wounds that throughout the war often rendered the skill of surgeons abortive, but the ravages of true contagious hospital gangrene were comparatively limited. Voluminous papers on this subject have been contributed. It has been discussed in its clinical relations by Medical Inspector Hamilton, and Surgeons McParlin, Brinton, Goldsmith, Breed, Weeks and Moses, and its pathological anatomy has been investigated by Assistant Surgeons Woodward and Thomson.

CONCLUDING OBSERVATIONS.

MISSILES.—The collection at the Army Medical Museum of over five hundred projectiles extracted from wounds, together with the numerous preparations of fractures and wounded viscera in which the missiles that produced the injuries have been preserved, afford opportunities for the comparison of the various forms of bullets and their effects. During the protracted siege operations in front of Petersburg, an artist of the Museum prepared upon the spot a large number of colored drawings, illustrating with singular fidelity the recent appearance of wounds inflicted at short range by shot and shell. The reports on gunshot wounds have specified the nature of the missile whenever it could be ascertained. From these different sources ample materials are available for the study of the modifications in gunshot wounds resulting from modern improvements in ordnance. The general employment in the late war of cylindro-conoidal projectiles, moving in low trajectories, largely increased the proportion of wounded to the troops engaged, and the frequency of the occurrence of several wounds in the same individuals. The projectiles for small arms chiefly used were those of the Springfield, Enfield, and Austrian rifled muskets. The rebels also used quite largely, for the Enfield rifle, an elongated bullet without grooves.

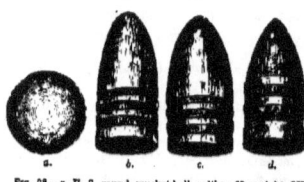

FIG. 95.—a. U. S. round musket-ball, calibre 69, weight 387 grains; b. Springfield rifled musket-ball, calibre 58, weight 500 grains; c. Enfield rifled musket-ball, weight 450 grains; d. Austrian rifle-ball, weight 460 grains.

WOUNDED ON THE BATTLE-FIELD.—Surgeon T. H. Squire, 89th New York Vols., has furnished this office with two instructive reports on the wounded that came under his observation during the battle of Antietam and in the engagements before Petersburg. Similar papers on the wounded at Chickamauga have been contributed by Surgeon John C. Norton, U. S. Vols., and Surgeon J. T. Wood, 99th Ohio Vols., and in relation to the wounded at Chattanooga by Surgeon A. McMahon, 64th Ohio Vols., and Surgeon C. H. Walton, 21st Kentucky Vols. Surgeon H. S. Hewit, U. S. Vols., and Surgeon E. Batwell, 14th Michigan Vols., have communicated valuable reports on the wounded in the engagements of the Atlanta campaign. Recorded observations on the primary attention given to the wounded in battle are, from the nature of things, rare, and these important memoirs therefore merit especial recognition.

In conclusion, it has been estimated that it will be possible, by judicious condensation, to include in one large quarto volume the statistics of the graver injuries, as fractures of the extremities and wounds implicating the joints or great cavities, and of the major surgical operations they have involved, the individual cases, their progress and results, being concisely recorded; while a second quarto volume could comprise numerical tables of the less serious injuries, an historical summary, and a discussion of the lessons derived from the statistical records of the war.

I have the honor to be, General,
Very respectfully,
Your obedient servant,
GEORGE A. OTIS,
*Brevet Lieut. Col. and Surgeon U. S. Vols.,
In charge of the Division of Surgical Records, S. G. O.,
and Curator of the Army Medical Museum.*

SURGEON GENERAL'S OFFICE,
WASHINGTON, D. C.,
October 20th, 1865.

BREVET MAJOR GENERAL JOSEPH K. BARNES,
SURGEON GENERAL U. S. ARMY.

GENERAL:—

IN reply to your inquiries as to the nature and extent of the data bearing on the health of the army during the war, which have accumulated in the branch of your office under my charge, and as to how far the labor of digesting this material for publication has advanced, I have the honor to present for your consideration the following statements.

The matter collected is partly statistical, partly pathological. The first category embraces the medical statistics of the several armies and general hospitals. The second consists of a number of memoirs and reports by medical officers on the causes, symptoms, and treatment of the more important camp diseases, of numerous histories of cases and autopsies, of the fine series of medical and microscopical specimens in the Army Medical Museum, and of the results of the pathological studies conducted under my direction on the basis of these collections. In addition, there are a large number of descriptions and plans of general hospitals, of reports on hospital organization, and some other miscellaneous matters.

The object kept steadily in view has been to collect all the information possible with regard to the sickness and mortality of the army during the war, and especially whatever related to the nature and causes of those affections which were the chief occasion of death and disability.

The importance of such a study cannot be overestimated. The happy exemption of our army from serious epidemics, an exemption which, under Providence, was the legitimate and necessary consequence of the liberality of our commissariat and of our medical supplies, is continually quoted in terms of the highest self-congratulation. Indeed, so far as can be judged from other recent wars, and from the careful study of such imperfect information as can be collected with regard to the health of troops prior to the nineteenth century, the mortality of our soldiers from disease has been far less than that of any other army in time of war.

But while our hearts are filled with gratitude at this fortunate result, it should not be forgotten that our losses from disease have, nevertheless, been enormous when contrasted with the usual mortality of men of military ages in time of peace. Not counting those of our soldiers who died while prisoners in the hands of the rebels—not counting those who were discharged for diseases contracted in the service, and who subsequently died at home,—the deaths of our men from disease were far more numerous than all the slain in all the battles, and all the wounded who have since died or are likely yet to die of the injuries received in the struggle. Judging from the statistics of the first two years, which have already been compiled, the mortality from disease during the war—not counting deaths among prisoners of war or discharged soldiers—was more than five times as great as the mortality of men of the same ages in civil life, and it is not to be disguised that the diseases which produced most mortality were precisely those which are most under the control of hygienic means.

At the commencement of the present struggle, the only important work which could serve to give correct notions as to the nature of the diseases of armies, and the direction to be given to the activity of those whose duty it is to combat them, was the Official Medico-Chirurgical History of the British Army in the Crimean War, laid before Parliament, in two folio volumes. This work refers to a comparatively small number of troops serving in a climate very different from our own, yet its study was of great value in giving direction to our efforts. What was the direction these efforts took—what were the results attained—why our soldiers died, and how this can be best and most economically prevented in future wars—are questions upon which the experience of the present struggle, as recorded in the official reports and documents, can throw a flood of light. Such a publication, therefore, becomes one of the most important duties of the Medical Department of the army; a duty the evasion or neglect of which would be a grave crime against the army of the United States, and against every American citizen who, in future wars, volunteers in the defence of his country.

The character and importance of the material available for such a publication, and the labor yet necessary to complete its preparation for the press, can be best appreciated after a brief description of each of the divisions mentioned at the commencement.

REMARKS ON THE STATISTICAL MATERIAL.

The statistical material embraces a mass of facts with regard to the several armies and general hospitals.

Tables are being prepared for each *army*, showing the monthly number of cases and of deaths from each form of disease or injury. Other tables give the numbers returned to duty, sent to general hospitals, discharged the service for disability, transferred to the Veteran Reserve Corps, died, and remaining at the close of each month.

The tables referring to the *general hospitals* show the number admitted into each hospital monthly and the causes of admission, the number of deaths from each disease or class of wounds, the number returned to duty, transferred to the Veteran Reserve Corps, transferred to other hospitals, discharged the service for disability, and remaining under treatment at the close of the month.

The data furnished by these tables render it possible to calculate ratios illustrating many important matters connected with the laws of the sickness and mortality of armies operating in the United States. By such ratios we shall be enabled to form an intelligent judgment as to the success of the means adopted by the government to preserve the health of our troops, and to compare the results attained with those which have occurred in other armies. The comparative prevalence of those diseases which are known to be preventable, or at least greatly under the influence of hygienic control, will indicate the path in which the further exercise of sanitary precautions should be directed. In fact, the medical history of the past four years, as recorded in the official figures, will be found full of meaning and of manifold suggestion for the future.

It is believed that no one would fail to recognize the importance of medical statistics, if confidence were placed in the data from which they are compiled; but it is often insinuated that these data are, from their nature, unreliable in all medical statistics, and that they are especially uncertain in the statistics of armies in time of war. The causes of error are twofold—on the one hand, mistakes in diagnosis; on the other, negligence, omissions, or falsehoods in the reports.

That errors of both kinds exist, is to be freely admitted. That they are sufficiently numerous and important to rob the medical statistics of our army of their practical value, may be emphatically denied.

Diagnostic errors can be largely eliminated from medical statistics by grouping together those allied affections which are most apt to be confounded. There is probably, for example, no army in the world among whose medical officers a sufficient number of men acquainted with the details of ophthalmic science can be found to give authenticity to its statistics of diseases of the eye, if the form required to be filled embraced the modern classification based upon observations with the ophthalmoscope. This fact, however, does not prevent them from being able to report correctly the total number of diseases of the eye, or even, with considerable accuracy, the proportion of these to be included under the designation "ophthalmia;" and these are practically the most important facts.

Like remarks apply to many similar cases in which there is difficulty in the diagnosis between allied affections; and it becomes therefore one of the most important duties of the medical statistician to group the several diseases together in such a way as to extinguish the greatest possible number of errors of this class.

But the chief cause which disturbs confidence in medico-military statistics is the belief that medical records are imperfectly and carelessly kept, especially in the case of troops in the field. It has been insinuated that their charge is often intrusted to ignorant subordinates, and even, that in extreme cases, no records were kept, and the monthly reports required by law filled up with no other guide than memory. The objection based upon this supposition has been considerably exaggerated in certain quarters, and it is not for a moment believed that medical officers were generally negligent of their duty, or that their reports were not, in the vast majority of instances, based upon records kept according to the best of their abilities. Even during campaigns, when it was impossible to keep the cumbersome books required by the regulations in force at the beginning of the war, surgeons had their pocket memorandum-books, which perfectly sufficed to preserve reliable data for the simple form of report required monthly. It was a knowledge of this fact that led to the issue of the "pocket register and prescription book" at present used by troops in the field. But the most conclusive answer to every objection of this kind is to be found in the character of the reports themselves as they exist in the official files; they contain internal evidence of the care with which they were prepared, and, it is believed, will compare favorably with any other set of statistical papers in existence.

It is true, indeed, that the duty of making reports was sometimes neglected, and that sometimes they were missing, from the absence of surgeons, the capture of records by the enemy, or the loss of the papers themselves during transmittal; but the deficiencies of this character became progressively less and less numerous and important, and, during the second, third, and fourth years of the war, the number of regiments and detachments not represented was comparatively small.

Deficiencies of this kind are very much to be deplored, but they in no way diminish the value of the reports received for the troops which they represent; and where the troops represented amount to hundreds of thousands, the results have probably a scientific value very nearly as great as would have been possessed by complete reports.

It has been deemed proper to present these considerations, because much has been said by persons unacquainted with statistical science as to the imperfection of the data which it has been possible to collect, and because it is nevertheless earnestly believed that to neglect the study of these data would be gravely prejudicial to the interests of military medicine and surgery in America. The circumstances interfering with the accuracy and completeness of our reports have operated in the case of all former military statistics in like degree, so that the results are fairly comparable; though it cannot be denied that the immense size of the figures in our case, and the consequent more perfect balancing of errors in opposite directions, lead us, on considerations which flow from the mathematical law of probabilities, to place greater confidence in the accuracy and importance of our results than in the figures collected under like circumstances by any other nation.

The statistical tables necessary to present the data collected in a convenient shape for study can, it is hoped, be compressed into one quarto volume. They are now fully prepared for the first and second years of the war. The work on the third is well advanced; while that on the fourth has but recently been commenced.

A few general considerations, based upon the manuscript of the tables for the first two years of the war, will here be presented, to give a general idea of the character and scope of the statistics in question. These considerations will have reference to the mortality rates, the prevalence of disease, and the comparative frequency of the several diseases, especially of those which have caused the chief mortality. A few remarks on the character of the latter affections will also be presented.

MORTALITY RATES.

The mortality of the armies of the United States from disease alone was 48·7 per 1000 of mean strength during the first year of the war, viz., the year ending June 30th, 1862, and 65·2 per 1000 during the second year, viz., that ending June 30th, 1863.[*]

In obtaining these ratios, the sum of the deaths reported by regiments and detachments, and by the general hospitals, is compared with the mean strength given by the

---

[*] The mortality rate here given for the first year of the war differs slightly from that published in Circular No. 15, Surgeon General's Office, September, 1863, the difference resulting in part from corrections made in completing the discussion of the statistics of that year, in part from the incorporation of material not accessible when the original computation was made.

reports as present in the field, in garrison, and in the hospitals. The sick reports furnishing the data employed do not give the deaths among those absent as prisoners of war, on furlough, or deserters; hence the mean strength of those thus absent is not considered in determining the ratios. These absentees may have had a very different mortality rate from that above given. In fact, in the case of those of our men who were absent as prisoners of war, the rate of mortality was terribly greater. An attempt will hereafter be made to estimate this rate on data other than that of the monthly sick reports. Such an attempt, however, would be premature at present. The figures given are therefore to be understood simply as the rate of deaths from disease among that portion of the troops which is represented in the sick reports received at the Surgeon General's Office. How far they may be regarded as applicable to the whole of the army of the United States (excepting always prisoners and absentees), may be inferred from the following considerations:

The reports for the first year are incomplete, still they represent a large part of the troops in every army and in hospitals throughout the country. The reports from troops in the field and in garrison for the first year represent an average strength constantly present during the year of 281,177 men. The reports from the hospitals represent an average strength constantly present of 9759 men. The total strength represented therefore is 290,936 men, among whom there were 14,183 deaths from disease. The average mean strength above given is much smaller than the real average for the year. The number of deaths therefore is less than the real number of deaths; but it is believed that the figures are quite large enough to make it in the highest degree probable that the rate obtained is true, or very nearly true, for the whole army of the United States, excluding always prisoners of war and other absentees.

The reports for the second year were less incomplete than those of the first. They represent an average mean strength in the field and in garrison of 598,821, and an average strength in hospital of 45,687 men. The total strength represented therefore is 644,508, among whom there were 42,010 deaths from disease. These figures are so large that it is to the last degree improbable that the reports of the comparatively small number of troops not represented would have made any perceptible change in the ratio, had it been possible to collect them.

The mortality rates thus obtained, and believed to represent accurately the facts of the case, are much smaller than is usual with armies in time of war. Thus, for example, according to the figures compiled by Assistant Surgeon (now Medical Inspector) R. H. Coolidge, the annual mortality of our troops in the Mexican war from disease alone was 103·8 per 1000. For the British army, during the Crimean war, according to the Parliamentary report, the annual mortality from disease was 232 per 1000. The losses of the French army from disease during the Crimean war were, it is probable, proportionately greater than those of the English army. It is difficult, however, to fix them precisely. In the long-expected volume of Chenu,* now just published, no computed ratios are presented. It is true, monthly statistical tables are given,

---

* Rapport au Conseil de Santé des Armées sur les Résultats du Service Médico-Chirurgical aux Ambulances de Crimée et aux Hôpitaux Militaires Français en Turquie, pendant la Campagne d'Orient en 1854, '55, and '56. Par J. C. Chenu. Paris, 1865.

which contain the number of deaths from disease and the mean strength of the army; but unfortunately, after the first few months, these tables, which are headed "Mouvement des Ambulances de Crimée," do not include the deaths in the general hospitals established by the French in Turkey. Separate tables for each hospital are given, but these consolidate the deaths from wounds with those from disease, under the general designation "Morts," and do not, therefore, render it possible to complete the computation. If, however, from the total mortality given in the report, the killed in battle and the deaths from wounds, as given in the tables on the several individual injuries, be deducted, it will be seen that the deaths from disease alone cannot be much short of 75,000 during the twenty-eight months, while the strength constantly present was about 100,000; this would indicate an annual ratio of over 300 per 1000 of mean strength.

It is thus seen that the losses of our troops from disease during the first half of the recent struggle were proportionately much less than those of the allied armies in the Crimea, or of our own army in the Mexican war; and although the present condition of the statistical work progressing under my direction does not permit me to present mortality rates for the third and fourth years of the war, yet, from the examinations I have thus far made, I am inclined to the belief that the proportion of deaths from disease rather diminished than otherwise during that period.

The mortality of our troops from disease was considerably greater during the second year of the war than during the first. It was also different in the different regions in which the troops operated. For the purposes of this comparison, which will also be made in the case of the several diseases, the United States may be regarded as divided into three great regions, designated severally the Atlantic, the Central, and the Pacific regions.

The Atlantic region will embrace all the slope between the Appalachian range and the sea. It will include the Northeastern and Middle Departments, the Army of the Potomac, the troops in North and South Carolina and in Florida. The Pacific region embraces all that lies west of the Rocky Mountains. It includes California, Oregon, and Washington Territory; to these, New Mexico[*] has been added, as more allied to this than to the Central region. The Central region embraces all the great basin of the continent between the Appalachian and the Rocky Mountains. It contains the valley of the Mississippi River and its tributaries, and includes the Northern and Northwestern Departments, Western Virginia, Kentucky, Missouri, Arkansas, the Army of the Tennessee, the Army of the Cumberland, and the Department of the Gulf.

The exposures of the troops in each of these regions presented certain well-marked characteristics. In the Pacific region, the conditions approached those of peace. The forces were mainly scattered in numerous small posts, and shared few of the active duties of war. In both the Atlantic and the Central regions, on the other hand, campaigns were conducted on a grand scale. In the Atlantic region were the several coast expeditions—the Army of the Potomac and its great battles; in the Central, the expeditions on the Tennessee and Mississippi Rivers, and conflicts like those of Shiloh and Stone River. One of the chief characteristics of the Central region would appear to

---

[*] In the tables given in Circular No. 15, S. G. O., above cited (see note to p. 92), New Mexico was included in the Central region.

have been the extent of territory over which the operations extended and the consequent embarrassment in the transportation of supplies; in addition, it is to be noted that the malarial miasms, under the influence of which intermittent and other malarial fevers are developed, have for many years been known, from the experience of civil life, to be much more intense in the Central region than on the Atlantic slope. As might be expected, therefore, we find the rates of disease and mortality very different in these three regions. Differences also exist between the different parts of each region, which, however, cannot be gone into in a brief paper like the present.

A comparison of the reports from the troops and hospitals in the three great regions shows the mortality rate of the Central region to be the greatest, and that of the Pacific region the least. In the Pacific region, the mortality from disease alone was about 12 per 1000 of mean strength for the first year and 8 for the second, the average for the two years closely corresponding with the rates for young men of military ages in civil life, and with the mortality of the British troops in Great Britain and Ireland, as given in their official reports for 1859, '60, '61, and '62. In the Atlantic region, the rates were nearly 33 for the first year and 41 for the second. In the Central region, 80 for the first year and nearly 90 for the second.

Tables I. and II. present the monthly mortality in each of these regions.

TABLE I.
Monthly Mortality of the Armies of the United States during the year ending June 30th, 1862, expressed in ratio per 1000 of mean strength.

	1861.						1862.						For the year.
	July.	August.	September.	October.	November.	December.	January.	February.	March.	April.	May.	June.	
Atlantic Region	1·96	2·03	1·77	2·02	2·65	3·20	2·88	2·37	2·50	3·04	3·12	8·85	32·54
Central Region	·98	2·96	3·52	4·63	6·25	6·54	8·69	8·78	10·06	6·46	7·10	5·90	80·18
Pacific Region	1·72	1 00	1·34	1·43	1·75	1·04	·19	·83	·89	·49	·75	·77	11·65

TABLE II.
Monthly Mortality of the Armies of the United States during the year ending June 30th, 1863, expressed in ratio per 1000 of mean strength.

	1862.						1863.						For the year.
	July.	August.	September.	October.	November.	December.	January.	February.	March.	April.	May.	June.	
Atlantic Region	3 03	5·69	4·27	4·58	4·52	4·82	3·79	2·96	2·55	2·00	1·25	1·73	41·40
Central Region	7·69	6·11	5·72	6·20	8·49	8·30	8·68	9·93	9·14	7·31	5·46	4·94	89·55
Pacific Region	·76	·00	·34	·77	·71	·96	·50	1·01	·82	1·24	·77	1·05	8 38

The monthly reports from which the foregoing rates of mortality from disease were computed give also a certain amount of information as to the mortality from wounds and injuries. The deaths from these causes, reported during the first year of the war, were 4857 out of the strength given above, or seventeen (16·7) per 1000 of mean strength; during the second year, 10,142, or sixteen (15·7) per 1000. These rates, however, by no means represent the real losses from wounds and injuries, since they do not include those slain in battle, or those who died of their wounds while prisoners of war or otherwise absent. To form a correct estimate of the total losses from wounds, I must therefore refer to the Surgical History of the War.

GENERAL PREVALENCE OF DISEASE.

The directions for making the monthly sick reports in the armies of the United States require every man excused from duty, on account of sickness, to appear on the report. The total number taken sick represents thus slight indispositions as well as severe illness, and the figures are therefore much larger than in those armies in which such only are reported as are received into hospital. It follows that the comparative health of the several divisions of our army is to be ascertained rather by considering the monthly number taken sick with serious diseases, such as fever and diarrhœa, than by merely observing the total number of cases reported.

The statistics show the ratio of cases to have been such, during the first two years of the war, that on the average each soldier must have been taken on sick report several times a year. The figures of the second year show a slight diminution in the number of cases. The ratio for the whole army was 2966 per 1000 of mean strength for the first year, 2694 for the second. In the Atlantic region, the number of cases was 2749 per 1000 of mean strength for the first year, 2563 for the second. In the Central region, 3422 for the first year, 2832 for the second. In the Pacific region, 2168 for the first year, 2123 for the second. Tables III. and IV. give the monthly rates for each of these regions.

TABLE III.

Monthly Sickness Rates of the Armies of the United States during the year ending June 30th, 1862, expressed in ratio per 1000 of mean strength.

	1861.						1862.						For the year.
	July.	August.	September.	October.	November.	December.	January.	February.	March.	April.	May.	June.	
Atlantic Region....	391·85	372·18	298·26	267·14	255·90	230·99	199·92	183·83	167·26	214·52	208·45	239·75	2748·83
Central Region.....	267·22	378·81	336·66	331·35	304·11	313·51	389·08	254·19	257·07	287·09	259·43	233·73	3421·93
Pacific Region......	163·15	199·67	197·48	187·10	286·80	153·68	128·99	210·57	193·97	140·77	220·84	187·06	2168·48

CONSTANT SICKNESS RATES.

TABLE IV.

Monthly Sickness Rates of the Armies of the United States during the year ending June 30th, 1863, expressed by ratio per 1000 of mean strength.

	1862.						1863.						For the year.
	July.	August.	September.	October.	November.	December.	January.	February.	March.	April.	May.	June.	
Atlantic Region.....	310.79	250.21	242.82	285.79	239.11	229.10	222.44	181.51	180.50	149.34	163.43	159.10	2563.25
Central Region......	244.21	220.26	263.22	271.47	202.23	244.14	255.76	236.18	239.26	207.46	192.60	219.82	2831.64
Pacific Region.......	182.43	230.73	211.15	180.10	189.35	166.87	173.39	145.63	152.49	172.23	150.60	188.20	2122.92

At first sight it might appear that these figures represent an extraordinary amount of disease; but if they be compared with those of the published statistics of the United States army in time of peace, it will be found that the effect of the war on the health of the troops is rather in the increased number of serious diseases and the consequent mortality than in the number taken on sick report. The average number taken on sick report annually in time of peace, from 1840 to 1859, was 2558 per 1000.

CONSTANT SICKNESS RATES.

In this connection, the constant sickness rates assume the highest interest, especially to the military authorities. As every regimental sick report contains a separate statement of the number of sick and wounded under treatment at the close of each month, it might be supposed that the sum of these reports would furnish the number sick in the whole army at the close of each month, and that this would give a fair notion of the constant sickness. But the rates thus deduced give no idea of the number "absent sick," and the proportion of sick "absent" or "present" is not uniform, but varies continually. An army lying in winter quarters generally makes provision for most of its sick with it, while on the march all serious cases are sent to the general hospitals at the base of operations; so that constant sickness rates, which do not include those absent in hospital, are of no value. Now, for the early part of the war, it has not been possible to compute reliable constant sickness rates, because very many of the reports received were the old "quarterly" form, and only show the remaining at the end of each quarter, which would hardly give a just idea of the constant rates; moreover, in these quarterly reports the "remaining" were not discriminated into "sick" and "wounded," but given in gross. The figures, therefore, give the constant sickness rates plus the number of wounded under treatment. Subsequently to the period named, however, it is possible to compile quite accurate constant sickness rates from the data of the Surgeon General's Office, by taking the number "remaining" in general hospitals into the count and carefully discriminating "sick" from "wounded."

It might perhaps be hoped that the monthly and tri-monthly returns of the Adjutant General's Office would supply the missing information for the early part of the war, but this is not the case. These returns are prepared for military, not for medical purposes. The monthly returns represent the number "present sick," but not the number "absent;" and under the head "present sick" (i.e. *on sick report*), they include those who are really "present wounded." The tri-monthly returns, indeed, represent the number "absent sick" as well as those "present sick;" but under the term sick, as in the monthly returns, both sick and wounded are included.

All ratios hitherto compiled, and published unofficially, which purport to be based on the returns in the Adjutant General's Office, are open to this objection, that they include the wounded with the sick, and are therefore to be regarded as wholly valueless in forming a notion of the health of the army. The following table of constant sickness rates extends only from October 1st, 1862, to June 30th, 1863. It compares the health of the troops in the three regions. The figures include only those under treatment for disease, and not those suffering from wounds.

TABLE V.

Constant Sickness Rates for a part of the year ending June 30th, 1863, expressed in ratio per 1000 of mean strength.

		Atlantic Region.	Central Region.	Pacific Region.
1862.	October	128	102	65
	November	134	106	77
	December	118	91	66
1863.	January	112	106	82
	February	108	109	71
	March	93	105	67
	April	79	88	71
	May	81	83	67
	June	104	97	62
	Average rate	106	98	70

The data from which this table was compiled are not as complete in all respects as could be desired: still the rates presented are believed to be close approximations. It will be observed the Atlantic region has a rate slightly higher than the Central, but that in both the rate is about 10 per cent. of the strength. The rate for the Pacific region, 7 per cent., is in striking contrast with the slight mortality of that region.

COMPARATIVE FREQUENCY OF THE SEVERAL DISEASES.

The monthly sick reports of the several regiments, detachments, and garrisons give the number taken sick during the month, and the number of deaths from each of the more important diseases; the reports of the general hospitals give the number of admissions and deaths from each disease. The form employed during the first year of the war differed in arrangement and in some other points from the improved form adopted in the summer of 1862. Among the changes may here especially be mentioned a change in classification and the omission of the designation unclassified—(morbi varii)—the diseases not embraced in the list being directed to be reported as "other diseases," under the heads of the several orders to which they belong. In compiling the statistical tables for the first year of the war, the material contained in the reports has been rearranged to make its classfication correspond with that adopted for the second and subsequent years. The classification adopted is, with some slight alterations, that proposed by Dr. Farr, and employed in the reports of the Registrar General of England, and in the annual reports of the British army. The chief points of difference are, that "parasitic diseases" have been made a separate class, instead of being included with "zymotic diseases;" that "diseases of the eye" and "of the ear" are made separate orders of "local diseases," instead of being included with "diseases of the nervous system;" that "developmental diseases" are omitted as having no special applicability to army statistics, and that the class of "wounds, accidents, and injuries" is subdivided in a less elaborate manner than in Farr's classification. To these may be added the minor point that Farr includes rheumatism and tonsillitis among miasmatic diseases, instead of which, in our classification, rheumatism is placed among "constitutional diseases," and tonsillitis with diseases of the digestive organs.

The classification has been adopted as a matter of convenience in grouping the facts, rather than as an expression of any well-considered natural relationship between diseases. Thus, at the very threshold, the question may be raised whether the fundamental notion which furnished the name "zymotic," is not a mere conjecture; but if, without thereby meaning to insist upon the idea of a ferment, we retain the term to indicate certain grave constitutional disorders determined by dietic errors, by inoculation or contagion, by epidemic or endemic influences, or by those groupings of conditions found in camps which act like epidemic influences on many at once, it may be asked whether many of the affections now placed under local diseases ought not to be transferred to this class?

Thus, for example, in the tables of Farr, simple coryza and catarrh, as well as epidemic catarrh, are placed in the first order of zymotic diseases; while acute bronchitis and pneumonia are placed among local diseases. It would appear, however, that all these affections belong in fact to one category, are developed by a like series of conditions, acting with different intensities or in constitutions of different resisting powers; that catarrh stands at one end of the scale, pneumonia at the other; and that, regarded as the expression of more or less exposure to unfavorable climatic influences, the proper place for all these affections is with miasmatic diseases.

Without entering into a further discussion as to the scientific accuracy of the English classification, it may be remarked that one of the arguments most frequently used in its favor is derived from a very different source. It is claimed that the various affections embraced under the class of zymotic diseases are to be regarded as essentially *preventable*, while diathetic, local, developmental, and violent diseases are more or less *inevitable*. The classification therefore has this special advantage for military and political purposes, that the amount of disease which, by proper sanitary precautions, might have been avoided, is kept constantly in view; a consideration which must undoubtedly act as a constant stimulant to sanitary effort. Unfortunately, however, our notions of the causation of disease are not sufficiently accurate to enable us to draw any sharp boundary between preventable and unavoidable affections; and, indeed, if such a

100   COMPARATIVE FREQUENCY OF THE SEVERAL DISEASES.

boundary were attempted, it would certainly not correspond with the classification under consideration; a large proportion of the "local" inflammatory affections being conditioned in frequency and severity at least, if not determined, by want of proper clothing and shelter, unnecessary exposure to cold and moisture, and other causes quite as well understood, and certainly more readily modified by hygienic means, than the causes of diphtheria, of enteric fever, or of epidemic cholera. But notwithstanding these critical objections, the English classification appears to be the most convenient and rational hitherto proposed, and, with the slight modifications above mentioned, it has been thought best to employ it.

The following tables give the number of cases and deaths in each of the three great regions for the several classes, orders, and individual diseases during the first and second years of the war. Under the head of "taken sick," in these tables, all cases occurring in the field and in garrison are included, but not the "admissions" into general hospitals; because this would have involved a repetition of cases previously reported in the field or in garrison. Under the head of deaths, however, the deaths in general hospitals are included.

In calculating the ratio of cases to strength in the following tables, then, the strength employed includes only the troops represented in the reports, and this because it was among them only that the cases occurred. In computing the ratio of deaths to strength, however, as already explained under the head of mortality rates, the strength in hospital is included.

The average annual strengths represented in the reports from which the following tables were compiled, are as follows:

For the first year—Atlantic region, 177,899 in field and garrison, 4687 in general hospitals; Central region, 96,583 in field and garrison, 5072 in general hospitals; Pacific region, 6695 in field and garrison,—no general hospitals. For the second year —Atlantic region, 283,703 in field and garrison, 27,802 in general hospitals; Central region, 306,405 in field and garrison, 17,885 in general hospitals; Pacific region, 8713 in field and garrison,—no general hospitals.

These strengths are those employed in computing all the ratios given in this paper.

The six tables now presented are arranged as follows: Table VI. shows the numbers taken sick and died for each class of disease in each of the three regions, and for the whole army, during the first year of the war. The ratio of cases and deaths to strength, in each region and for the whole army, is also given.

Table VII. contains similar figures for the second year.

Tables VIII. and IX. are arranged in the same manner, and give the number taken sick and died, and the ratio to strength for each order.

Tables X. and XI. contain the number taken sick and died from each individual disease and injury for the two years.

The years spoken of here, and throughout the paper, are congressional fiscal years, beginning on the 1st of July and terminating on the 30th of June following.

TABLE VI

Summary of Cases and Deaths, by the several Classes of Diseases and Injuries, for the year ending June 30th, 1862.

CLASSES.	ATLANTIC REGION.				CENTRAL REGION.				PACIFIC REGION.				TOTAL.			
	Taken sick.	Died.	Ratio per 1000 of cases to strength.	Ratio per 1000 of deaths to strength.	Taken sick.	Died.	Ratio per 1000 of cases to strength.	Ratio per 1000 of deaths to strength.	Taken sick.	Died.	Ratio per 1000 of cases to strength.	Ratio per 1000 of deaths to strength.	Taken sick.	Died.	Ratio per 1000 of cases to strength.	Ratio per 1000 of deaths to strength.
I. Zymotic diseases........	249,120	4,032	1400·34	22·08	207,799	5,269	2151·51	51·73	6,561	32	979·99	4·75	463,480	9,333	1648·36	32·08
II. Constitutional diseases	35,177	285	201·11	1·56	15,090	367	156·24	3·61	1,607	14	240·03	2·00	52,474	666	186·62	2·29
III. Parasitic diseases......	640	......	3·60	......	408	......	4·22	......	10	...	1·49	......	1,058	......	3·76	......
IV. Local diseases...........	198,951	1,375	1118·34	7·53	105,054	2,341	1087·71	23·03	5,917	26	883·79	3·88	309,922	3,742	1102·23	12·66
V. Wounds and injuries..	27,562	2,410	156·62	13·20	15,149	2,336	156·85	23·47	1,875	61	280·06	9·11	44,586	4,857	158·64	16·60
VI. Unclassified diseases...	4,526	262	25·44	1·43	2,149	175	22·25	1·72	423	5	63·18	0·75	7,098	442	25·24	1·52
Total......................	515,876	8,364	2905·45	45·81	345,649	10,558	3578·78	103·66	16,393	138	2448·54	20·51	878,918	19,040	3125·85	65·44

TABLE VII.

Summary of Cases and Deaths, by the several Classes of Diseases and Injuries, for the year ending June 30th, 1863.

CLASSES.	ATLANTIC REGION.				CENTRAL REGION.				PACIFIC REGION.				TOTAL.			
	Taken sick.	Died.	Ratio per 1000 of cases to strength.	Ratio per 1000 of deaths to strength.	Taken sick.	Died.	Ratio per 1000 of cases to strength.	Ratio per 1000 of deaths to strength.	Taken sick.	Died.	Ratio per 1000 of cases to strength.	Ratio per 1000 of deaths to strength.	Taken sick.	Died.	Ratio per 1000 of cases to strength.	Ratio per 1000 of deaths to strength.
I. Zymotic diseases........	428,503	9,579	1510·76	30·59	586,329	20,158	1913·55	62·16	10,317	23	1164·09	2·64	1,025,149	29,710	1712·11	66·10
II. Constitutional diseases	62,560	812	220·90	2·81	49,135	1,736	160·36	5·35	1,943	8	223·00	0·92	113,138	2,556	189·94	5·07
III. Parasitic diseases......	5,103	1	10·94	0·003	4,218	......	13·77	......	33	...	3·78	......	7,354	1	12·28	0·002
IV. Local diseases...........	232,836	2,555	820·70	9·20	227,947	7,146	743·94	22·04	6,204	42	712·04	4·82	466,987	9,743	779·84	16·12
V. Wounds and injuries..	54,431	5,344	191·96	17·18	41,903	4,757	136·76	14·67	2,141	41	245·72	4·71	98,475	10,142	164·45	16·74
Total......................	781,633	18,341	2755·71	58·56	909,532	33,797	2968·40	104·22	20,638	114	2368·64	13·08	1,711,803	52,152	2858·62	80·92

COMPARATIVE FREQUENCY OF THE SEVERAL DISEASES.

TABLE VIII.
Summary of Cases and Deaths, by the several Orders of Diseases and Injuries, for the year ending June 30th, 1862.

ORDERS.	ATLANTIC REGION.				CENTRAL REGION.				PACIFIC REGION.				TOTAL.			
	Taken sick.	Died.	Ratio per 1000 of cases to strength.	Ratio per 1000 of deaths to strength.	Taken sick.	Died.	Ratio per 1000 of cases to strength.	Ratio per 1000 of deaths to strength.	Taken sick.	Died.	Ratio per 1000 of cases to strength.	Ratio per 1000 of deaths to strength.	Taken sick.	Died.	Ratio per 1000 of cases to strength.	Ratio per 1000 of deaths to strength.
I. 1. Miasmatic Diseases	231,671	3,989	1302·28	21·95	201,291	5,216	208·13	51·21	3,755	30	580·97	4·48	436,717	9,235	1553·17	31·74
2. Enthetic Diseases	15,504	5	87·15	·02	3,786	8	59·91	·08	2,511	...	375·06	...	23,801	13	81·65	·04
3. Dietic Diseases	1,045	38	10·93	·21	722	45	7·47	·44	295	2	44·08	·30	2,062	85	10·53	·30
II. 1. Diathetic Diseases	35,589	38	199·37	·21	14,094	62	145·43	·61	1,556	9	232·41	·89	49,839	106	175·47	·82
2. Tubercular Diseases	2,083	247	11·74	1·35	996	305	10·31	3·09	51	8	7·63	1·16	3,135	590	11·75	1·92
III. Parasitic Diseases	640	...	3·60	...	408	...	4·22	...	10	...	1·49	...	1,058	...	3·76	...
IV. 1. Diseases of Nervous System.	17,970	232	101·01	1·27	8,844	233	91·57	2·29	461	9	68·86	1·34	27,275	474	97·00	1·63
2. Diseases of the Eye	5,553	...	31·37	...	4,457	1	46·15	·01	355	...	53·17	...	10,376	1	39·90	·003
3. Diseases of the Ear	3,263	...	18·34	...	1,721	4	17·81	·04	95	...	14·19	...	5,079	4	18·06	·01
4. Diseases of Organs of Circulation	2,231	68	12·54	·37	821	61	8·50	·60	35	4	5·23	·60	3,087	133	10·98	·46
5. Diseases of Respiratory Organs	29,375	866	508·20	4·74	48,440	1,797	501·54	17·67	2,058	8	307·39	1·19	140,373	2,671	499·23	9·18
6. Diseases of Digestive Organs	61,215	183	344·10	1·00	33,406	225	349·81	2·21	2,202	5	328·90	·75	96,913	413	344·67	1·42
7. Diseases of the Urinary and Genital Organs	2,839	22	15·96	·12	1,220	8	12·63	·08	85	...	12·70	...	4,144	30	14·74	·10
8. Diseases of the Bones and Joints	350	...	2·02	...	198	1	1·95	·01	7	...	1·05	...	554	1	1·97	·003
9. Diseases of the Integumentary System	15,536	4	87·89	·02	5,937	11	60·75	·11	618	...	92·31	...	22,121	15	78·67	·05
V. Wounds, Accidents and Injuries	27,362	2,410	159·62	13·20	15,149	2,388	156·85	23·47	1,975	61	280·96	9·11	44,586	4,857	159·84	16·69
VI. Unclassified Diseases	4,508	282	25·44	1·43	2,119	175	22·25	1·72	423	5	63·13	·75	7,098	442	23·24	1·52
Total	516,976	8,384	2905·45	45·61	345,949	10,538	3578·75	103·66	16,363	136	2448·04	20·61	878,918	19,040	3125·85	65·44

TABLE IX.
Summary of Cases and Deaths, by the several Orders of Diseases and Injuries, for the year ending June 30th, 1863.

ORDERS.	ATLANTIC REGION.				CENTRAL REGION.				PACIFIC REGION.				TOTAL.			
	Taken sick.	Died.	Ratio per 1000 of cases to strength.	Ratio per 1000 of deaths to strength.	Taken sick.	Died.	Ratio per 1000 of cases to strength.	Ratio per 1000 of deaths to strength.	Taken sick.	Died.	Ratio per 1000 of cases to strength.	Ratio per 1000 of deaths to strength.	Taken sick.	Died.	Ratio per 1000 of cases to strength.	Ratio per 1000 of deaths to strength.
I. 1. Miasmatic Diseases	406,433	9,395	1432·02	30·15	560,637	19,968	1829·72	61·57	5,888	17	767·59	1·96	973,758	29,380	1629·23	45·58
2. Enthetic Diseases	17,868	13	62·98	·04	20,347	29	66·41	·09	2,793	...	330·56	·46	41,008	46	58·48	·07
3. Dietic Diseases	4,302	121	15·16	·39	3,345	161	17·44	·50	836	2	96·95	·25	10,483	284	17·51	·44
II. 1. Diathetic Diseases	59,046	167	208·13	·54	44,953	301	146·61	·93	1,881	...	213·59	...	105,880	468	179·83	·73
2. Tubercular Diseases	3,514	645	12·74	2·27	4,152	1,435	13·55	4·43	82	8	9·41	·92	7,848	2,088	13·11	3·24
III. Parasitic Diseases	3,108	1	10·93	·003	4,218	...	13·77	...	33	...	3·78	...	7,354	1	12·28	·002
IV. 1. Diseases of Nervous System	25,084	567	88·42	1·82	26,147	917	85·33	2·83	605	7	69·14	·80	51,836	1,491	86·66	2·31
2. Diseases of the Eye	7,480	...	26·37	...	16,294	...	53·18	...	527	...	60·50	...	24,301	...	40·58	...
3. Diseases of the Ear	4,611	2	16·25	·009	5,727	1	18·69	·003	168	...	19·28	...	10,506	3	17·54	·005
4. Diseases of Organs of Circulation	6,018	266	21·21	·85	4,416	320	14·42	·99	70	6	8·03	·57	10,504	591	17·54	·92
5. Diseases of Respiratory Organs	61,836	1,189	217·95	3·81	58,761	4,818	191·78	14·85	881	13	101·11	1·49	121,278	6,019	202·53	9·34
6. Diseases of Digestive Organs	96,769	415	341·09	1·43	91,675	914	299·20	2·82	2,906	15	333·52	1·72	191,350	1,374	319·54	2·13
7. Diseases of the Urinary and Genital Organs	5,862	63	20·66	·20	5,406	63	17·64	·20	163	2	18·71	·23	11,431	158	19·09	·25
8. Diseases of the Bones and Joints	1,711	4	6·03	·01	1,351	25	4·41	·08	27	...	3·10	...	3,089	29	5·16	·05
9. Diseases of Integumentary System	23,665	20	83·41	·06	18,168	58	59·29	·19	857	...	98·36	...	42,690	78	71·29	·12
V. Wounds, Accidents and Injuries	54,431	5,344	191·86	17·18	41,903	4,797	136·76	14·67	2,141	41	245·72	4·71	98,475	10,142	164·45	15·74
Total	781,533	18,241	2755·11	58·56	909,532	33,797	2968·40	104·22	20,638	114	2368·64	13·05	1,711,803	52,152	2858·62	80·92

TABLE X.

Showing the Number of Cases and Deaths, by Individual Diseases and Injuries, for the year ending June 30th, 1862.

LIST OF DISEASES.	ATLANTIC REGION.		CENTRAL REGION.		PACIFIC REGION.		TOTAL.	
	Taken sick.	Died.	Taken sick.	Died.	Taken sick.	Died.	Taken sick.	Died.
Class I.—Zymotic Diseases.								
ORDER I. *Miasmatic Diseases.*								
Typhus Fever	463	101	359	89	2	1	824	191
Yellow Fever	......	......	......	......	......	...	....	......
Typhoid Fever	12,616	2,736	9,312	2,864	49	8	21,977	5,608
Common Continued Fever	7,645	40	4,008	105	118	1	11,771	146
Remittent Fever	21,792	182	17,934	187	321	1	40,047	370
Quotidian Intermittent Fever	18,145	1	21,622	81	608	...	40,375	82
Tertian Intermittent Fever	13,666	5	12,776	28	308	...	26,750	33
Quartan Intermittent Fever	1,546	3	1,855	1	50	...	3,451	4
Congestive Intermittent Fever	1,500	201	727	160	7	...	2,234	361
Acute Diarrhœa	90,472	40	72,715	187	1,864	...	164,551	227
Chronic Diarrhœa	4,881	52	10,876	440	58	1	15,815	493
Acute Dysentery	18,392	116	13,472	230	373	1	32,237	347
Chronic Dysentery	1,180	30	1,407	94	24	3	2,611	127
Asiatic Cholera	......	......	......	......	......	...	....	......
Erysipelas	1,309	39	1,292	81	51	1	2,652	121
Small-pox and Varioloid	678	210	464	190	168	12	1,310	412
Measles	10,055	173	11,558	377	63	1	21,676	551
Scarlet Fever	93	7	40	3	......	...	188	10
Mumps	4,536	2	6,660	7	20	...	11,216	9
Epidemic Catarrh	6,649	2	4,649	3	16	...	11,314	5
Debility	11,670	89	6,529	116	125	...	18,324	155
Other diseases of this order	4,383	10	3,036	23	30	...	7,449	33
ORDER II. *Enthetic Diseases.*								
Syphilis	6,139	5	1,628	7	1,244	...	9,011	12
Gonorrhœa	7,416	......	3,185	......	1,037	...	11,638	......
Orchitis	1,631	......	906	......	185	...	2,722	......
Stricture of the Urethra	309	......	56	......	43	...	408	......
Serpent-bite	9	......	11	1	......	...	20	1
Other diseases of this order	......	......	......	......	2	...	2	......
ORDER III. *Dietic Diseases.*								
Scurvy	933	6	321	3	74	...	1,328	9
Delirium Tremens	426	21	178	35	52	2	656	58
Inebriation	586	11	223	7	169	...	978	18
Class II.—Constitutional Diseases.								
ORDER I. *Diathetic Diseases.*								
Gout	45	......	51	......	......	...	96	......
Acute Rheumatism	17,686	7	7,435	19	1,136	3	26,257	29
Chronic Rheumatism	10,204	9	3,701	10	311	...	14,216	19
Lumbago	2,848	2	1,367	......	74	...	4,289	2
Anæmia	636	8	590	4	3	1	1,229	13
General Dropsy	259	11	491	22	8	1	758	34
Cancer	14	......	18	4	1	1	33	5
Tumors	360	......	75	......	12	...	447	......
Other diseases of this order	1,637	1	366	3	11	...	2,014	4
ORDER II. *Tubercular Diseases.*								
Consumption	1,678	243	795	299	35	8	2,508	550
Scrofula	410	4	201	6	16	...	627	10
Class III.—Parasitic Diseases.								
Worms	640	......	408	......	10	...	1,058	......
Carried forward	285,537	4,317	223,297	5,636	8,178	46	517,012	9,999

TABLE X.—Continued.

LIST OF DISEASES.	Atlantic Region.		Central Region.		Pacific Region.		Total.	
	Taken sick.	Died.	Taken sick.	Died.	Taken sick.	Died.	Taken sick.	Died.
Brought forward	285,537	4,317	223,297	5,636	8,178	46	517,012	9,999
Class IV.—Local Diseases.								
Order I. Diseases of Nervous System.								
Apoplexy	124	60	68	58	4	3	196	121
Headache	5,307	1	1,711	......	116	...	7,134	1
Inflammation of Brain	92	43	57	49	4	2	153	94
St. Vitus Dance	49	1	28	1	1	...	78	2
Epilepsy	843	19	326	18	30	1	1,199	38
Sun-stroke	253	7	163	9	4	1	420	17
Spinal Irritation	271	3	281	5	7	...	559	8
Insanity	162	4	55	4	10	...	227	8
Melancholy	152	1	111	2	3	...	266	3
Inflammation of Membranes of Brain	113	58	51	47	6	...	170	105
Nostalgia	331	1	241	......	......	...	572	1
Neuralgia	4,418	......	2,915	1	183	...	7,546	1
Toothache	4,997	......	2,449	......	71	...	7,517	......
Paralysis	200	10	117	11	13	1	330	22
Other diseases of this order	658	24	241	28	9	1	908	53
Order II. Diseases of Eye.								
Amaurosis	109	......	33	......	5	...	147	......
Cataract	52	......	18	......	1	...	71	......
Inflammation of Iris	205	......	66	......	11	...	282	......
Night Blindness	97	......	11	......	1	...	109	......
Ophthalmia	4,269	......	3,969	1	326	...	8,564	1
Inflammation of Retina	66	......	63	......	3	...	132	......
Other diseases of this order	765	......	297	......	9	...	1,071	......
Order III. Diseases of Ear.								
Earache	1,137	......	600	......	34	...	1,771	......
Inflammation of Internal Ear	913	......	504	1	43	...	1,460	1
Otorrhœa	926	......	479	1	5	...	1,410	1
Deafness	182	......	71	......	10	...	263	......
Other diseases of this order	105	......	67	2	3	...	175	2
Order IV. Diseases of Organs of Circulation.								
Aneurism	21	2	13	3	1	1	35	6
Angina Pectoris	167	3	55	3	11	...	233	6
Inflammation of Heart	114	11	30	10	5	...	149	21
Inflammation of Endocardium	75	10	34	5	......	...	109	15
Inflammation of Pericardium	167	20	55	20	3	2	225	42
Inflammation of Veins	36	1	37	2	......	...	73	3
Varicocele	726	......	258	......	4	...	988	......
Varicose Veins	534	......	236	1	6	...	776	1
Other diseases of this order	391	21	103	17	5	1	499	39
Order V. Diseases of Respiratory Organs.								
Asthma	881	4	288	7	1	...	1,170	11
Acute Bronchitis	18,247	48	7,857	54	97	...	26,201	102
Chronic Bronchitis	2,588	21	1,295	15	19	...	3,902	36
Catarrh	58,721	1	28,455	4	1,661	...	88,837	5
Hæmorrhage from Nose	293	1	112	2	1	1	406	4
Hæmorrhage from Lungs	745	13	294	9	13	...	1,052	22
Dropsy of Chest	15	3	8	2	......	...	23	5
Inflammation of Larynx	1,671	22	885	11	41	1	2,597	34
Inflammation of Pleura	3,023	40	1,964	42	92	2	5,079	84
Inflammation of Lungs	4,562	601	6,368	1,529	113	4	11,061	2,134
Other Diseases of this order	4,109	112	916	122	20	...	5,045	234
Order VI. Diseases of Digestive Organs.								
Abdominal Dropsy	77	5	69	7	4	...	150	16
Cholera Morbus	2,818	12	1,464	21	26	...	4,308	33
Colic	7,524	3	3,695	8	155	...	11,374	11
Constipation	17,895	1	8,631	4	1,172	...	27,198	5
Dyspepsia	4,265	1	1,719	......	165	...	6,149	1
Carried forward	436,518	5,509	303,158	7,772	12,705	67	752,381	13,348

COMPARATIVE FREQUENCY OF THE SEVERAL DISEASES.

TABLE X.—Concluded.

LIST OF DISEASES.	ATLANTIC REGION.		CENTRAL REGION.		PACIFIC REGION.		TOTAL.	
	Taken sick.	Died.	Taken sick.	Died.	Taken sick.	Died.	Taken sick.	Died.
Brought forward	436,518	5,509	303,158	7,772	12,705	67	752,381	13,348
ORDER VI. *Diseases of Digestive Organs—Continued.*								
Inflammation of Bowels	455	43	695	48	4	1	1,154	92
Inflammation of Stomach	1,033	15	868	20	55	...	2,556	35
Fistula	263	......	99	......	13	...	375	......
Hæmorrhage from Stomach	137	1	40	2	10	...	187	3
Piles	3,861	......	1,823	3	89	...	5,773	3
Acute Inflammation of Liver	1,018	9	1,042	12	19	...	2,079	21
Chronic Inflammation of Liver	538	7	585	12	15	2	1,138	21
Hernia	2,516	3	1,259	3	34	...	3,809	6
Jaundice	5,110	9	5,795	31	24	...	10,929	40
Prolapsus Ani	219	......	121	......	4	...	344	......
Inflammation of Peritoneum	161	44	260	23	4	1	425	68
Inflammation of Spleen	98	......	180	2	3	...	281	2
Inflammation of Tonsils	7,782	5	3,488	3	197	1	11,467	9
Other diseases of this order	5,345	21	1,663	26	209	...	7,217	47
ORDER VII. *Diseases of Urinary and Genital Organs.*								
Stone and Gravel	56	......	34	......	8	...	98	......
Inflammation of Bladder	258	5	135	......	8	...	401	5
Diabetes	89	1	35	1	......	...	124	2
Incontinence of Urine	136	1	33	......	1	...	170	1
Retention and Difficulty of Urination	641	1	239	......	8	...	888	1
Inflammation of Kidneys	506	6	410	4	16	...	932	10
Hydrocele and Hæmatocele	194	......	99	......	10	...	303	......
Sarcocele	91	......	35	......	1	...	127	......
Non-Syphilitic Ulcer of Penis	255	......	66	......	15	...	336	......
Other diseases of this order	613	8	134	3	23	...	770	11
ORDER VIII. *Diseases of Bones and Joints.*								
Anchylosis	67	......	56	......	2	...	125	......
Exostosis	68	......	41	......	2	...	111	......
White Swelling	77	......	33	1	1	...	111	1
Necrosis	147	......	58	......	2	...	207	......
ORDER IX. *Diseases of the Integumentary System.*								
Abscess	3,648	1	1,474	6	171	...	5,293	7
Carbuncle	976	......	198	1	13	...	1,187	1
Whitlow	944	......	306	......	48	...	1,298	......
Boil	2,752	......	651	......	132	...	3,535	......
Skin Diseases	3,111	1	1,961	1	114	...	5,186	2
Ulcers	2,878	2	1,092	3	121	...	4,091	5
Other diseases of this order	1,327	......	185	......	19	...	1,531	......
Class V.—Wounds, Accidents, and Injuries.								
Burns	656	1	292	1	50	...	998	2
Concussion of Brain	81	8	48	8	17	2	146	18
Compression of Brain	25	10	34	6	1	...	60	16
Contusion	4,730	17	1,675	7	494	...	6,899	24
Fracture	761	24	426	24	59	1	1,246	49
Frost-bite	102	1	69	3	19	...	190	4
Dislocation	874	......	224	......	40	...	638	......
Sprain	2,249	......	717	1	185	...	3,151	1
Incised Wounds	3,178	5	704	11	179	...	4,061	16
Contused and Lacerated Wounds	3,162	48	1,769	64	319	...	5,250	112
Punctured Wounds	1,024	19	317	16	47	2	1,388	37
Gunshot Wounds	9,270	2,205	7,837	2,167	389	49	17,406	4,421
Poisoning	183	11	89	8	21	...	293	19
Suicide	....	25	....	15	......	5	....	45
Others of this class	2,067	36	948	55	55	2	3,070	93
Unclassified Diseases	4,526	262	2,149	175	423	5	7,098	442
Total	516,876	8,364	345,649	10,538	16,393	138	878,918	19,040

TABLE XI.

Showing the Number of Cases and Deaths, by Individual Diseases and Injuries, for the year ending June 30th, 1863.

LIST OF DISEASES.	ATLANTIC REGION.		CENTRAL REGION.		PACIFIC REGION.		TOTAL.	
	Taken sick.	Died.	Taken sick.	Died.	Taken sick.	Died.	Taken sick.	Died.
Class I.—Zymotic Diseases.								
ORDER I. *Miasmatic Diseases.*								
Typhoid Fever	17,050	4,356	14,218	6,106	106	5	31,374	10,467
Typhus Fever	469	128	424	252	6	1	899	381
Typho-Malarial Fever	12,093	489	10,426	640	133	...	22,652	1,129
Yellow Fever	256	100	......	......	......	...	256	100
Remittent Fever	35,056	332	48,219	828	441	...	83,716	1,167
Quotidian Intermittent Fever	28,968	29	67,087	115	606	...	96,653	144
Tertian Intermittent Fever	22,295	20	57,380	96	378	...	80,053	116
Quartan Intermittent Fever	2,687	5	6,698	73	54	...	9,434	78
Congestive Intermittent Fever	1,098	243	2,728	776	21	1	3,847	1,020
Acute Diarrhœa	175,152	210	197,089	659	1,686	1	373,927	870
Chronic Diarrhœa	28,062	1,974	34,900	5,510	121	4	63,083	7,488
Acute Dysentery	24,597	249	39,637	671	470	2	64,704	922
Chronic Dysentery	3,753	309	4,941	777	53	...	8,747	1,086
Asiatic Cholera	......	......	......	......	......	...	......	......
Erysipelas	1,996	75	4,512	759	68	1	6,576	835
Small-pox and Varioloid	802	375	1,974	757	46	...	2,822	1,132
Measles	5,106	110	11,217	1,203	22	...	16,345	1,313
Scarlet Fever	115	7	89	19	2	...	206	26
Diphtheria	1,046	143	1,317	136	81	...	2,444	279
Mumps	3,005	13	10,291	17	133	...	13,429	30
Epidemic Catarrh	28,391	3	32,915	21	1,896	...	63,202	24
Other diseases of this order	14,336	213	14,580	558	363	2	29,279	773
ORDER II. *Enthetic Diseases.*								
Syphilis	6,118	4	6,439	20	1,224	3	13,781	27
Gonorrhœa	9,348	......	10,982	6	1,302	...	21,632	6
Orchitis	1,537	......	1,580	3	199	...	3,316	3
Stricture of the Urethra	441	2	279	......	37	1	757	3
Purulent Ophthalmia	222	......	878	......	4	...	1,104	......
Serpent-bite	9	......	17	......	3	...	29	......
Other diseases of this order	193	7	172	......	24	...	389	7
ORDER III. *Dietic Diseases.*								
Scurvy	3,090	36	3,774	53	531	1	7,395	90
Purpura	85	14	217	17	2	...	304	31
Delirium Tremens	314	40	385	70	73	1	772	111
Inebriation	437	11	560	11	224	...	1,221	22
Chronic Alcoholism	101	3	120	7	5	...	226	10
Other diseases of this order	275	17	289	3	1	...	565	20
Class II.—Constitutional Diseases.								
ORDER I. *Diathetic Diseases.*								
Gout	42	......	78	......	6	...	126	......
Acute Rheumatism	25,723	27	18,887	57	1,067	...	45,677	84
Chronic Rheumatism	26,571	25	18,483	40	704	...	45,758	65
Anæmia	4,596	59	4,746	106	17	...	9,359	165
General Dropsy	725	18	1,564	27	5	...	2,294	45
Cancer	92	4	53	5	5	...	150	9
Tumors	306	2	279	1	23	...	608	3
Dry Gangrene	58	11	7	13	1	...	66	24
Other Diseases of this order	933	21	886	52	33	...	1,852	73
ORDER II. *Tubercular Diseases.*								
Consumption	2,566	630	2,983	1,402	50	8	5,599	2,040
Scrofula	957	9	1,075	23	32	...	2,064	32
Other diseases of this order	91	6	94	10	......	...	185	16
Class III.—Parasitic Diseases.								
Itch	2,435	......	3,790	......	7	...	6,232	......
Tape-worm	85	......	49	......	6	...	140	......
Other intestinal worms	550	1	336	......	20	...	906	1
Other diseases of this order	33	......	43	......	......	...	76	......
Carried forward	494,386	10,342	639,682	21,894	12,298	31	1,146,341	32,267

COMPARATIVE FREQUENCY OF THE SEVERAL DISEASES.

TABLE XI.—Continued.

LIST OF DISEASES.	ATLANTIC REGION.		CENTRAL REGION.		PACIFIC REGION.		TOTAL.	
	Taken sick.	Died.	Taken sick.	Died.	Taken sick.	Died.	Taken sick.	Died.
Brought forward....................................	494,366	10,842	639,682	21,894	12,293	81	1,146,341	32,267
Class IV.—Local Diseases.								
ORDER I. *Diseases of Nervous System.*								
Apoplexy...	170	107	221	146	7	2	398	255
Epilepsy...	1,386	44	1,166	61	33	...	2,585	105
Headache...	11,059	......	9,384	......	202	...	20,645	......
Insanity...	407	8	410	12	14	...	831	20
Inflammation of Brain............................	175	137	271	307	4	2	450	446
Inflammation of Membranes of Brain.........	130	69	165	139	2	...	297	208
Inflammation of Spinal Cord.....................	319	10	713	32	5	...	1,037	42
Nostalgia...	806	5	1,207	7	3	...	2,016	12
Neuralgia...	8,188	2	10,060	6	285	...	18,533	8
Paralysis...	561	42	584	57	19	2	1,164	101
Sun-stroke...	651	15	547	42	1	...	1,199	57
Other diseases of this order.....................	1,232	128	1,419	108	30	1	2,681	237
ORDER II. *Diseases of Eye.*								
Amaurosis...	280	......	226	......	7	...	513	......
Cataract..	106	......	192	......	3	...	301	......
Inflammation of Conjunctiva....................	5,540	......	14,490	......	448	...	20,478	......
Inflammation of Iris...............................	295	......	294	......	30	...	619	......
Night Blindness....................................	691	......	451	......	5	...	1,147	......
Other diseases of this order.....................	568	......	641	......	34	...	1,243	......
ORDER III. *Diseases of Ear.*								
Earache...	2,454	......	3,020	......	47	...	5,521	......
Inflammation of Internal Ear....................	537	1	1,000	......	54	...	1,591	1
Deafness...	439	......	316	......	20	...	775	......
Otorrhœa..	1,057	1	1,310	1	39	...	2,406	2
Other diseases of this order.....................	124	......	81	......	8	...	213	......
ORDER IV. *Diseases of Organs of Circulation.*								
Aneurism...	50	10	48	10	1	1	99	21
Valvular Disease of Heart........................	789	97	424	85	4	...	1,217	182
Dropsy from Heart Disease......................	123	16	109	31	......	...	232	47
Dropsy of Pericardium............................	62	14	57	21	......	...	119	35
Inflammation of Pericardium....................	279	24	263	71	11	2	553	97
Inflammation of Endocardium...................	122	15	133	32	4	...	259	47
Inflammation of Veins............................	58	4	70	2	4	...	132	6
Varicose Veins.....................................	2,070	1	1,270	......	4	...	3,344	1
Varicocele...	1,929	......	1,566	......	9	...	3,504	......
Other diseases of this order.....................	536	85	478	68	33	2	1,047	155
ORDER V. *Diseases of Respiratory Organs.*								
Asthma..	1,987	8	1,455	21	26	...	3,468	29
Bronchitis Acuta...................................	29,727	48	20,815	139	257	...	50,799	187
Bronchitis Chronica...............................	4,695	31	4,771	170	52	...	9,518	201
Dropsy of Chest....................................	63	6	128	24	......	...	191	30
Hæmorrhage from Nose..........................	528	1	478	2	7	...	1,013	3
Inflammation of Larynx..........................	2,822	31	3,011	121	86	...	5,919	152
Inflammation of Lungs...........................	5,894	933	14,450	4,014	122	10	20,466	4,957
Inflammation of Pleura...........................	4,986	37	5,252	130	121	2	10,359	169
Hæmorrhage from Lungs.........................	923	24	1,066	39	27	...	2,016	63
Other diseases of this order.....................	10,011	69	7,335	158	183	1	17,529	228
ORDER VI. *Diseases of Digestive Organs.*								
Colic...	12,195	5	12,094	11	139	2	24,428	18
Constipation..	20,720	1	18,630	5	1,408	...	40,758	6
Cholera Morbus....................................	4,010	42	4,553	54	60	...	8,623	96
Cirrhosis of Liver..................................	46	3	67	2	1	...	114	5
Dropsy from Hepatic Disease....................	569	24	897	50	1	1	1,467	75
Dyspepsia...	7,466	4	5,574	6	191	1	13,231	11
Diseases of Pancreas.............................	22	......	18	......	15	...	55	......
Diseases of Spleen................................	167	2	741	10	4	...	912	12
Fistula in Ano......................................	410	......	457	5	10	...	877	5
Hernia...	5,573	7	4,329	15	75	1	9,977	23
Hæmorrhage from Stomach.....................	150	3	211	5	7	...	368	8
Carried forward....................................	650,523	12,456	798,600	28,113	16,455	61	1,465,578	40,630

COMPARATIVE FREQUENCY OF THE SEVERAL DISEASES.

TABLE XI.—Concluded.

LIST OF DISEASES.	Atlantic Region.		Central Region.		Pacific Region.		Total.	
	Taken sick.	Died.	Taken sick.	Died.	Taken sick.	Died.	Taken sick.	Died.
Brought forward...............................	650,523	12,456	798,600	28,113	16,455	61	1,465,578	40,630
ORDER VI. *Diseases of Digestive Organs—Continued.*								
Hæmorrhage from Bowels..............................	336	13	407	32	......	...	748	45
Inflammation of Tonsils................................	9,680	17	7,751	22	304	...	17,735	39
Inflammation of Stomach..............................	1,582	48	2,141	185	39	...	3,762	173
Inflammation of Bowels................................	859	92	1,292	176	26	3	2,177	271
Inflammation of Peritoneum..........................	147	62	297	97	102	3	546	162
Acute Inflammation of Liver.........................	1,467	22	2,477	58	52	4	3,996	84
Chronic Inflammation of Liver......................	1,307	15	2,285	49	48	...	3,590	64
Jaundice...	16,858	28	14,702	98	85	...	31,640	121
Piles...	10,252	2	9,551	20	229	...	20,032	22
Other diseases of this order.........................	3,008	60	3,251	69	60	...	6,319	129
ORDER VII. *Diseases of Urinary and Genital Organs*								
Stone and Gravel...	431	......	430	6	6	...	867	6
Diabetes..	158	7	266	11	8	...	432	18
Bright's Disease...	298	18	197	19	3	...	498	37
Diseases of Prostate.....................................	39	......	86	1	2	...	127	1
Diseases of Testis..	486	......	397	3	2	...	885	3
Inflammation of Kidneys..............................	1,744	18	1,877	34	20	1	3,641	53
Inflammation of Bladder..............................	602	7	544	9	16	...	1,162	16
Incontinence of Urine..................................	859	......	419	2	2	...	1,280	2
Hydrocele..	256	1	256	......	8	...	522	1
Other diseases of this order.........................	939	12	932	8	96	1	2,017	21
ORDER VIII. *Diseases of Bones and Joints.*								
Anchylosis...	152	......	179	......	7	...	338	......
Caries..	166	1	69	1	1	...	236	2
Inflammation of Joints.................................	756	1	473	3	7	...	1,236	4
Inflammation of Bones................................	46	......	42	1	1	...	89	1
Inflammation of Periosteum........................	252	......	190	3	1	...	443	3
Necrosis..	223	......	249	16	3	...	475	16
Other diseases of this order.........................	116	2	149	1	7	...	272	3
ORDER IX. *Diseases of Integumentary System.*								
Abscess...	8,665	17	7,624	52	544	...	16,833	69
Boils..	8,101	......	5,807	......	80	...	13,488	......
Carbuncle..	1,096	1	1,046	2	24	...	2,166	3
Ulcers..	206	1	......	4	......	...	206	5
Whitlow...	1,998	......	1,800	......	79	...	3,877	......
Skin Diseases..	3,599	1	2,891	......	130	...	6,620	1

Class V.—Wounds, Accidents, and Injuries.

ORDER I. *Wounds, Accidents, and Injuries.*

Burns...	1,510	6	1,122	29	47	...	2,679	35
Contusions...	5,911	15	4,067	19	728	...	10,726	34
Concussion of Brain....................................	109	22	167	38	12	1	288	61
Drowning..	....	50	....	69	....	4	....	123
Dislocation..	424	2	432	1	35	...	891	3
Simple Fractures...	743	15	807	28	68	...	1,618	43
Compound Fractures...................................	105	78	190	54	......	...	295	132
Gunshot Wounds...	31,185	4,782	24,599	3,946	210	27	55,974	8,755
Incised Wounds...	3,595	6	1,759	75	182	...	5,536	81
Lacerated Wounds.......................................	1,591	39	2,335	222	321	1	4,247	262
Punctured Wounds......................................	803	54	770	54	47	1	1,620	109
Poisoning...	461	10	346	15	50	...	857	25
Asphyxia...	8	4	28	1	......	...	31	5
Sprains..	5,972	......	3,730	......	293	...	9,995	......
Other accidents and injuries........................	2,033	204	1,534	138	148	5	3,715	347
ORDER II. *Homicide*...................................	....	12	....	13	....	1	....	26
ORDER III. *Suicide*.....................................	*1	39	*2	48	......	1	*3	88
ORDER IV. *Execution of Sentence*............	....	6	....	7	......	...	....	13
Total..	781,638	18,241	909,532	33,797	20,633	114	1,711,803	52,152

* Attempted.

In order to facilitate the appreciation of the foregoing tables, a few considerations, derived partly from the statistical facts, partly from contributed papers and from pathological observations conducted in this branch of the office, are presented with regard to some of the more important affections.

CAMP FEVER—(TYPHO-MALARIAL FEVER).

On account of the great mortality resulting from it, camp fever has been, during the two years under consideration, the most important of the diseases of the army.

Under the general designation of Camp Fever, all those cases are here included which were reported, during the first year of the war, under the heads of Typhus, Typhoid, Common Continued, and Remittent Fevers, and, during the second year, under the heads of Typhus, Typhoid, Typho-Malarial, and Remittent.

This grouping is by no means intended to express a doubt as to the propriety of regarding typhus, typhoid or enteric and remittent fevers as distinct affections. The enteric lesion characteristic of typhoid fever enables a ready distinction to be effected between it and a genuine typhus or a true remittent, on the autopsy at least. But as the diseases have occurred in our army during the present war, the phenomena of these two affections have continually complicated each other in the same patient: so that, in fact, the enteric fevers have broken out among men campaigning in a malarial region, with constitutions more or less thoroughly impregnated with the malarial poison; the remittents among soldiers, peculiarly prone by their exposures and mode of life to enteric disease; and both have occurred, almost without exception, in men whose health has been more or less modified by camp diet, and who were therefore suffering in some degree from a condition best characterized as the scorbutic taint.

These three modifying conditions or tendencies, each of which, acting alone, might produce simple enteric fever, periodic fever, or scurvy, when acting simultaneously produce mixed types of disease that vary infinitely in accordance with the predominance of one or another of the three sets of determining conditions. For these variable resulting fevers I proposed the general name of Typho-Malarial Fever, which, in June, 1862, was, at my suggestion, adopted in the statistical nomenclature of the monthly reports of sick and wounded.

Typho-malarial fever is then the most important and frequent of the diseases included here under the head of CAMP FEVER, and its several varieties embrace the great majority of the continued fevers of the army. Undoubtedly cases of simple enteric and simple remittent fevers did occur, especially among recruits not yet brought under camp influences, and among the attendants in hospitals or others not exposed to them. It would be difficult to state the real frequency of such uncomplicated cases, and when the extreme diversity of opinion existing among physicians on the subject of fevers is considered, it will be understood that the number of cases reported as Typhoid and Remittent Fevers are, to a great extent, to be regarded simply as those in which the typhoid or the paroxysmal phenomena predominated.

Using then the term Camp Fever in the broad sense above indicated, the following statistical facts may be presented:

The whole number of cases during the first year of the war was 74,619, the deaths

6315; during the second year, 138,641 cases and 13,144 deaths,—the total for the two years being 213,260 cases and 19,459 deaths.

The distribution among the several affections included in the statistical reports is shown in Table XII.

TABLE XII.

Number of Cases and Deaths, from the several forms of Camp Fever, during the first two years of the war.

	Year ending June 30, 1862.		Year ending June 30, 1863.	
	Taken sick.	Died.	Taken sick.	Died.
Typhus	824	191	899	381
Typhoid	21,977	5,608	31,374	10,467
Typho-Malarial	....	......	22,652	1,129
Common Continued	11,771	146	....	......
Remittent	40,047	370	83,716	1,167
Total	74,619	6,315	138,641	13,144

The ratio of cases and deaths to strength is very similar for both years. In a general way, it may be said that each year about one-quarter of the men suffered from some form of the fever, and that the deaths amounted to about two per cent. of the strength. The whole number of deaths from these fevers during the first year was nearly one-half the total mortality from disease; during the second year, owing to the increased mortality from other diseases, and especially from diarrhœa and dysentery, only about one-third the total mortality from disease, though still maintaining nearly the same ratio to strength.

The ratio of cases and deaths to strength for each year, and for the average of the two years, is shown in the following table:

TABLE XIII.

Total Number of Cases and Deaths from Camp Fever for the first two years of the war, with the annual ratio per 1000 of mean strength.

	Taken sick.	Died.	Annual ratio of cases per 1000 of mean strength.	Annual ratio of deaths per 1000 of mean strength.
Year ending June 30, 1862	74,619	6,315	265·45	21·71
Year ending June 30, 1863	138,641	13,144	231·52	20·39
For the two years	213,260	19,459	242·34	20·80

A comparison of the reports from the three great regions shows camp fever to have been far more frequent in the Atlantic and Central regions than in the Pacific. In the Atlantic region, during both years, the number of cases was somewhat less than one-fourth the strength; the deaths for each year about seventeen per 1000 of strength.

CAMP FEVER. 111

In the Central region, the ratio of both cases and deaths was much greater during the first year than the second. During the first, the cases amounted to nearly one-third the strength; the deaths to about thirty-two per 1000 of strength. During the second year, the cases were somewhat less than one-fourth the strength; the deaths twenty-four per 1000 of strength. In the Pacific region, the cases for each year amounted only to between seventy and eighty per 1000 of strength; the deaths somewhat over one per 1000 during the first year, somewhat less than one per 1000 during the second. These relations are here presented in detail.

TABLE XIV.
Number of Cases and Deaths from Camp Fever in each of the three regions.

	YEAR ENDING JUNE 30, 1862.				YEAR ENDING JUNE 30, 1863.			
	Taken sick.	Died.	Ratio per 1000 of mean strength taken sick.	Ratio per 1000 of mean strength died.	Taken sick.	Died.	Ratio per 1000 of mean strength taken sick.	Ratio per 1000 of mean strength died.
Atlantic Region	42,516	3,059	238.99	16.75	64,668	5,312	227.94	17.05
Central Region	31,613	3,245	327.31	31.92	73,287	7,826	239.16	24.13
Pacific Region	490	11	73.19	1.64	686	6	78.74	0.69
Total	74,619	6,315	265.38	21.71	138,641	13,144	231.52	20.39

The modifying influence of region on the mortality is shown still more strikingly when, instead of comparing the deaths with strength, they are compared with the number of cases. It is then seen that the disease is not only more frequent, but more fatal in proportion to the number of cases, in the Central region than in the Atlantic, and in this more than in the Pacific. In the Central region there was one death to every 9.7 cases for the first year; one for every 9.3 for the second. In the Atlantic region one to 14 cases for the first year; one to 12 for the second. In the Pacific region, as there were but eleven deaths in the first year and six in the second, much importance cannot be attached to its ratios. The relationship of deaths to cases for each year and region is shown in the following table:

TABLE XV.
Relation between Cases and Deaths of Camp Fever.

	YEAR ENDING JUNE 30, 1862.		YEAR ENDING JUNE 30, 1863.		ANNUAL AVERAGE FOR THE TWO YEARS.	
	Ratio of deaths per 1000 cases.	Number of cases to each death.	Ratio of deaths per 1000 cases.	Number of cases to each death.	Ratio of deaths per 1000 cases.	Number of cases to each death.
Atlantic Region	71.95	13.90	82.14	12.17	78.10	12.80
Central Region	102.65	9.74	106.79	9.36	105.54	9.48
Pacific Region	22.57	44.31	8.75	114.29	14.46	69.16
Total	84.63	11.82	94.81	10.55	91.25	10.96

A comparison of the monthly ratios of cases to strength in each region indicates the autumnal character of many of these fevers, and confirms the idea of a malarial element in their causation, as already indicated. In fact, the season wave for camp fever during the first year of the war is similar in many respects to that of the intermittent fevers, the malarial origin of which is universally admitted. During the second year, the season wave, which in other respects is similar, is somewhat masked by the large figures for July and August in the Atlantic and Central regions. How far this deviation is due to the character of the campaigns of the great armies in these regions and the location in which they operated, is a question the discussion of which must be postponed for the present.

Tables XVI. and XVII. give the monthly ratio of cases to strength in each of the three regions for the first and second years of the war.

TABLE XVI.

Monthly Rates of Camp Fever in the Armies of the United States during the year ending June 30th, 1862, expressed in ratio per 1000 of mean strength.

	1861.						1862.						For the year.
	July.	August.	September.	October.	November.	December.	January.	February.	March.	April.	May.	June.	
Atlantic Region	8·80	18·78	25·60	27·64	27·88	19·74	13·85	13·81	10 00	17·42	24·88	27·07	288·00
Central Region	15·87	38·26	39·98	37·60	36·25	26·80	23·28	18·59	16·97	28·96	29·33	27·70	327·31
Pacific Region	1·72	5·81	5·85	6·67	4·81	4·90	2·15	3·45	6·34	9·19	20·44	12·50	73·19

TABLE XVII.

Monthly Rates of Camp Fever in the Armies of the United States during the year ending June 30th, 1863, expressed in ratio per 1000 of mean strength.

	1862.						1863.						For the year.
	July.	August.	September.	October.	November.	December.	January.	February.	March.	April.	May.	June.	
Atlantic Region	36·20	28·59	19·54	27·67	21·72	18·51	17·61	14 32	14·06	12·29	13·87	14·87	227·04
Central Region	28·18	27·18	24·81	24·14	19·24	16·94	18·77	20 16	19·28	16·83	16·74	18·76	230·18
Pacific Region	4·21	9·45	18·92	9·83	0·19	6·74	2·29	1·01	2·79	5·00	4·10	5·85	78·74

The upper diagram of the plate facing this page represents the monthly fluctuations indicated in these tables.

Materials for an elaborate discussion of the subject of camp fever have been collected, and a careful investigation of its pathological anatomy has been conducted under my direction at the Army Medical Museum. The space to which it has been thought best to limit this paper does not, however, permit the presentation of further

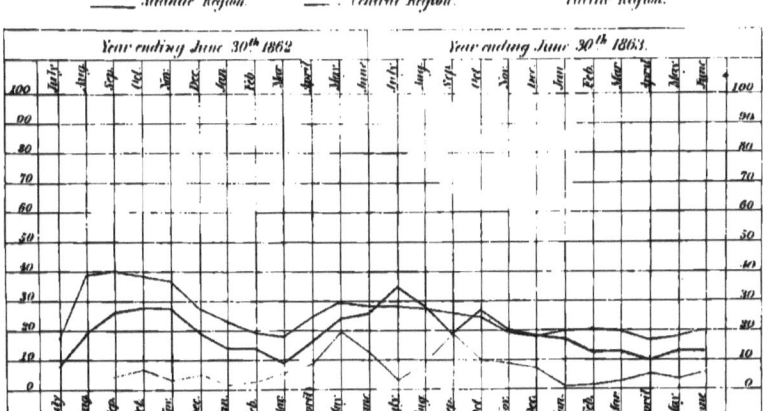

Diagram shewing Monthly rates of Camp Fever
—— Atlantic Region.   — — Central Region.   ······ Pacific Region.

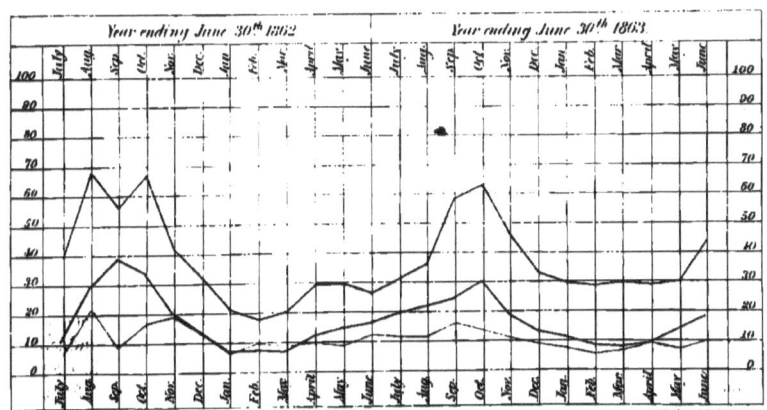

Diagram shewing Monthly rates of Intermittent Fever
—— Atlantic Region.   — — Central Region.   ······ Pacific Region.

details than the foregoing remarks, and the brief sketch of the pathological specimens of the affection now in the Museum, which will be given in the account of the medical and microscopical sections of that collection.

Besides the forms of continued fever which may be properly included under the general designation of Camp Fever, three other forms, which have occurred during the war, deserve a brief mention in this place, viz.: True Typhus Fever, Spotted Fever, and Yellow Fever.

Of typhus fever, 824 cases and 191 deaths are reported during the first year; 899 cases and 381 deaths during the second. There is evidence, however, which will be presented in the Medical History of the War, that many of these cases were not true typhus, but rather cases of typho-malarial, or of ordinary enteric fever of an adynamic character, with strongly marked typhous symptoms, or complicated with scurvy; congestive intermittents occurring in scorbutic patients, and perhaps other diseases, were also occasionally diagnosed as typhus. These facts led me for a long while to doubt whether true typhus fever had ever occurred in our army during the rebellion, and inclined me to look upon the few hundred cases above quoted as belonging chiefly to typho-malarial fever; they have therefore been included in the foregoing statistics of camp fever. Subsequent facts, however, have been brought to my knowledge, which induce me to admit the occasional occurrence of a limited number of cases of true typhus, in connection with overcrowded and ill-policed camps, and especially in the case of those of our soldiers who were detained as prisoners in the enemy's hands.

Spotted fever, called also cerebro-spinal meningitis, attracted attention chiefly at a period later than that embraced in the present paper. Large numbers of cases, autopsies and other interesting materials on this subject have been contributed, with the mere mention of which I must here content myself.

Yellow fever, from which the army wholly escaped during the first year of the war, made its appearance at Key West, Florida, in July, 1862, and subsequently at Hilton Head, South Carolina. The outbreak was limited to a few hundred cases and the deaths to a hundred. In both places, there was the most decisive evidence that the disease was imported in consequence of the neglect or violation of quarantine regulations. The fear that yellow fever would prove a terrible obstacle to the operation of our troops in the Southern States has proved wholly unfounded. It may here be mentioned that the only subsequent outbreak of importance which has occurred up to the date of writing was the epidemic at Newbern, North Carolina, in the summer of 1864. But even here the mortality, so far as our troops were concerned, was limited to a few hundred men. In the case of this outbreak, Surgeon D. W. Hand, U. S. Vols., Medical Director of the Department, expresses the belief that the fever was not imported, but that it originated on the spot in consequence of the neglect of hygienic precaution by the citizens of the place and by the refugees who had made it an asylum. There is now in the possession of this office a most interesting set of papers, contributed by surgeons who were eye-witnesses, giving the whole history of the several outbreaks of yellow fever during the war, with descriptions of the disease, of the treatment employed, etc. etc. It is proposed to publish these papers in extenso in the Medical History of the War.

INTERMITTENT FEVER.

The several forms of intermittent fever played a conspicuous part among the diseases of the army, as might indeed have been anticipated, from a consideration of the frequency of these affections in the United States. They were not the source of any very great mortality; nevertheless the malarial influence, of which the frequency of these simple manifestations may be regarded as the measure, played a part in so many more serious and more fatal affections, that the rate of the occurrence of intermittents assumes a high significance in the appreciation of the comparative mortality of the several regions.

Intermittent fevers were reported under the several heads of Quotidian, Tertian, Quartan, and Congestive. The total number of all forms reported was 72,810 during the first year, 189,997 during the second; making a total during the two years of 262,807 cases reported. The mortality, however, was extremely small, with the exception of the so-called congestive form—(the Pernicious Fever of Dr. Wood). The whole number of deaths, including this more fatal variety, was 430 during the first year and 1358 during the second, or 1788 during the two years. Excluding the congestive cases, the mortality of the other varieties was but 407 deaths for the two years, or one death to every 631 cases. It has not, however, been thought proper to omit these cases, as, after all, in the present state of our knowledge they are to be regarded simply as extremely intense cases of intermittent fever, and are therefore a proper element to be included in considering the mortality of this affection. Embracing them in the computation, it will be found that there was one death to every 147 cases during the two years. It may be remarked, however, that possibly a certain number of cases of spotted fever and of cerebro-spinal meningitis may have been erroneously included under the head of Congestive Fever.

The following table shows the number of cases and deaths reported from each variety of intermittent fever. It will be seen that, according to the reports, Quotidian was somewhat the most frequent form, next comes the Tertian: the Quartan is comparatively rare, the Congestive still rarer.

TABLE XVIII.

Number of Cases and Deaths from the several forms of Intermittent Fever during the first two years of the war.

	Year ending June 30, 1862.		Year ending June 30, 1863.	
	Taken sick.	Died.	Taken sick.	Died.
Quotidian Intermittent	40,375	32	96,603	144
Tertian Intermittent	26,750	33	80,053	116
Quartan Intermittent	3,451	4	9,434	78
Congestive Intermittent	2,234	361	3,847	1,020
Total	72,810	430	189,937	1,358

INTERMITTENT FEVER. 115

Intermittent fever was more frequent during the second year than the first. In both, however, the total number of cases during the year amounted to considerably more than one-fourth of the strength. The mortality for the first year was a little over one per 1000 of strength, for the second a little over two per 1000.

TABLE XIX.

Total Number of Cases and Deaths from Intermittent Fever for the first two years of the war, with the annual ratio per 1000 of mean strength.

	Taken sick.	Died.	Annual ratio of cases per 1000 of mean strength.	Annual ratio of deaths per 1000 of mean strength.
Year ending June 30, 1862	72,810	430	258·95	1·15
Year ending June 30, 1863	189,997	1,358	817·29	2·11
For the two years	262,807	1,788	298·64	1·91

Intermittent fever was more frequent and fatal in the Central than in the Atlantic, and in this than in the Pacific region. In the Pacific region, there were no deaths during the first year and but one during the second. In the Atlantic region, the deaths were somewhat over one per 1000 of strength the first year, somewhat less than one per 1000 during the second; while in the Central region, the deaths were somewhat over two per 1000 during the first year, somewhat over three per 1000 during the second. These relations are exhibited in detail in Table XX.

TABLE XX.

Number of Cases and Deaths from Intermittent Fever in each of the three regions.

	Year ending June 30, 1862.				Year ending June 30, 1863.			
	Taken sick.	Died.	Ratio per 1000 of mean strength taken sick.	Ratio per 1000 of mean strength died.	Taken sick.	Died.	Ratio per 1000 of mean strength taken sick.	Ratio per 1000 of mean strength died.
Atlantic Region	34,857	210	195·94	1·15	55,048	297	194·03	0·95
Central Region	36,980	220	382·88	2·16	133,888	1,060	436·96	3·27
Pacific Region	973	000	145·33	0·00	1,061	1	121·77	0·11
Total	72,810	430	258·95	1·48	189,997	1,358	817·29	2·11

The proportion of deaths to cases was slightly greater in the Central than in the Atlantic region, especially during the second year. In the Pacific region, for the two years, the proportion was over two thousand cases to each death.

TABLE XXI.

Relation between Cases and Deaths of Intermittent Fever.

	Year ending June 30, 1862.		Year ending June 30, 1863.		Annual Average for the Two Years.	
	Ratio of deaths per 1000 cases.	Number of cases to each death.	Ratio of deaths per 1000 cases.	Number of cases to each death.	Ratio of deaths per 1000 cases.	Number of cases to each death.
Atlantic Region................................	6·02	166·11	5·39	185·58	5·64	177·80
Central Region	6·22	160·77	7·91	126·42	7·49	133·51
Pacific Region...................................	0·00	000·00	0·94	1063·88	0·49	2040·82
Total	5·91	169·20	7·20	138·89	6·80	147·06

The influence of season on the frequency of the disease is shown in Tables XXII. and XXIII. It will be seen that intermittents occur at all seasons of the year, but that they are most frequent in the latter portion of the summer, and during the autumn months. In the Atlantic region, the maximum was attained in September during the first year, in October during the second; in the Central region, in August and October during the first year, October during the second; in the Pacific region, in August during the first year and September during the second.

The curve formed by the monthly ratios in each region is an autumnal one, and, on the whole, September and October would appear to be the months of greatest frequency. To appreciate fully, however, the effects of season, it would be necessary to study the detailed statistics of the several armies in each region, with their location and exposures, which is out of the question in a brief pamphlet. Full materials for such a comparison are in course of compilation.

The lower diagram of the plate facing page 112 represents these fluctuations, and may be advantageously compared with the diagram showing the monthly rates of camp fever, which occupies the upper part of the same plate and is constructed on the same scale.

TABLE XXII.

Monthly Rates of Intermittent Fever in the Armies of the United States during the year ending June 30th, 1862, expressed in ratio per 1000 of mean strength.

	1861.						1862.						For the year.
	July.	August.	September.	October.	November.	December.	January.	February.	March.	April.	May.	June.	
Atlantic Region	10·97	27·96	39·32	34·46	22·06	14·08	7·87	6·43	7·00	12·01	15·25	16·88	195·94
Central Region	39·19	66·93	56·46	66·77	42·13	30·60	21·37	17·37	19·07	27·68	28·09	26·25	382·88
Pacific Region	6·46	21·56	9·36	17·17	18·99	13·54	7·29	10·20	8·67	10·01	8·72	12·97	145·33

TABLE XXIII.

Monthly Rates of Intermittent Fever in the Armies of the United States during the year ending June 30th, 1863, expressed in ratio per 1000 of mean strength.

	1862.						1863.						For the year.
	July.	August.	September.	October.	November.	December.	January.	February.	March.	April.	May.	June.	
Atlantic Region....	20·12	22·85	25·40	30·98	19·35	13·67	11·54	8·74	9·89	10·48	15·87	19·16	194·03
Central Region.....	31·39	36·38	56·85	63·05	45·59	33·38	28·46	26·93	29·25	28·37	29·20	44·02	436·96
Pacific Region......	11·87	12·51	15·66	13·91	11·19	8·67	8·27	5·94	7·39	8·94	8·26	9·90	121·77

Before passing from the subject of intermittents, a word may be said with regard to some other manifestations of malarial poisoning, and especially with regard to *jaundice*.

Besides developing intermittent fever and complicating other diseases, such as camp fever and diarrhœa, the malarial influence manifests itself with considerable frequency among troops exposed to its action by the development of a peculiar form of anæmia, which may be designated Chronic Malarial Poisoning. This condition, attended usually with enlargement of the spleen and frequently with an increase in the number of the white corpuscles of the blood, manifests itself externally by languor, feebleness, and pallor, attended commonly with neuralgic pains, and, as it actually occurred among our troops, often complicated by slight scorbutic symptoms. Attacks of fever, pneumonia, or other acute diseases occurring among patients in this condition are peculiarly apt to prove fatal. A yellowish complexion is a frequent phenomenon in the form of anæmia here referred to, and often amounts to decided jaundice.

Mild epidemics of jaundice, running a course of from two to six or eight weeks, and usually terminating in recovery, have also been of frequent occurrence among our troops in malarial regions. That this form of the affection also stands related to the malarial poison, is shown by the fact that, as a general rule, it was most common in those localities in which intermittents were most frequent. In Tables X. and XI. jaundice will be found reported among diseases of the digestive organs. The number of cases reported during the first year was 10,929, during the second year 31,640, making in all 42,569 cases. The deaths were only 40 during the first year and 121 during the second, or 161 in all, which is but one death in 264 cases. Of the large number of cases reported, only 24 during the first year and 85 during the second occurred in the Pacific region; none of these cases died.

DIARRHŒA AND DYSENTERY.

These disorders were reported under the four heads—Acute Diarrhœa, Chronic Diarrhœa, Acute Dysentery, and Chronic Dysentery. The words diarrhœa and dysentery were somewhat loosely used during the war. The disease most generally called Chronic Diarrhœa was, in fact, usually an affection of the large intestine, which was thickened, softened, and often ulcerated. The term dysentery would have been more exact, and was bestowed by many surgeons on the same affection which others called diarrhœa. Hence it has been thought advisable, in considering the figures, to group together all cases reported under these heads.

The extreme frequency of diarrhœa and dysentery makes it most important to understand these disorders. They constitute more than one-fourth of all the cases of disease reported during the period under consideration. The annual number of cases for the whole army was greater than three-fourths of the mean strength, and next, after camp fever, they were the chief cause of mortality from disease. The total number of cases reported during the first year was 215,214, with 1194 deaths; during the second year 510,461 cases and 10,366 deaths—the total, 725,675 cases and 11,560 deaths. It will be seen that the proportionate mortality of the second year is by far the greatest, showing the prevalence of cases of a more formidable type.

The following table presents the number of cases and deaths as actually reported under each of the heads above mentioned:

TABLE XXIV.

Number of Cases and Deaths from the several forms of Diarrhœa and Dysentery during the first two years of the war.

	Year ending June 30, 1862.		Year ending June 30, 1863.	
	Taken sick.	Died.	Taken sick.	Died.
Acute Diarrhœa	164,551	227	373,927	870
Chronic Diarrhœa	15,815	493	63,083	7,488
Acute Dysentery	32,237	347	64,704	922
Chronic Dysentery	2,611	127	8,747	1,086
Total	215,214	1,194	510,461	10,366

Taking the total of these several forms, it will be seen the ratio of cases was 765 per 1000 of mean strength during the first year and 852 per 1000 for the second; so that considerably more than three-fourths of the whole strength was attacked each year. The mortality was 4 per 1000 of strength during the first year and 16 during the second; the disease being just four times more fatal during the second year than the first.

TABLE XXV.

Total Number of Cases and Deaths from Diarrhœa and Dysentery for the first two years of the war, and the annual ratio per 1000 of mean strength.

	Total sick.	Died.	Annual ratio of cases per 1000 of mean strength.	Annual ratio of deaths per 1000 of mean strength.
Year ending June 30, 1862	215,214	1,194	765·40	4·10
Year ending June 30, 1863	510,461	10,366	852·44	16·08
For the two years	725,675	11,560	824·63	12·36

DIARRHŒA AND DYSENTERY. 119

The greatly increased mortality during the second year will be at once understood if the acute cases of diarrhœa and dysentery, as given in Table XXIV., are added together for each year and their mortality compared with that of the chronic cases. Of acute diarrhœa and dysentery, 196,788 cases and 574 deaths were reported during the first year, 438,631 cases and 1792 deaths during the second; the mortality being one death to every 331 cases in the first year and one to every 245 in the second. It appears, therefore, that the acute forms remained comparatively mild. Of chronic diarrhœa and dysentery, there were 18,426 cases and 620 deaths during the first year, 71,830 cases and 8574 deaths during the second; the mortality increasing, therefore, from one death in every 30 cases for the first year to one in every 8 for the second.

This increased mortality, which shows that the chronic forms assumed a more formidable type during the second year, becomes at once intelligible on the presumption that a certain length of time is required before the influences to which a soldier is exposed culminate in chronic diarrhœa. Indeed, individual experience shows that the same soldier has frequently, perhaps usually, repeated attacks of acute diarrhœa, which terminate in temporary recovery, and which, of course, are each reported as a separate case, before the more serious and continuous disorder sets in, on which the term "chronic" is usually bestowed.

Like camp fever and intermittents, diarrhœa and dysentery were most frequent in the Central region; less so in the Atlantic, and least in the Pacific region. In the Central region, the cases were more numerous than the strength during the first year and nearly equal to the strength during the second; in the Atlantic, they were more than half the strength during the first year and more than three-quarters during the second; in the Pacific region, during each year somewhat over one-quarter the strength. The differences between the ratio of mortality to strength in the three regions was still more striking: in the Central region, the mortality was 9 per 1000 of mean strength during the first year, 23 per 1000 during the second; in the Atlantic, 1 per 1000 during the first year, 9 per 1000 during the second; in the Pacific region, less than 1 per 1000 during each year.

TABLE XXVI.

Number of Cases and Deaths from Diarrhœa and Dysentery in each of the three regions.

	YEAR ENDING JUNE 30, 1862.				YEAR ENDING JUNE 30, 1863.			
	Taken sick.	Died.	Ratio per 1000 of mean strength taken sick.	Ratio per 1000 of mean strength died.	Taken sick.	Died.	Ratio per 1000 of mean strength taken sick.	Ratio per 1000 of mean strength died.
Atlantic Region	114,925	238	646·01	1·30	231,504	2,742	810·22	8·80
Central Region	98,470	951	1019·54	9·86	276,567	7,617	902·02	28·49
Pacific Region	1,819	5	271·10	0·75	2,330	7	267·42	0·80
Total	215,214	1,194	765·40	4·10	510,461	10,366	852·44	16·08

DIARRHŒA AND DYSENTERY.

The ratio of deaths to cases shows the influence of region in a striking manner.

TABLE XXVII.
Relation between Cases and Deaths of Diarrhœa and Dysentery.

	YEAR ENDING JUNE 30, 1862.		YEAR ENDING JUNE 30, 1863.		ANNUAL AVERAGE FOR THE TWO YEARS.	
	Ratio of deaths per 1000 cases.	Number of cases to each death.	Ratio of deaths per 1000 cases.	Number of cases to each death.	Ratio of deaths per 1000 cases.	Number of cases to each death.
Atlantic Region	2·07	483·09	11·84	84·46	8·60	116·28
Central Region	9·66	103·52	27·54	36·31	22·85	43·77
Pacific Region	2·75	363·64	3·00	333·33	2·89	346·02
Total	5·55	180·18	20·31	49·24	15·93	62·77

If now we consider the influence of *season* in each of the regions, it will be found that diarrhœa and dysentery were by far most frequent in the summer and autumnal months. In the Atlantic region, the greatest monthly ratio was during July, 1861, after which it diminished through the fall and winter, but again increased from March to June, 1862; July, 1862, was the maximum month for the second year. The cases greatly diminished in August—after the Army of the Potomac had withdrawn from the Peninsula to near Washington; but increased in September, and attained a second maximum in October, which is the month in which intermittents were most frequent in this region; it then diminished steadily till April, 1863, increasing again in May and June. In the Central region, the maximum month is August, 1861, after which there is a gradual diminution till December; an increase in January, 1862; a falling off in February, and a great increase in March and April. The monthly ratio became gradually less during May, June, July, and August, but increased considerably in September, after which it gradually diminished until January, 1863, when it increased again, and made subsequently but slight fluctuations. On the Pacific coast, the disease was most frequent during the summer and autumnal months. The following tables give the rates, and the upper diagram of the plate facing this page represents them to the eye:

TABLE XXVIII.
Monthly Rates of Diarrhœa and Dysentery in the Armies of the United States during the year ending June 30th, 1862, expressed in ratio per 1000 of mean strength.

	1861.						1862.						For the year.
	July.	August.	September.	October.	November.	December.	January.	February.	March.	April.	May.	June.	
Atlantic Region	166·23	116·29	70·80	62·66	46·06	28·54	23·20	22·20	35·22	67·20	70·92	87·06	646·01
Central Region	93·06	139·99	97·94	94·68	70·91	63·34	71·87	55·53	70·73	107·12	97·99	83·78	1019·54
Pacific Region	28·41	40·96	29·63	27·03	30·85	13·54	10·74	16·54	18·13	16·57	22·93	35·82	271·70

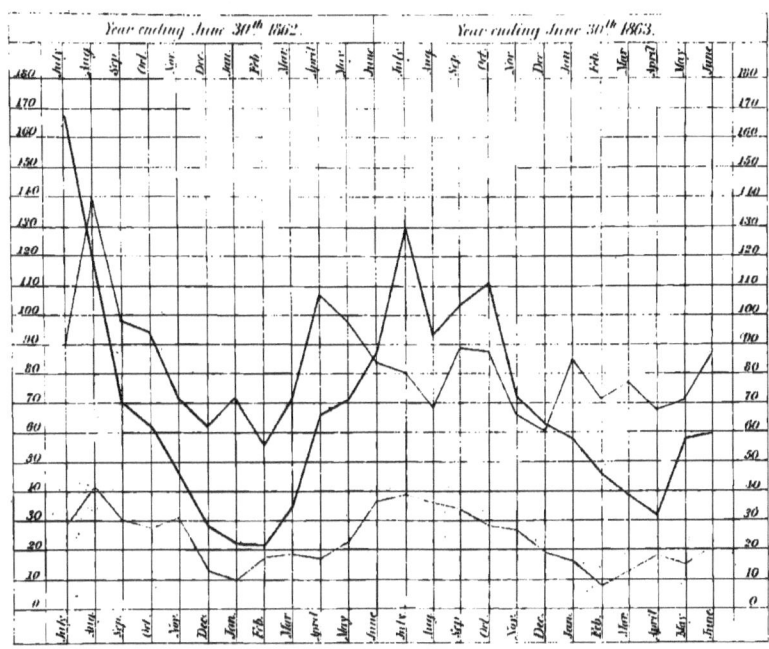

Diagram shewing the Monthly rates of Diarrhoea and Dysentery.
——— Atlantic Region.   ——— Central Region.   ——— Pacific Region.

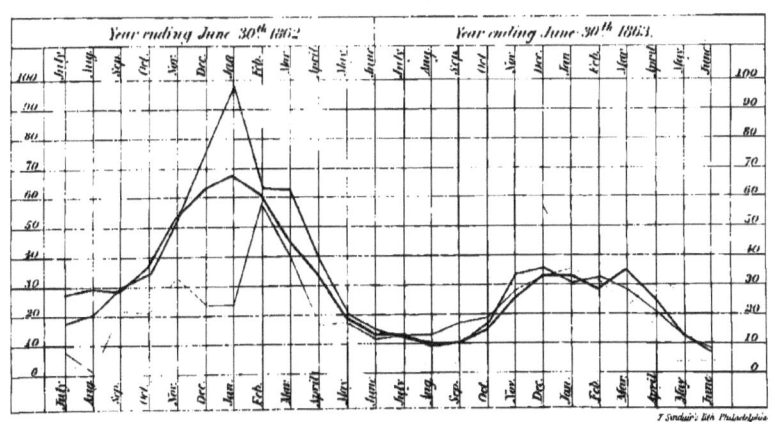

Diagram shewing the Monthly rates of Inflammatory affections of the Respiratory Organs.
——— Atlantic Region   ——— Central Region   ——— Pacific Region.

TABLE XXIX.

Monthly Rates of Diarrhœa and Dysentery in the Armies of the United States during the year ending June 30th, 1863, expressed in ratio per 1000 of mean strength.

	1862.						1863.						For the year.
	July.	August.	September.	October.	November.	December.	January.	February.	March.	April.	May.	June.	
Atlantic Region	129.56	94.40	105.00	111.22	73.47	63.64	58.50	45.52	38.67	31.85	58.02	59.96	816.22
Central Region	79.76	67.64	88.45	86.93	66.27	60.03	84.54	70.84	76.73	67.86	71.48	80.36	902.62
Pacific Region	38.43	36.21	33.53	28.38	26.97	18.66	14.65	7.55	12.54	18.38	15.09	21.16	267.42

Much interesting material has been collected bearing on the causes, symptoms, nature and treatment of these formidable affections. This consists, besides detailed statistics, of a number of papers on the subject by medical officers, of numerous histories of cases and accounts of autopsies, of pathological specimens, drawings, and microscopical preparations, and of the records of microscopical investigations in the Army Medical Museum. The subject is one of such general interest that, although it is utterly impossible to present in this place even an outline of the material collected, it may not be amiss to make a few remarks suggested by these studies.

The origin of the diarrhœa and dysentery of troops is to be sought in no one condition, but in the co-operation of several, each of which should be the subject of hygienic precautions, if the health of an army is to be preserved. Some of the chief of these, but assuredly not the only ones, are the scorbutic taint dependent upon camp diet, the malarial influences operating in certain seasons and regions, the overcrowding and filth of camps and barracks, the heat of summer, the exhaustion and fatigue of campaigns, and the use of water containing saline or organic impurities. Whether there has ever existed, in addition to these intelligible conditions, any specific causative momentum deserving the designation of epidemic influence, is a grave question which receives no affirmative reply from any experience reported during this war. The causation of *chronic* diarrhœa and dysentery is to be found in the long-continued action of the influences above mentioned, and in the consequent frequency and duration of attacks, but not in any specific cause or set of causes different from those which induce the acute form.

The influence of the scorbutic taint in the production of diarrhœa and dysentery is shown not only by the increased frequency of these disorders whenever supplies of fresh meat and vegetables have been deficient, but also by the presence of readily-recognized scorbutic symptoms in the patients. When, on marches or active campaigns, the diet is reduced to a minimum, often consisting chiefly of hard bread and coffee, with but a scanty supply of salt pork, and of beef on the hoof, the number of acute attacks of a mild form, as also of attacks which become chronic, is always greatly increased. It would be a grave error, however, to suppose, as has been done for example by Dr. J. H. Salisbury, of Ohio,* that this is the efficient cause of the disorder, and to reject the consideration of other momenta. To neglect the influence of climate in the production

---

* Annual Report of the Surgeon General of Ohio for the year 1864.

of the disease, for example, would be almost as unfortunate as to neglect the consideration of diet.

The influence of climate, in this connection, is abundantly proved by the detailed statistics of individual armies and localities, too voluminous to be presented in this place, but which will appear in the official volumes. It is also worthy of note that the month of the greatest prevalence of diarrhœa and dysentery in any army is often also the month of the greatest prevalence of intermittent fever. But since it is not possible, in campaigning in malarial countries, to avoid exposure to malaria, the chief interest here attaches to the connection of climate with treatment. This connection is of such a nature, that the number of recoveries bears a direct relation to the latitude of the climate in which the patients are treated and to its freedom from malaria. Passing by the figures of the first year of the war, during which the deaths from chronic diarrhœa and dysentery were comparatively few, the second year gives the following results, which are of especial significance.

During the second year of the war, the proportion of deaths from chronic diarrhœa and chronic dysentery in the general hospitals of New England was one to every forty-nine (48·8) patients admitted for these disorders; in the general hospitals of New York City and State, including the hospital at Newark, New Jersey, one to every nineteen (18·7) cases; in the general hospitals of Philadelphia and at other places in Pennsylvania and Delaware, one to every fifteen cases; in the general hospitals of Maryland and the District of Columbia, including those of Washington, Georgetown, Alexandria, Frederick, Baltimore, Annapolis, etc., one to every eleven cases (11·4); in the general hospitals at Fortress Monroe and on the coast of North and South Carolina, one to every seven cases (7·1).

The mortality was greater in the Central region of the continent, but the relative influence of latitude was still observed. In the general hospitals of Ohio, Indiana, Illinois, Iowa, Missouri, Kansas and Kentucky, including those at Cincinnati, Louisville and St. Louis, the mortality was one death to every nine (8·53) cases; in those of Tennessee, Northern Mississippi and Arkansas, including among others the hospitals of Nashville, Memphis and Helena, one in five (5·4); in the hospitals of Louisiana, including New Orleans and Baton Rouge, one in four.

Nor will a separate consideration of the mortality from these affections in the hospitals of the great cities on the Mississippi River be less instructive. In the hospitals of Keokuk, Ia., the mortality was one in nine cases (9·1); in St. Louis, one in five (5·2); in Cairo, one in four (3·98); in Memphis, one in five (5·4); and at New Orleans, somewhat less than one in five (4·7). The extreme mortality, it may be noted, is not at the point farthest south, but at Cairo, situated on the alluvial peninsula formed by the junction of the Mississippi and Ohio Rivers, where, as is well known, most intense malarial influences prevail.

It is impossible to escape the conviction, based upon the foregoing observations, that a change of climate is one of the most important elements in the treatment of these diseases. The value of such a change, familiarly known to those surgeons of our army who had enjoyed the experience of the Mexican war, did not escape the attention of the Surgeon General's Office; and throughout the war, patients suffering from the fevers and bowel affections of southern latitudes were, as far as the exigencies of the service would permit, transferred to the North. In October, 1863, Surgeon C. McDougall, Medical Director of the Department of the East, recommended the transfer of patients suffering from chronic diarrhœa in the Atlantic region to the hospitals in the State of Vermont, where the freedom from malaria and the fine mountain air would, it was hoped, afford the most favorable results. The experiment was tried, as far as practicable, and with much success. In the West, also, such cases were sent, as far as possible, to hospitals in high northern regions, as at Keokuk, Ia., Madison, Wis., Chicago, Detroit, etc. etc. It was never possible to give the full benefit of climatic influences to all those patients who needed it; but the Medical Department was fully alive to the advantages to be derived from this source, and availed itself of them as far as, at the time, with a full knowledge of all the circumstances of the case, it was believed to be practicable.

Papers have been contributed by various surgeons, detailing the history, symptoms, and treatment of numerous cases of diarrhœa and dysentery. These reports, properly elaborated, will be a most important contribution to our knowledge of those diseases. An analysis which should do justice to them is quite out of the question in the present paper; but a few salient points, in connection with the chronic form, will be briefly touched upon.

The most common and characteristic chronic form, as already intimated, was anatomically a chronic ulcerative colitis, occasionally an entero-colitis. Designated correctly chronic dysentery by many surgeons, it was most generally known as chronic diarrhœa, or chronic camp diarrhœa; and it is to this form that the few remarks here offered are limited. Among its most striking phenomena may be mentioned the usual absence of fever throughout the greater part of its course, the progressive and ultimately often extreme emaciation, the dry, harsh condition of the skin, and the presence of complicating phenomena of malarial and scorbutic nature. The frequent complication of the disease with camp fever is also notable. Sometimes the attack of fever begins the disorder, and diarrhœa is left subsequently as a result. Often, however, camp fever occurs in patients who have already long suffered from chronic flux. In fatal cases of either variety, the anatomical lesions characteristic of diarrhœa are found variously combined with those of camp fever, as will be seen in the brief description of the specimens of this sort in the Museum, which is given in a subsequent paragraph.

Chronic flux, unaccompanied by camp fever, may run its course to its own natural termination in extreme emaciation, with death from debility and exhaustion; or, as perhaps happens more frequently, terminate at an earlier period, in consequence of the occurrence of some disastrous complication. Often, for example, after the disease has lasted a long time without fever, the stools varying from two or three to twenty or more daily, the patient still walking about and suffering little pain, acute dysenteric symptoms set in with fever, delirium, abdominal tenderness, tormina, tenesmus, rapid sinking and death in a few days. An autopsy shows the colon, which is more or less ulcerated according to the previous duration and severity of the flux, to be coated with a yellowish or greenish-yellow, sometimes brownish-yellow, pseudo-membrane, which often extends also through the small intestines. The nature of this pseudo-membrane has been made the subject of careful investigation in the Museum, and the examination of a large number of cases leaves no doubt on the matter. It is simply the croupous lymph, pseudo-plastic lymph, caco-plastic lymph, or false membrane of medical writers. The examination by the microscope of properly prepared sections shows it to be composed of innumerable round cells (lymph cells, pus cells), held together by an adhesive granular matrix more or less resembling coagulated fibrin. With such sections, there is no difficulty in tracing the origin of this membrane to a rapid multiplication of the epithelial cells and superficial connective tissue corpuscles of the diseased mucous membrane. The condition thus described is not always fatal, tubular casts of false membrane having been found in the stools of patients, with the above-described symptoms, who have subsequently recovered.

Another grave complication is diphtheria, with the formation of a similar false membrane in the fauces and respiratory passages. The membrane does not differ from that formed in ordinary diphtheria in civil life. The Museum contains several fine specimens. I have made a careful examination of the false membrane in a number of cases of this sort. It is anatomically similar to the false membrane of the intestine, and its origin is as readily traced to the epithelium of the mucous membrane, the connective tissue of which is, however, less frequently involved in the cell multiplication. The early stage of the diphtheritic affection, in these cases, is often associated with œdema of the glottis, which sometimes suddenly proves fatal before the formation of the false membrane. It may be mentioned in this place, that œdema of the glottis, with or without the formation of a diphtheritic false membrane, has been a not unfrequent mode of death in cases of protracted suffering from gunshot wounds. Other fatal complications of common occurrence in chronic diarrhœa are pneumonia, congestion of the lungs, serous apoplexy, Bright's disease of the kidneys, etc. etc.

An interesting complication which has several times been brought to my notice in autopsies is the formation of metastatic foci, generally in the liver, but sometimes also in the lungs and spleen. These foci precisely resemble those which occur in pyæmia after gunshot wounds. I have met them in the bodies of men dead of diarrhœa, who had received no wound or injury, but who had extensive ulceration of the colon. These are the only cases in which, with propriety, "*embolism*" can be spoken of as a complication of chronic diarrhœa. The heart clots (death polypi), observed in the autopsies of this disease, differ in no respect from those so frequently occurring in patients dead of the most diverse affections, and even, under certain circumstances, in animals killed by violence; and all the evidence which careful investigation has hitherto accumulated on the subject is in favor of the opinion that they are formed during the death agony—consequences and not causes of the fatal issue. Ordinary abscesses of the liver, sometimes of great size, were not very rare, and a number of illustrative specimens have been received at the Museum.

Considerable interest attaches to the examination of the fæces in chronic diarrhœa, and especially to their examination with the microscope. The naked eye at once recognizes as a prominent fact the presence in the stools of undigested portions of the food, the characters of which are often but little altered. This, however, is also frequent in ordinary acute diarrhœa, and is simply an expression of diminished digestive power. In the case of soldiers in the field using hard bread as a part of the ration, lumps of this article but little altered by their passage through the alimentary canal are very commonly present. The most various substances derived from the food are frequently observed; the microscopic appearances of some of them being well calculated to deceive the unwary pathologist, especially if he attempts the microscopical study of the excreta without a prior knowledge of the minute structure of the articles of diet likely to be encountered. Besides such undigested fragments, mucus, blood and pus, in variable quantities, are commonly met, with excess, deficiency, or absence of the products of the intestinal transformation of the hepatic secretions. For the recognition of blood and pus, when they exist in small quantity, the microscope is necessary; in large amounts they can be recognized by the naked eye. Especial significance is to be attached to the presence of pus, which, in moderate quantities, can be recognized in a vast number of cases, probably in all those in which there are ulcers of any size in the colon. Of course, it may happen that though pus exists, its corpuscles have been destroyed by the peculiar form of putrefaction which the intestinal contents sometimes undergo; for, coincident with the diminished activity of the digestive processes, forms of fermentation and even of putrefaction occur, which are not usually met with in the healthy human body. The frequent occurrence in the stools of torula cells, indicative of the setting up of fermentation among the saccharine and starchy elements of the undigested food, has been mentioned by Dr. Salisbury in the paper before referred to. This quite accords with my own observations; but the account given in his paper of the presence of other "algoid forms," etc. is, I presume, based upon some misinterpretation.

For a brief statement of some facts as to the pathological anatomy of this disease, see subsequent remarks on the specimens in the Museum.

The papers above referred to contain also much interesting detail as to the *treatment* of these affections, which cannot be here introduced on account of its bulk. A few remarks may, however, be made in reference to the chronic variety. In this form, the two most important elements of treatment would appear to be diet and climate. The diet should be antiscorbutic. Fresh meat and broth made from it, eggs, milk, oysters, etc. are of the greatest value; but fresh vegetables also exercise a favorable influence. If the disease remains obstinate under this diet and suitable medication, the patient should be transported to a non-malarial northern locality. As to medication, the whole range of vegetable and mineral tonics, astringents and alteratives have been employed with variable success. Among the remedies which have been brought into extensive use in this country for the first time during the present war, I may briefly mention subnitrate of bismuth, strychnia and arsenic.

Subnitrate of bismuth is perhaps the most generally available of these articles. The first paper published on its use in camp diarrhœa was that of Acting Assistant Surgeon J. B. Trask,[*] who recommended it in both the acute and chronic forms. Dr. Trask advised the bismuth to be given daily in one large dose of from one to four scruples, which he regarded as more efficacious than its use in divided doses. He was very sanguine as to its success in all cases in which the patient was not actually dying when the treatment was commenced. He says: "In not a case of the two hundred and seventy treated at Finley Hospital during the period named, and by this agent, was there a failure in promptly and radically arresting the disease, when given in the quan-

---

[*] Report on the Treatment of Acute and Chronic Diarrhœa with Subnitrate of Bismuth at Camp Downey, California, and Finley Hospital, Washington, D. C., by J. B. Trask, M.D., Acting Assistant Surgeon U. S. A. San Francisco, 1863.

tities and time as stated." In September, 1863, Surgeon T. Rush Spencer, U. S. Vols., made an official report on the use of the remedy in seventy-six cases, sixty of which were chronic and sixteen acute. Seventy-one of these cases were cured and five still under treatment at the date of his report. The treatment in the successful cases lasted from one to eight days. Influenced by these and other reports, I myself tried the remedy quite extensively, and was cognizant of its use in a large number of cases of both acute and chronic diarrhœa. It generally showed itself a most valuable agent. In a few cases, however, tormina, tenesmus, and other dysenteric phenomena, with an aggravation of all the symptoms, followed its use, and in a very considerable proportion of the severe chronic cases it appeared to be wholly without effect. The subsequent experience of many surgeons in the field and in hospital gave similar results; so that while it must be admitted to be a quite useful remedy, especially when given in large doses, the extravagant expectations which were at first entertained with regard to it by some must be abandoned.

Strychnia was also extensively used by some surgeons. It was given in the form of sulphate, or as extract of nux vomica. Very generally it was combined with quinine, or with quinine and iron, and proved valuable in many atonic and paralytic conditions of the bowels, but was far from being of general availability in the treatment of severe chronic cases.

Arsenic in pill, or in the form of Fowler's solution, was more frequently useful, and by some surgeons this remedy was regarded almost as a specific. So far as I have been able to learn, it was chiefly available in cases complicated with chronic malarial poisoning. The utter failure of these, or indeed any therapeutic agents, to command general confidence, or to come into general use, will serve to show how subordinate their effect is to be regarded to that of proper dietic and climatic conditions.

Asiatic cholera did not make its appearance during the war, nor was any similar affection of a severe type frequent. The whole number of deaths from cholera morbus was 33 during the first year and 96 during the second.

SMALL-POX.

From a very early period in the war the attention of the Medical Bureau was directed to the subject of vaccination, and strenuous efforts were made to render this method of protection universal. That these efforts were to a great extent successful, is shown by the comparatively small number of cases reported: 1310 cases of small-pox and varioloid were reported during the first year and 2822 during the second—making a total of 4132; the deaths were 412 during the first year and 1132 during the second—being 1544 in all. According to these figures, the mortality would be one death to about every three (2·67) cases. Since, however, a certain number of cases of variolous disease originated in the general hospitals themselves, and upon the statistical system employed the deaths from among these cases would be included in the above figures, it is probable that the ratio of deaths to cases thus obtained is somewhat too high. If, however, the experience of some of the larger small-pox hospitals, in which it is known that the cases received were treated to their termination, be compared, it will be found that the mortality shown in their reports closely approximates the above. Thus, in the two largest establishments of the kind, the Small-pox Hospital at St. Louis, Missouri, and that at Washington, D. C., the total number of cases of small-pox and varioloid treated during the two years was 2319; the number of deaths 597, or one in four (3·88) cases.

A considerable amount of material is on file concerning the frequency and fatality of variolous disease among those who have been vaccinated, as compared with the unprotected, and on other matters of interest connected with this subject. Most of this material belongs, however, to a period subsequent to that referred to in this paper. I will only mention here the occurrence in many instances, especially in the Central region, of foul or gangrenous ulcers as an accident attendant upon vaccination. The earliest cases of the sort referred to in the official reports occurred in the latter part of 1863 in the District of the Frontier, and are reported by Surgeon George H. Hubbard, U. S. Vols., Medical Director of the district. They were supposed to be caused by the accidental admixture of syphilitic matter with the virus employed. Other cases subsequently occurred in Missouri, the Northern Department, Kentucky, Tennessee, etc., and were made the subject of careful inquiry by Colonel C. S. Tripler, Medical Director of the Northern Department, and other surgeons. The opinion generally arrived at was, that they were the expression of scorbutic or other cachectic conditions of the patients, and not due to any poisonous admixture with the vaccine virus; and it was frequently observed that the same scab which had produced a number of successful vaccinations would, in other men vaccinated at the same time, produce the ulcers referred to. An exceedingly interesting paper which illustrates this point, as observed in a number of cases among citizens at Horicon, Wisconsin, has been contributed by Surgeon Howard Culbertson, U. S. Vols. The subject is one which deserves a full discussion hereafter.

CAMP MEASLES.

Epidemic measles was one of the characteristic affections of the war. It occurred chiefly in regiments recently raised, and among recruits, and appeared to be due wholly to the incidental exposure of men brought up in rural districts who had hitherto escaped the contagion: 21,676 cases and 551 deaths were reported during the first year of the war, 16,345 cases and 1313 deaths during the second; but there is reason to believe that the actual number of cases was considerably greater, since it is well known that the disease frequently prevailed epidemically in new regiments, after the men began to come together in the State to which they belonged, but before they were mustered into the service of the United States, and therefore before their medical officers began to report to the Surgeon General's Office. The disease resembled ordinary measles in adults, except when aggravated by the effects of crowd poisoning or other depressing influences. The direct mortality was not great, being only one death to every twenty cases, but tedious catarrh, pneumonia, and pleuro-pneumonia were frequent sequelæ; and a part of the mortality from these affections was due indirectly to measles.

EPIDEMIC MUMPS.

Another affection, which prevailed extensively, was Epidemic Mumps (parotitis). It occurred both as an independent affection and as a complication of other diseases. It was seldom fatal. During the first year 11,216 cases and 9 deaths were reported; during the second 13,429 cases and 30 deaths. The inflammation of the gland seldom terminated in abscess, except in those cases which occurred as complications of camp fever. Metastasis to the testicle was not unfrequent. The disease appeared to spread by contagion, affecting almost exclusively those who had never previously suffered.

INFLAMMATORY DISEASES OF THE RESPIRATORY ORGANS.

The last of the miasmatic group of zymotic affections on which remarks will here be made is Epidemic Catarrh, of which 11,314 cases and 5 deaths were reported during the first year, and 63,202 cases and 24 deaths during the second. Considerable confusion, however, appears to have existed as to the precise signification and limits of the terms Catarrh, Epidemic Catarrh, and Acute Bronchitis; precisely similar cases being reported by different surgeons under each of these heads. It appears probable, moreover, that the causes determining inflammatory affections of the several portions of the respiratory apparatus are intimately allied, the total number of cases representing the effect of exposure to unfavorable climatic influences, such as cold, dampness, etc.; while the mortality is determined partly by the intensity of the cause, partly by the hygienic surroundings and constitutional condition of the patients. Influenced by these and other reasons, it has been considered advisable to bring together into a single group all the disorders of this class. This group will be designated *Inflammatory Diseases of the Respiratory Organs*, and will include all the cases reported as Epidemic Catarrh, Catarrh, Acute and Chronic Bronchitis, Laryngitis, Pleurisy, and Pneumonia.

The whole number of the cases of this group reported during the first year of the war was 143,991 cases and 2400 deaths; during the second year, 160,263 cases and 5690 deaths—making a total for the two years of 304,254 cases and 8090 deaths. These cases were distributed among the several affections included in the group, as shown in the following table:

TABLE XXX.

Number of Cases and Deaths from Inflammatory Diseases of the Respiratory Organs during the first two years of the war.

	Year ending June 30, 1862.		Year ending June 30, 1863.	
	Taken sick.	Died.	Taken sick.	Died.
Catarrh	83,837	5	....	......
Epidemic Catarrh	11,314	5	63,202	24
Laryngitis	2,597	34	5,919	152
Acute Bronchitis	26,201	102	50,790	187
Chronic Bronchitis	3,902	36	9,518	201
Pleurisy	5,079	84	10,350	169
Pneumonia	11,061	2,134	20,466	4,957
Total spoken of as Inflammatory Diseases of the Respiratory Organs	143,991	2,400	160,263	5,690

The total number of cases during the first year amounted to more than one-half the mean strength; during the second year, however, to not much more than one-quarter of the strength. The deaths were between 8 and 9 per 1000 of strength during each year.

INFLAMMATORY DISEASES OF THE RESPIRATORY ORGANS. 129

TABLE XXXI.

Total Number of Cases and Deaths from Inflammatory Diseases of the Respiratory Organs for the first two years of the war, with the annual ratio per 1000 of mean strength.

	Taken sick.	Died.	Annual ratio of cases per 1000 of mean strength.	Annual ratio of deaths per 1000 of mean strength.
Year ending June 30, 1862	148,991	2,400	512·10	8·25
Year ending June 30, 1863	160,263	5,690	267·68	8·83
For the two years	304,254	8,090	345·74	8·65

It will thus be seen that the ratio of cases to strength during the second year is only about one-half that during the first while the ratio of deaths to strength is about the same; so that while the proportionate number of cases greatly diminished during the second year, their comparative fatality increased and the proportion of mortality to strength remained about the same. The greater prevalence of slight cases during the first year thus indicated is probably to be attributed, to a certain extent at least, to the large number of men taken suddenly, during the fall and winter, from the shelter and comforts of civil life and subjected to the exposure of camps. The greater number of cases of measles during the first year is also undoubtedly connected with the greater prevalence of catarrhal cases.

Unlike camp fever and diarrhœa, the inflammatory affections of the respiratory organs occurred with nearly equal frequency in the three regions, the only exception being in the case of the Pacific region, which suffered somewhat less than the others during the first year, somewhat more during the second. The proportion of mortality to strength, however, followed the same general law as the other important camp diseases, being most frequent in the Central and least so in the Pacific region. In the Central region it was 16 per 1000 of strength during the first year, 14 during the second; in the Atlantic about 4 per 1000 of strength during both years; in the Pacific about 1 per 1000 during both. Table XXXII. gives the details.

TABLE XXXII.

Number of Cases and Deaths from Inflammatory Diseases of the Respiratory Organs in each of the three regions.

	YEAR ENDING JUNE 30, 1862.				YEAR ENDING JUNE 30, 1863.			
	Taken sick.	Died.	Ratio per 1000 of mean strength taken sick.	Ratio per 1000 of mean strength died.	Taken sick.	Died.	Ratio per 1000 of mean strength taken sick.	Ratio per 1000 of mean strength died.
Atlantic Region	90,481	785	508·61	4·08	76,515	1,083	209·67	3·48
Central Region	51,471	1,658	582·92	16·31	81,214	4,595	265·05	14·17
Pacific Region	2,089	7	304·56	1·04	2,534	12	290·88	1·38
Total	148,991	2,400	512·10	8·25	160,263	5,690	267·68	8·83

130   INFLAMMATORY DISEASES OF THE RESPIRATORY ORGANS.

The proportion of deaths to cases was likewise greater in the Central than in the Atlantic, and in this than in the Pacific region, and, as already intimated, it was greater during the second year than during the first. In the Atlantic region there was one death to every 123 cases during the first year, one to every 71 during the second; in the Central region one to every 31 cases during the first year, one to every 18 during the second; in the Pacific region one to every 291 cases during the first year, one to every 211 during the second. The average for all regions and both years was one death to every 38 cases.

TABLE XXXIII.
Relation between Cases and Deaths of Inflammatory Diseases of the Respiratory Organs.

	Year ending June 30, 1862.		Year ending June 30, 1863.		Annual Average for the Two Years.	
	Ratio of deaths per 1000 cases.	Number of cases to each death.	Ratio of deaths per 1000 cases.	Number of cases to each death.	Ratio of deaths per 1000 cases.	Number of cases to each death.
Atlantic Region	8·15	122·70	14·15	70·67	10·91	91·66
Central Region	32·21	31·05	56·58	17·67	47·13	21·22
Pacific Region	3·44	290·70	4·74	210·97	4·15	240·96
Total	16·70	59·88	35·50	28·17	26·62	37·57

The effect of season on the development of these diseases is indicated, as might be expected, by the occurrence of the greatest number of cases during the winter. On the Atlantic coast the number of cases taken sick each month gradually increased from July, 1861, to January, 1862, after which it diminished to August, 1862, increased till December, and then diminished through 1863 till the close of the fiscal year in June, with the exception of an irregular increase in March. In the Central region the disease pursued an essentially parallel wave, and this was the case during the second year in the Pacific region. In the Pacific region during the first year, however, the wave was less regular. The following tables exhibit these relationships in detail:

TABLE XXXIV.
Monthly Rates of Inflammatory Diseases of the Respiratory Organs in the Armies of the United States during the year ending June 30th, 1862, expressed in ratio per 1000 of mean strength.

	1861.						1862.						For the year.
	July.	August.	September.	October.	November.	December.	January.	February.	March.	April.	May.	June.	
Atlantic Region	27·06	29·17	28·32	35·75	52·95	64·32	67·17	59·64	44·51	32·73	17·86	13·27	506·86
Central Region	16·88	21·41	30·45	35·37	53·40	75·89	98·29	62·92	68·37	38·37	19·87	15·88	532·92
Pacific Region	7·53	1·01	22·18	21·46	32·73	23·86	24·38	56·80	40·44	15·75	17·45	12·19	304·56

* The Table of Catarrhal Affections published for this year in the Circular of September 8, 1863, before alluded to, did not include Pneumonia or Pleurisy, and hence differs considerably from the above.

INFLAMMATORY DISEASES OF THE RESPIRATORY ORGANS. 131

TABLE XXXV.

Monthly Rates of Inflammatory Affections of the Respiratory Organs in the Armies of the United States during the year ending June 30th, 1863, expressed in ratio per 1000 of mean strength.

	1862.						1863.						For the year.
	July.	August.	September.	October.	November.	December.	January.	February.	March.	April.	May.	June.	
Atlantic Region....	13·46	9·37	10·34	13·87	24·55	32·82	33·12	28·13	35·19	24·51	12·44	7·21	269·70
Central Region......	12·01	10·03	10·14	17·07	33·10	35·08	30·75	32·84	28·30	20·49	11·29	8·28	265·05
Pacific Region	12·63	13·18	16·05	18·66	27·67	32·90	35·38	31·10	22·72	32·06	25·78	18·00	290·63

The rates contained in the foregoing tables are presented also in the lower diagram of the plate opposite page 120, where they may be instructively contrasted with the course of diarrhœa and dysentery.

A reference to Table XXX. will show that by far the greatest number of deaths from the inflammatory affections of the respiratory organs were reported under the head of Pneumonia. Out of a total of 8090 deaths from respiratory affections, 7091 are reported as due to this cause. It might perhaps be claimed that this mortality is too great, on account of a certain number of cases of fatal pleurisy and bronchitis having been erroneously included. But the same deficient knowledge of auscultation and percussion which would lead to this error, would produce also an error in the opposite direction, and cause the slight cases of pneumonia to be reported as bronchitis. While then it is possible that the ratio of deaths from pneumonia to strength is somewhat too great, the probabilities are in favor of the approximative correctness of the proportion of deaths to cases; and this proportion is so great, as compared with the results in modern civil hospitals, as to direct attention to the general want of success which appears to have attended the treatment of this disorder. The experience of the two years gives a mortality of one death to every seven (6·8) cases in the Atlantic region and one to every four (3·8) in the Central, as is shown in the following table:

TABLE XXXVI.
Ratio of Deaths from Pneumonia to Cases in the three regions.

	First Year.			Second Year.			For the two Years.		
	Cases.	Deaths.	Number of cases to each death.	Cases.	Deaths.	Number of cases to each death.	Cases.	Deaths.	Number of cases to each death.
Atlantic Region................	4,582	601	7·6	5,894	933	6·3	10,476	1,534	6·8
Central Region.....................	6,366	1,529	4·2	14,450	4,014	3·6	20,816	5,543	3·8
Pacific Region	113	4	28·3	122	10	12·2	235	14	16·8
Total	11,061	2,134	5·1	20,466	4,957	4·1	31,527	7,091	4·4

The great proportion of deaths to cases thus indicated was undoubtedly connected to a certain extent with the character of the disorder. The two chief types to which, as far as can be learned, the majority of the cases belonged, were Typhoid Pneumonia and Adynamic Pleuro-Pneumonia; the first characterized in fatal cases by the condition of the lung designated Splenization, the second, besides the lung lesion, by the presence on the pleura of considerable masses of yellow opaque lymph, with fluid in the pleural cavity.

Both these forms occurred in a large number of cases as sequelæ to measles, or intercurrent affections in the course of chronic diarrhœa and chronic malarial poisoning. In many instances, moreover, what was called pneumonia proved, on the autopsy, to be camp fever, in which the usual intestinal lesions were associated with congestion of the lungs, with capillary bronchitis, or with pneumonia: of course these circumstances would lead to the expectation of a greater mortality than is found among uncomplicated cases occurring in civil practice. The mortality from pneumonia in the British army in the Crimea was still greater than our own figures, being one death to every 3·6 cases.

A considerable amount of valuable material has been contributed on the symptoms, post-mortem appearances, and treatment of this disorder, a careful analysis of which will be presented at the proper time. With regard to treatment, it may be stated that the use of alcoholic stimulants, supporting diet, quinine in large doses, and the expectant plan found numerous advocates, as well as opium, ipecacuanha, veratrum viride, antimony, cupping, and mercurials. The attempt to appreciate these methods must be postponed for the present.

CERTAIN OTHER DISEASES.

The most important affections reported under the head of *Enthetic Diseases* were the several forms of venereal. The reports give separate figures for syphilis, gonorrhœa, orchitis, and stricture of the urethra. The latter two affections being gonorrhœal sequelæ, may be grouped under the head of Gonorrhœa. Of syphilis, there were 9011 cases and 12 deaths during the first year; 13,781 cases and 27 deaths during the second—total, 22,792 cases and 39 deaths. Of gonorrhœa and its sequelæ, 14,768 cases and no deaths during the first year; 25,705 cases and 12 deaths during the second—total, 40,473 cases and 12 deaths. The number of cases of all kinds of venereal was 23,779 for the first year and 39,486 for the second, being 85 cases per 1000 of strength for the first year and 66 per 1000 for the second. The ratio of venereal to the total amount of disease was one case of venereal to every 35 taken sick during the first year; one to every 41 taken sick during the second.

If these figures be compared with the experience of other armies, we cannot fail to congratulate ourselves on the comparative exemption of our troops from these loathsome affections. The published statistics of the English army, for example, show that in 1859 there were 422 admissions to hospital for venereal among every 1000 men serving in the United Kingdom; in 1860, 369 per 1000; in 1861, 354, and in 1862, 330—being thus between one-third and one-half the whole number of admissions to hospital. It may be thought, perhaps, that the active occupations of a war carried on in an extensive and comparatively thinly-populated country will account for this difference in our favor; but the published statistics of the United States army from 1840 to 1859 give a mean annual rate of only 99 cases of venereal per 1000 of mean strength during that period; and this, though larger than the rates above given for the first two years of the war, is less than one-third of the most favorable rate above quoted from the English statistics.

When the frequency of venereal among the troops of the three regions is made the subject of comparison, it is found that in the Atlantic region the rate was 87 cases per 1000 of strength for the first year, 61 for the second; in the Central region, 60 per 1000 for the first year, 63 for the second; in the Pacific region rates are, however, attained which closely approximate those of the English army, viz.: 375 per 1000 for the first year and 317 for the second.

TABLE XXXVII.
Prevalence of Syphilis and Gonorrhœa in the several regions.

	YEAR ENDING JUNE 30, 1862.					YEAR ENDING JUNE 30, 1863.						
	ATLANTIC REGION.		CENTRAL REGION.		PACIFIC REGION.		TOTAL.		ATLANTIC REGION.		CENTRAL REGION.		PACIFIC REGION.		TOTAL.
	Cases.	Ratio per 1000 of mean strength.	Cases.	Ratio per 1000 of mean strength.	Cases.	Ratio per 1000 of mean strength.	Cases.	Ratio per 1000 of mean strength.	Cases.	Ratio per 1000 of mean strength.	Cases.	Ratio per 1000 of mean strength.	Cases.	Ratio per 1000 of mean strength.	Cases.	Ratio per 1000 of mean strength.
Syphilis	6,139	34·51	1,628	16·86	1,244	185·81	9,011	32·05	6,118	21·56	6,439	21·01	1,224	140·48	13,781	23·05
Gonorrhœa and its sequelæ	9,356	52·59	4,147	42·94	1,265	188·95	14,768	52·52	11,326	39·92	12,841	41·91	1,538	176·52	25,705	42·93
Total	15,495	87·10	5,775	59·79	2,509	374·76	23,779	84·57	17,444	61·49	19,280	62·92	2,762	317·00	39,486	65·94

The annual rate of venereal in the Pacific region, as given in this table, is greater than that deducible from the published statistics of eighteen years of peace. But even during that period it was about twice as great as in the rest of the army.

Among the documents connected with syphilis which have been received for publication, may be mentioned certain interesting papers with regard to the attempts made by the military authorities in the Cities of Nashville and Memphis to limit the spread of syphilis among the troops stationed near those places, by regulating prostitution after the plan practised by the French government in Paris—a plan which is reported to have produced the most salutary results in both places.

Under the head of *Dietic Diseases*, the chief affections included are scurvy and the abuse of alcohol. As to the latter of these causes of disease, the activity of the campaigns, and the stringent regulations very generally enforced with regard to sutlers, reduced the frequency of intoxication to a comparatively low figure in the large armies of the Atlantic and Central regions.

During the first year, 656 cases of delirium tremens and 978 cases of drunkenness (ebrietas) are reported—drunkenness here including only those cases in which, in consequence of the debauch, the man was obliged to go on sick report; during the second year, 772 cases of delirium tremens, 1221 of drunkenness, and 226 of chronic alcoholism were reported. This would give a ratio of 6 cases of all kinds per 1000 of mean strength for the first year; 4 per 1000 for the second. It is worthy of remark that the proportional number of cases was much greater on the Pacific coast, where the conditions of peace being more nearly approximated to, the men must of course have had more opportunity and more leisure for debauch. In the Atlantic region, the ratio of cases from the abuse of alcohol was 6 per 1000 of mean strength for the first year of the war; 3 for the second. In the Central region, 4 per 1000 for both years; while in the Pacific region it was 33 per 1000 for the first year and 35 for the second.

The amount of SCURVY reported was comparatively small: 1328 cases and 9 deaths for the first year; 7395 cases and 90 deaths for the second. To this may probably be added the greater part of the 304 cases and 31 deaths of purpura reported during the second year. This extremely small number of cases of scurvy is unparalleled in the history of armies, being but 5 per 1000 of mean strength for the first year and 13 for the second. It undoubtedly stands related to the quantity and comparatively good quality of the army ration,—to the immense supplies of antiscorbutics, of medical stores and comforts issued to the men by the Government, and to the large pay of the private soldier, which is very many times greater than in any other army in the world, and which, in part at least, was often spent at the sutler's on pickles, apples, pies containing dried fruit, etc. From all these sources, ours have undoubtedly been the best-fed soldiers in the world; and besides all this, they received at various times and localities, stores collected and distributed by several benevolent and patriotic associations, whose supplies, though of course comparatively small when contrasted with those of the Government, were yet of considerable value in aiding to form the sum total of the soldiers' resources.

Still it is not claimed that the alimentation of our troops was all that could have been desired; for recognizable scurvy existed to a limited extent, and a scorbutic taint, more or less pronounced, was a prominent phenomenon in most of the diseases of the war. The open question of the army ration, and of its possible economical improvement, is one of great importance, which will not be here discussed. That some alteration is needed, cannot be denied.

The scorbutic taint manifested itself very generally in the form of rheumatic pains in the back and limbs, associated with the scorbutic clay-like appearance of the skin, sometimes even with sponginess of the gums, much more rarely with petechiæ, scorbutic discolorations about the flexure of the knee, etc.

Most of the physicians called upon to treat these cases, having had in their previous private practice little experience with scurvy, reported them as rheumatism, lumbago, or neuralgia. It is by no means insinuated that all the cases reported under these heads were of a scorbutic nature. Many of malarial neuralgia and many of malingering were thus reported. Undoubtedly also a great deal of true rheumatism existed; certainly, however, the latter affection formed but a small part of the enormous number of rheumatic cases reported. During the first year of the war 26,257 cases of acute rheumatism, 14,216 of chronic, and 4289 of lumbago were reported, making a total of 44,762 rheumatic cases; during the second year 45,677 cases of acute rheumatism, 45,758 of chronic, making 91,435 rheumatic cases; of neuralgia, 7546 during the first year, 18,533 during the second. The sum is 162,276 cases of rheumatism and neuralgia for the two years, being 186 per 1000 of mean strength for the first year; 184 for the second. How many of these were rightly named? What proportion of them were in fact, as a vast number unquestionably were, simply the outward manifestation of incipient scurvy? What proportion of malingerers was there among those lame backs which were so common? These are questions which, unfortunately, cannot be answered with any approach to precision from our statistics, but in connection with which there exists some valuable material for future discussion.

Under the head of *Tubercular Disease*, the most important is pulmonary consumption, the number of cases of which, however, was not great: 2508 cases and 550 deaths are reported during the first year; 5599 cases and 2040 deaths during the second—being 8·9 cases per 1000 of mean strength for the first year; 9·3 for the second. The deaths were one to every 4·5 cases during the first year; one to every 2·7 during the second. In the British troops in the United Kingdom, the number of cases of pulmonary consumption reported in 1861 was 9 per 1000 of mean strength; in 1862, 10 per 1000; the deaths for both years, one in every three cases.

Space does not permit further or more extended comments in this direction. It is trusted, however, that enough has been said to give an idea of the scope and character of the statistical work in progress. The figures hitherto presented refer wholly to the white troops of our army. Separate statistical tables are projected for our *colored troops* and for *the prisoners of war* in our military prisons. Good data for these tables are on file. Elaborate tables are also being prepared on the subject of *discharges from service on surgeon's certificate of disability;* these are reported by name to the Surgeon General's Office, with the cause specified in each case, so that data exist for a complete and trustworthy discussion of the subject.

DISCHARGES ON SURGEON'S CERTIFICATE OF DISABILITY.

The monthly reports of sick and wounded from hospitals, garrisons, and troops in the field contain in the general summary a statement of the number of soldiers discharged the service during the month on surgeon's certificate of disability. On the reverse of the report, a nominal list is given setting forth, precisely as in the case of deaths, the name, company, regiment, date of discharge, and nature of disability in each case. From these nominal lists, the number of discharges for disability and the nature of the disabilities can be computed with great accuracy.

The various duties devolving upon this branch of the office during the progress of the war were such that it was not possible, until a few months since, to attempt the reduction of this voluminous material; and although the work is now fairly under way, the figures for the second year of the war could not be completed in time for the present publication. The statistical tables here offered, therefore, are limited to the first year. The total number of men reported to the Surgeon General's Office as having been discharged the service on surgeon's certificate of disability during the year ending June 30th, 1862, was 28,620, or 98·3 per 1000 of mean strength. Of this number, 1937 were discharged for wounds and injuries, and 26,683, or 91·7 per 1000, for disease. These discharges were apportioned as follows among the several States:

TABLE XXXVIII.

Showing the Number of Men discharged the Service for Diseases and Wounds, during the year ending June 30th, 1862, for each State.

State.	Discharged for disease.	Discharged for wounds and injuries.	State.	Discharged for disease.	Discharged for wounds and injuries.
Maine	1,119	59	Brought forward	22,164	1,500
New Hampshire	509	27	Wisconsin	1,095	59
Vermont	370	27	Iowa	1,050	111
Massachusetts	1,825	143	Minnesota	179	30
Connecticut	387	16	Missouri	796	62
Rhode Island	194	13	Kentucky	330	14
New York	7,051	441	Arkansas	1	
New Jersey	401	46	Kansas	115	32
Pennsylvania	3,160	169	Nebraska	59	4
Delaware	73	4	Colorado	4	1
Maryland	85	1	New Mexico	4	8
District of Columbia	6	1	California	33	1
Virginia	125	10	Oregon	8	
Ohio	2,317	142	Washington Territory	2	
Indiana	1,638	166	Regulars	754	114
Illinois	1,719	182	Miscellaneous	94	6
Michigan	1,185	53			
Carried forward	22,164	1,500	Total	26,683	1,937

It will be extremely interesting to compute the ratio of discharges per 1000 of strength actually in service from each State, but the above table has been too recently constructed to afford time for the necessary comparisons, which, moreover, will be still more instructive when the tables for the remaining years of the war are completed.

The following tables show the number of discharges from the several classes, orders, and individual diseases and injuries. They may be instructively compared with Tables VI. VIII. and X., the last columns of which give the total taken sick and died for the same year. In making the comparison it must be remembered that the column "taken sick" in the tables referred to does not include secondary affections or sequelæ.

TABLE XXXIX.

Showing the Number of Discharges for Disability by Classes of Diseases and Injuries, for the year ending June 30th, 1862.

Class.		Number discharged.
I.	Zymotic Diseases	5,194
II.	Constitutional Diseases	7,298
III.	Parasitic Diseases	000
IV.	Local Diseases	9,904
V.	Wounds, Accidents, and Injuries	1,937
VI.	Developmental Diseases	678
	Unclassified and cause not stated	3,609
	Total	28,620

DISCHARGES ON SURGEON'S CERTIFICATE OF DISABILITY. 137

TABLE XL.

Showing the Number of Discharges for Disability by Orders of Diseases and Injuries, for the year ending June 30th, 1862.

Class.	Order.		Number discharged.
I.	1	Miasmatic Diseases	4,645
	2	Enthetic Diseases	518
	3	Dietic Diseases	31
II.	1	Diathetic Diseases	3,960
	2	Tubercular Diseases	3,338
IV.	1	Diseases of the Nervous System	1,480
	2	Diseases of the Eye	529
	3	Diseases of the Ear	319
	4	Diseases of the Organs of Circulation	1,410
	5	Diseases of the Respiratory Organs	1,764
	6	Diseases of the Digestive Organs	3,011
	7	Diseases of the Urinary and Genital Organs	377
	8	Diseases of the Bones and Joints	660
	9	Diseases of the Integumentary System	354
V.	....	Wounds, Accidents, and Injuries	1,937
VI.	....	Developmental Diseases	678
....	....	Unclassified and cause not stated	3,009
		Total	28,020

TABLE XLI.

Showing the Number of Discharges for Disability by Individual Diseases, during the year ending June 30th, 1862.

LIST OF DISEASES.	Number discharged.	LIST OF DISEASES.	Number discharged.
Class I.—Zymotic Diseases.		Brought forward	5,194
ORDER I. *Miasmatic Diseases.*			
Typhoid Fever	258	**Class II.—Constitutional Diseases.**	
Remittent Fever	70	ORDER I. *Diathetic Diseases.*	
Intermittent Fever	56		
Diarrhœa	865	Gout	4
Dysentery	118	Rheumatism	3,585
Erysipelas	17	Anæmia	42
Small-pox	12	Cancer	5
Varioloid	13	Tumors	40
Measles	81	Obesity	2
Diphtheria	4	Marasmus	6
Debility	3,139	Dropsy	237
Other diseases of this order	12	Other diseases of this order	39
ORDER II. *Enthetic Diseases.*		ORDER II. *Tubercular Diseases.*	
Syphilis	399	Consumption	3,161
Gonorrhœa	9	Scrofula	177
Orchitis	49		
Stricture of the Urethra	60	**Class IV.—Local Diseases.**	
Other diseases of this order	1	ORDER I. *Diseases of Nervous System.*	
		Apoplexy	1
ORDER III. *Dietic Diseases.*		Epilepsy	669
		Headache	8
Scurvy	7	Insanity	246
Delirium Tremens	4	Inflammation of the Brain	25
Inebriation	20		
Carried forward	5,194	Carried forward	13,441

138   DISCHARGES ON SURGEON'S CERTIFICATE OF DISABILITY.

TABLE XLI.—*Concluded.*

LIST OF DISEASES.	Number discharged.	LIST OF DISEASES.	Number discharged.
Brought forward.............................	13,441	Brought forward.............................	21,005
ORDER I. *Diseases of Nervous System—Continued.*		ORDER VII. *Diseases of Urinary and Genital Organs.*	
Nostalgia..	8	Diabetes...	13
Neuralgia...	39	Diseases of Testis................................	7
Paralysis..	252	Gravel..	8
Sun-stroke...	21	Inflammation of the Kidneys...............	112
Chorea...	18	Inflammation of the Bladder................	5
Other diseases of this order................	193	Incontinence of Urine...........................	36
ORDER II. *Diseases of Eye.*		Bright's Disease...................................	33
Amaurosis..	109	Other diseases of this order................	163
Ophthalmia..	189	ORDER VIII. *Diseases of Bones and Joints.*	
Other diseases of this order................	281	Anchylosis...	199
ORDER III. *Diseases of Ear.*		Caries..	25
Deafness..	260	Inflammation of Joints.........................	93
Otalgia...	8	Inflammation of Bones........................	1
Otorrhœa...	1	Inflammation of Periosteum................	20
Other diseases of this order................	55	Necrosis...	161
ORDER IV. *Diseases of Organs of Circulation.*		Exostosis..	22
Heart Diseases.....................................	824	Diseases of Spine.................................	39
Varicose Veins.....................................	200	Other diseases of this order................	100
Varicocele..	287	ORDER IX. *Diseases of Integumentary System.*	
ORDER V. *Diseases of Respiratory Organs.*		Abscess..	39
Asthma..	244	Ulcers..	268
Bronchitis..	803	Skin Diseases......................................	85
Aphonia...	42	Other diseases of this order................	12
Inflammation of the Larynx................	27	Class V.—Wounds, Accidents, and Injuries.	
Inflammation of the Lungs.................	253	Burns and Scalds.................................	3
Inflammation of the Pleura.................	97	Contusions...	69
Hæmorrhage from the Lungs..............	151	Concussion of the Brain......................	2
Other diseases of this order................	147	Sprains...	57
ORDER VI. *Diseases of Digestive Organs.*		Dislocations...	103
Colic...	3	Frost-bite...	10
Constipation..	2	Fractures...	277
Dyspepsia..	69	Gunshot Wounds.................................	825
Diseases of the Spleen........................	13	Incised Wounds...................................	37
Fistula in Ano.....................................	82	Lacerated Wounds...............................	3
Hernia..	2,300	Wounds (unspecified)..........................	179
Prolapsus ani.......................................	38	Amputations..	85
Hæmorrhage from the Bowels............	2	Other accidents and injuries...............	287
Inflammation of the Tonsils................	1		
Inflammation of the Stomach.............	37	Class VI.—Developmental Diseases.	
Inflammation of the Bowels...............	21	Atrophy...	25
Inflammation of the Peritoneum........	14	Hypertrophy..	9
Inflammation of the Liver...................	136	Deformities..	238
Jaundice..	17	Old Age...	274
Piles...	215	Under Age...	128
Loss of Teeth......................................	37	Feebleness...	4
Other diseases of this order................	24	Unclassified and cause not stated......	3,609
Carried forward.................................	21,005	Total..	28,620

An inspection of Table XLI. shows that the diseases from which the greatest number of discharges were reported were: Rheumatism, 3585; Consumption, 3161; Debility, 3139; Hernia, 2300; Diarrhœa, 865; Heart Diseases, 824; Bronchitis, 803; and Epilepsy, 669. It will be perceived that the discharges reported under these headings constitute over two-thirds of those discharges for disease the causes of which are specified in the reports. The large proportion of discharges indicated by these figures would appear to justify some of the criticisms that have been made on the manner in which recruits were examined and discharges granted during the early part of the war. It certainly cannot be denied that these criticisms had a certain foundation, and that many men found their way into the service who were either physically disqualified at the time, or whose constitutions were so feeble from youth, age, or predisposition to disease, that they soon broke down under the labors and exposures of actual campaigns. But when it is considered with what haste it was necessary to organize those large armies, this fact ceases to be surprising, and it becomes rather a matter of wonder that the discharges for disease should be represented by a figure no greater than nine per cent. of the strength. It is also to be remarked that it is well known that numbers of those who were discharged for curable diseases recovered and re-enlisted; so that while the humane policy of releasing promptly from military restraint those who were not likely to recover if they continued in service was doubtless the means of saving thousands of lives, it is probable that the army rather gained than lost in actual strength by this liberality.

The statistics of the several drafts and of the Veteran Reserve Corps belong to the Bureau of the Provost Marshal General.*

ARMY MEDICAL MUSEUM.

Besides the statistical material and the documents accompanying it, such as the reports of medical directors of armies, etc. etc., much valuable material of a strictly pathological nature has been collected. To this category belong numerous valuable memoirs on subjects connected with the leading diseases of the troops, histories of cases, autopsies, etc., and the work done in connection with the Army Medical Museum. The portions of this institution under my charge are the medical and microscopical collections.

The *Medical Series* of the Museum, which is still growing, consists at present of about 700 specimens, chiefly wet preparations preserved in alcohol. Each preparation, after careful dissection, in order that the lesion to be exhibited may be as clearly displayed as possible, is suspended in alcohol from a glass hook in the stopper of a fine glass jar. The jar has tied on its neck a parchment label, with the number of the preparation, and the name of the lesion shown. Besides a number of miscellaneous pathological preparations, the Museum contains good collections on valvular disease of the heart,

---

* For interesting information on this subject, reference may be made to the published reports of the Provost Marshal General for 1864 and 1865.

diphtheria, pleurisy and pleuro-pneumonia, camp fever, and camp diarrhœa and dysentery. A collection illustrating the diseases of the freedmen has lately been commenced, and promises to be of considerable interest. The manuscript catalogue, containing the description of these specimens and the histories of the cases, occupies 350 pages folio.

A few words may be said with reference to the specimens illustrative of fever and diarrhœa. The series illustrative of *camp fever* consists of about 160 specimens, chiefly preparations exhibiting the condition of the intestine in this form of disease. The pieces have been mounted upon frames of glass rod, and suspended in alcohol, so that they can be viewed by either reflected or transmitted light. The specimens in this series are arranged in several groups.

In the first, the characteristic lesion is enlargement of the solitary follicles of the small intestine, and especially of the ileum. Thickening of Peyer's patches may be quite absent, or may be present to a variable extent. All degrees of enlargement have been noticed, from the slightest change to cases in which the follicle attains the size of a pea. The most characteristic specimens may be thus described: In the fresh intestine, as received at the Museum, the ileum presents patches of deep congestion of variable extent; the solitary follicles, enlarged to the size of large pin-heads, are frequently black with pigment deposits. The Peyer's patches, sometimes quite healthy, are more generally the seat of pigment deposits in the individual follicles composing the patch, which appears of a gray color, dotted over with blackish points, presenting a resemblance to the freshly-shaven chin. The name "shaven-beard appearance" has been quite currently bestowed upon this condition. In other cases, the Peyer's patches are somewhat thickened, and occasionally as much so as in ordinary cases of enteric fever. In the preparations, as preserved in the Museum, the color of the piece, including that of the pigment deposit, gradually disappears. The enlarged solitary follicles, and the alterations in the Peyer's patches, are, however, well preserved. The solitary follicles are not ulcerated in these cases, except rarely some of the largest, which may present a minute point of ulceration on the apex. The form of fever from which these specimens are obtained is that which attracted attention in 1862, under the designation of Chickahominy Fever, but which, before and since, has prevailed whenever our armies have operated in malarial regions. It is a continued fever, which presents also a more or less decidedly remittent type, at the beginning at least. It is accompanied by diarrhœa and abdominal tenderness, but usually without tympanites. Cerebral and pulmonary complications are common, as in ordinary enteric fever. Enlargement of the spleen is frequent, and often excessive. The fever usually lasts from three to five weeks, and terminates in a lingering and protracted convalescence. This variety I have proposed to designate as the Malarial form of Typho-Malarial Fever.

The second group of specimens are less numerous, and represents, so far as I have been able to learn, a rarer form of disease. As first received at the Museum, the ileum presents intense reddish-black patches of congestion, which sometimes extend throughout its whole length. The patches of Peyer are converted into livid, blackish, pulp-like sloughs, which are often remarkable for their size and fungoid appearance. Petechia-like blotches in the mucous membrane of the colon, the small intestine, and the stomach are of frequent occurrence. Similar discolorations are at times observed in other organs. The cadaver often presents petechiæ on the external surface of the body and scorbutic alterations of the mouth. During life, these cases are marked by the extremely adynamic character of the symptoms, by petechiæ, at times even by the characteristic scorbutic lesions of the mouth, by hæmorrhage from the bowels, and other hæmorrhages which complicate the disorder and often prove fatal. The specimens preserved in the Museum, although they have lost their color, show satisfactorily the pulpy slough-like transformation of Peyer's patches. This variety I have proposed to designate the Scorbutic form of Typho-Malarial Fever. It occurred chiefly at times when other scorbutic diseases were prevailing among the troops.

Specimens of the third group are quite identical with those obtained from the typhoid or enteric fever of civil life, and the cases in many instances are undoubtedly that affection in its ordinary form. As it occurred among the troops, however, the course of the disease was so generally more or less modified by the influence on the soldier of malaria, or of the scorbutic taint, or both, that I have proposed to indicate such cases as the Enteric variety of Typho-Malarial Fever.

Besides these groups, there is a fine series of preparations showing the several forms of ulceration left by the softening and destruction of the patches and solitary glands in each of the varieties, the different methods of perforation, of cicatrization, etc.

A few brief abstracts of cases, selected from the foregoing series, are here presented in illustration, especial prominence being given to the conditions observed in the autopsies:

Private C——, 61st New York Vols., was admitted to Satterlee Hospital, West Philadelphia, Pa., July 10th, 1862, from the Army of the Potomac, then on the Peninsula. His disease was registered Typhoid Fever. He died August 24th, 1862. Autopsy, August 25th: Organs generally healthy, except that the solitary glands were thickened, and both these and Peyer's glands of a black color, resembling the bluish-black of tattooing. The surrounding parts of the mucous membrane were pale and devoid of anything like congestion. No. 270, Medical Series, is a piece of the ileum, showing numerous solitary glands the size of large pin-heads, and a Peyer's patch, which is not perceptibly diseased. The whole ileum was received at the Museum in alcohol, and none of the Peyer's patches were prominent Contributed by Prof. J. Leidy, then Acting Asst. Surgeon U. S. A.

Private D——, 17th U. S. Infantry, was admitted to Satterlee Hospital, West Philadelphia, Pa., August 10th, 1862, from the Army of the Potomac. His disease was registered Typhus Fever. He died August 22d. Autopsy: Age about twenty-two; body moderately emaciated; ecchymoses on the surface of the trunk. There were a number of minute ulcers in the lesser curvature of the stomach; the ileum was of a dark color; most of Peyer's glands were healthy, a few of them slightly thickened, but none ulcerated; the solitary glands were enlarged; the colon was slate-colored, with patches of congestion, a number of spots of ecchymosis, and in the descending portion a few small ulcers. Nos. 273 to 276, Medical Series, are successive portions of the ileum, showing the enlarged solitary follicles and a few slightly-thickened Peyer's patches No. 272 is the stomach, with minute ulcers in the lesser curvature. Contributed by Prof. J. Leidy.

Private B——, 7th Maine Vols., was admitted to Satterlee Hospital, West Philadelphia, August 10th, 1862, from the Army of the Potomac. His disease was registered Diarrhœa. He died October 8th. Autopsy: Age about twenty-seven years; body much emaciated; skin ecchymosed. There was continuous congestion throughout the small intestine, which was most intense in its lower part; the ileum was of a deep maroon color; Peyer's glands were not perceptibly altered; the solitary glands numerous and conspicuous from enlargement; the ascending colon was also congested, and presented a few spots of ecchymosis with pigment in some of its solitary follicles. Nos. 237 and 238, Medical Series, are successive portions of the ileum of this patient; each presents a normal Peyer's patch and a number of enlarged solitary follicles. Contributed by Prof. J. Leidy.

Private W——, 20th Michigan Vols., was admitted to Satterlee Hospital, West Philadelphia, December 13th, 1862, from the Army of the Potomac. His disease was registered Diarrhœa. He died December 26th, 1862. Autopsy, December 27th: Age about twenty-two years. Body rather emaciated; spots of purpura on the trunk; recent pleurisy on both sides, most marked on the right; pneumonia in the lower lobes of both lungs; bronchitis; liver and spleen enlarged; moderate congestion diffused throughout ileum and colon; enlargement of the solitary glands in lower part of ileum; Peyer's glands reddened; slight enlargement of the solitary follicles of large intestine. Nos. 107 and 108, Medical Series, are successive portions of ileum. No. 108 taken from just above the ileo-cœcul valve;

both exhibit well-marked enlargement of the solitary follicles, many of which are as large as bird-shot. Each piece exhibits a Peyer's patch, in which, in the alcoholic specimens, nothing abnormal is visible. No. 109, Medical Series, is the enlarged spleen of this patient, 7½ inches long, 5 wide by 3 thick. Contributed by Prof. J. Leidy.

Corporal S——, 9th Wisconsin Vols., was admitted to Satterlee Hospital, West Philadelphia, December 16th, 1862, from the Army of the Potomac. His disease was registered Diarrhœa. He died December 24th. Autopsy the same afternoon: Age about thirty years; cadaver rather emaciated; spots of purpura on chest and abdomen; lobular pneumonia in lower lobes of both lungs; the inflamed portions numerous, from the size of a marble to that of a walnut, and in a state of gray hepatization; bronchitis; stomach much contracted; patches of congestion in small intestines; Peyer's patches congested and dark red in color, with, however, only the slightest degree of thickening in some of the lowest of them; the solitary glands looked like yellow mustard-seeds sprinkled on a red ground; large intestine streaked with ash color and dark red, and with purpura-like spots of ecchymosis. Nos. 93 to 98, Medical Series, are successive portions of the ileum of this patient. As preserved in the Museum, Peyer's patches are not perceptibly diseased, except the large patch in No. 98, which was taken from just above the ileo-cœcal valve, and which is slightly thickened. The solitary follicles in all the pieces are enlarged to the size of mustard-seeds. Contributed by Prof. J. Leidy.

Private D——, 100th Pennsylvania Vols., aged eighteen, was admitted to Carver Hospital, Washington, D. C., July 5th, 1864, from hospital at City Point, Va. He was considerably emaciated; his tongue thickly coated; pulse rapid and feeble; there was headache, anorexia, and diarrhœa; the left parotid gland was swollen and painful. July 15th. The parotitis has terminated in suppuration; the abscess was opened to-day; the febrile symptoms continue; there are distinct remissions during the forenoon of each day; persistent diarrhœa. July 22d. Patient has grown gradually worse; the integument over the parotid has sloughed; diarrhœa continues; there is deafness and low delirium, especially at night; the remissions have not been so distinct for the last few days; died this evening. Autopsy: Emaciation; lungs congested; heart pale and flabby; Peyer's patches congested, but not thickened; the solitary follicles of the ileum considerably enlarged; several very minute ulcers in the vermiform appendix and the ascending colon. Nos. 385, 386, and 387, Medical Series, are successive portions of the ileum, showing marked enlargement of the solitary follicles. Peyer's patches are not perceptibly diseased. Contributed by Acting Assistant Surgeon O. P. Sweet.

Private V——, 126th Ohio Vols., was admitted to Carver Hospital, Washington, D. C., from Field Hospital, Army of the Potomac, July 4th, 1864. He was much emaciated, and suffering from symptoms resembling typhoid fever. Tongue coated with thick, dry, brown fur, teeth with dark sordes; tympanites; petechiæ on abdomen and chest; the diarrhœa was severe, but the stools feculent; the patient at first improved, but July 25th the diarrhœa began to grow worse and delirium set in; death July 30th. Autopsy: Old pleuritic adhesions on both sides; two ounces of serum in pericardium; liver large and pale; spleen large and firm; the solitary follicles of small intestine enlarged to the size of large pin-heads; Peyer's patches congested, but not thickened; the colon thin, presenting a number of ulcers, which, in the descending colon. were large and irregular. No. 416, Medical Series, is a portion of the ileum of this patient, taken from just above the ileo-cœcal valve, showing pin-head enlargement of the solitary follicles. The whole ileum (preserved in alcohol) was received at the Museum. No disease of Peyer's patches was visible. Nos. 417 and 418, Medical Series, are from the transverse and descending colon, and present a number of irregular ulcers. Contributed by Acting Assistant Surgeon O. P. Sweet.

Private W——, 7th Western Virginia Vol. Cav., aged nineteen, was admitted to Carver Hospital, Washington, D. C., from the Army of Western Virginia, August 21st, 1864. He was considerably emaciated, and had been sick for some time with fever, diarrhœa, and vomiting. When admitted, he appeared exhausted; his pulse was frequent and feeble; he had slight diarrhœa and incessant vomiting; under treatment, the vomiting disappeared, and the diarrhœa greatly improved, but he remained in a typhoid condition, and died August 25th. Autopsy: Hypostatic congestion of posterior part of lungs; the right side of heart contained a large fibrinous clot; the ileum presented patches of congestion, with enlargement of the solitary follicles; there were numerous ulcers of Peyer's patches, which, however, presented this peculiarity, that three, four, or more small oval ulcers, a few lines in diameter, were seated in each patch, but the remaining portions were nearly normal. This condition is well shown in the portions preserved in the Museum, Nos. 407 and 408, Medical Series. In the colon, the solitary follicles were the seat of pigment deposits. Contributed by Acting Assistant Surgeon O. P. Sweet.

Private C—— was admitted to Hospital No. 3, Alexandria, Va., from the Field Hospital at City Point, November 30th, 1864. He was in an extremely typhoid condition, with sordes about the mouth, muttering delirium, petechial spots on the surface, and hæmorrhage from the nostrils and bowels. He died December 3d. Autopsy: Peyer's patches converted into black, pultaceous sloughs; the solitary follicles enlarged, near the ileo-cœcal valve some of them ulcerated; a few small ulcers in the cæcum. No. 468, Medical Series, is the lower part of the ileum, which well exhibits the sloughs described. After nearly a year's immersion in alcohol, they have not yet lost their dark color. Contributed by Acting Assistant Surgeon W. Miner.

Private F——, 42d Massachusetts Vols., was admitted to Hospital No. 3, Alexandria, Va., October 29th, 1864. He was taken sick about a week before with a decided chill, followed by hot skin, severe headache, thirst, and diarrhœa; has had no epistaxis or tympanites; is wakeful, with hot skin, pulse 120, thirst, scanty urine, coated dry tongue, and some bronchial irritation. November 12th. Improved under treatment until this morning; his respiration is now hurried; there is a renewal of all the febrile symptoms, more cough, and dark flushed cheeks, but none of the physical signs of pneumonia. November 15th. Better. November 16th. Feeble, skin cool. November 17th. Bilious vomiting several times last night; some pain in the epigastric region; no tympanites; pulse feeble; the stomach continues irritable, with frequent vomiting, the matters vomited resembling coffee-grounds towards the last; death at 8 P.M. Autopsy: Not much emaciation; intestines glued together with pasty yellow lymph; abdominal cavity contained two pints of yellow turbid fluid, with fæcal odor; a perforation about ¼ of an inch in diameter near middle of ileum; Peyer's glands much enlarged; spleen enlarged and softened. No. 439, Medical Series, is a piece of the ileum of this patient, presenting two deep typhoid ulcers quite like those encountered in ordinary enteric fever. One of the ulcers has perforated, and the peritoneal surface of the piece is coated with pseudo-membrane. Contributed by Surgeon E. Bentley, U. S. Vols.

The series illustrative of diarrhœa and dysentery consists of over 200 specimens, grouped as follows:

The first group embraces the examples of follicular ulceration of the colon. The specimens present all the transition forms of simple enlargement of the solitary follicles of the colon, the rupture of the same, and the formation of punched-out ulcers of moderate size. The colon is usually more or less thickened, the thickening, in some cases, amounting to a quarter of an inch. The ulcers are usually rounded or oval, extending nearly or quite to the muscular coat, and looking much as if they had been cut out with a punch; when received fresh at the Museum, the appearances varied with the stage of the process. In the few cases in which the solitary follicles were simply enlarged, without ulceration, the intestine was seldom thickened. It was often normal in color; sometimes, however, slate or ash colored; sometimes it presented patches of congestion. The enlarged solitary follicles were often the seat of pigment deposits; sometimes also an areola of pigment, deposited in and among the glands of Lieberkühn, surrounded the enlarged and blackened solitary follicles. These patients had generally died of some other disease, as of camp fever supervening upon the diarrhœa, with lesions of the small intestine—of gunshot wounds, etc. In the more serious cases of diarrhœa, the colon was more or less thickened, and presented punched-out ulcers which had originated in the solitary follicles. The colon was then seldom normal in its color. Sometimes it was red, reddish brown, or reddish black; at other times greenish, slate, or ash colored; at others, again, unnaturally pale. Its texture, when cut into, was sometimes tough and lardaceous; sometimes it was softened. The ulcers usually presented a grayish or yellowish-gray base. They were sometimes filled with mucus, at other times contained pus. In the majority of the cases of this class, the small intestine was not involved, unless camp fever had existed as a complication.

In the second group of cases, the follicular ulcers have extended until, in extreme instances, the greater part of the mucous membrane of the colon is destroyed by the vast erosions thus produced. The follicular ulcers usually extend by burrowing in the submucous connective tissue; in this way, in some of the specimens, several of these ulcers communicate with each other in the submucous tissue, though still retaining distinct orifices. The mucous layer containing the glands of Lieberkühn, undermined by the extension of the ulcer, not unfrequently hangs in shreds like a fringe from its edge; the undermined portion being occasionally destroyed by ulceration, but more frequently perishing by sloughing. In such specimens, when received fresh at the Museum, the mucous membrane was generally of a dark-red, brownish, greenish-brown, or slate color. The ulcers presented yellowish-brown or yellowish bases, often with blackish or brown sloughs adhering to their surface or edges. It would appear that this second group of cases represents simply a more advanced stage of the disease shown in the first group; and that the conditions determining the degree of ulceration are the duration of the disorder on the one hand, on the other, the constitutional condition of the patients; those who labored under the scorbutic taint, or who were otherwise brought to an extremely adynamic condition, presenting the most extensive ulcers.

In the third group, the cases present more or less ulceration of the bowel, similar to that seen in the first and second group; but, in addition, the surface of the gut is more or less coated with a yellowish or greenish-yellow pseudo-membranous layer, like that observed in the air-passages in diphtheria. This condition is generally the result of an acute dysenteric process supervening upon a previous diarrhœa of long standing. The appearances of the gut, when fresh, are masked by the plastered layer of greenish-yellow or yellowish pseudo-membrane which coats its surface.

The fourth group includes those cases in which the small intestine is diseased as well as the large. Most of these are examples of the complications of diarrhœa with camp fever, and the lesions in the small intestine are therefore similar to the lesions already described as existing in fever cases. In some instances the history of the case shows fever to have been the primary disorder, from which, however, the patient never wholly convalesced, but finally succumbed to the diarrhœa which supervened. In other cases, the fever occurred after the patient had suffered from diarrhœa for months. The character of the lesions in the small intestine and colon usually corresponds to this history.

But besides these cases, in which the affection of the small intestine is evidently the result of fever, the Museum contains several specimens in which, from the character of the lesion, it must be inferred that the affection of the small intestine is simply an extension of the disease upwards from the colon. In these cases, the ileum is more or less thickened,—the thickening being greatest near the ileo-cœcal valve. The thickened ileum presents ulcers of variable size, which appear, as a rule, to have their origin in the solitary follicles, and not in the patches of Peyer.

The fifth group embraces tubercular ulceration of the bowels. The ulcers are more characteristic in the small intestine than in the large; but both small and large intestines are usually affected. The patients have tubercles in the lungs; cheesy transformation of the mesenteric glands; at times, other tubercular lesions. In the small intestine, Peyer's patches appear to determine the position of the ulcers, which are usually irregular ovals, with their long diameter transverse to the gut, as has been observed in tubercular ulceration of the bowels in civil practice. Frequently also small tubercles can be seen on the peritoneal surface of the piece opposite the ulcers. Of this condition, fine specimens exist in the Museum. With this lesion of the small intestine, thickening and ulceration of the colon are associated. The ulcers are quite similar always to some one of the forms above described. Usually they are extensive and deep, the colon being much thickened. I have not been able to satisfy myself that they originate in tubercular deposits. On the contrary, they seem quite like the colon ulcers of other patients from the same command who have no tubercular disease whatever. Besides the foregoing groups, there are specimens of perforating ulcers of the colon, cicatrices of colon ulcers, etc. etc.

Abstracts of a few cases are here very briefly presented in illustration of the foregoing series:

Private R——, 4th Iowa Cavalry, was admitted to Hospital No. 3, Vicksburg, Miss., October 10th, 1863. He had suffered from diarrhœa for nine months previous to his decease. The attack began as dysentery, with frequent bloody stools, which, in a day or two, greatly diminished in number, becoming mucoid and gelatinous. After five weeks, the disease assumed the characters of chronic diarrhœa, which continued till his admission; the dysenteric symptoms, however, recurring from time to time. He died November 17th. Autopsy: A few calcareous tubercles and cicatrices at the apex of each lung; patches of congestion in small intestine; at the lower end of the ileum a few of Peyer's glands were slightly prominent; cæcum of a deep red color, its mucous coat softened; the rest of the colon much thickened, cutting like cartilage, pale, with livid spots or stains, and presenting great numbers of small punched-out follicular ulcers; spleen small. Nos. 119 to 123, Medical Series, are successive portions of the colon, which show very well its thickness and the follicular ulcers. Contributed by Surgeon George F. French, U. S. Vols.

Private B——, 5th Illinois Cavalry, aged twenty-one, was admitted to Hospital No. 3, Vicksburg, Miss., October 10th, 1863. Has been sick eight months. His disease began with an attack of intermittent fever, which was succeeded by dysentery for a few days, when the stools became watery, and the complaint assumed the character of chronic diarrhœa, which it retained, with occasional dysenteric symptoms, until the date of his admission. Death, November 19th. Autopsy: Old pleuritic adhesions; patches of congestion in small intestine; solitary glands enlarged to the size of small shot; Peyer's glands healthy; cæcum inflamed; descending colon and rectum extensively ulcerated. No. 145, Medical Series, is a piece of the ileum, with enlarged solitary follicles. No. 146, of the ulcerated colon. Contributed by Surgeon George F. French, U. S. Vols.

Private C——, 2d Battalion, Veteran Reserve Corps, on duty at the Fairfax Seminary Hospital, near Alexandria, Va., applied for treatment August 6th, 1864. He stated that he had suffered from frequent attacks of diarrhœa during the previous six months. He was pale and sallow, with furred tongue, quick pulse, and dry skin. The stools were from ten to fifteen daily, consisting of thin frothy mucus mixed with blood. He died November 25th. Autopsy: Small intestine normal; colon extensively ulcerated, and coated with a dark-colored pseudo-membrane, which hung in shreds from the edges of the ulcers. Nos. 383 and 384, Medical Series, are successive portions of the colon, exhibiting the conditions described. Contributed by Assistant Surgeon H. Allen, U. S. A.

Private M——, 108th New York Vols., was admitted to Douglas Hospital, Washington, D. C., February 13th, 1863. Had been taken sick in the Army of the Potomac, and was brought from Aquia Creek in a very feeble condition. He was greatly emaciated, pulse 110, tongue red, stools frequent and liquid. He gradually sank, the abdomen became tender and tympanitic, and he died March 20th. Autopsy: Pleuritic adhesions of lower lobe of right lung; nutmeg liver; patches of inflammatory congestion in small intestine; the colon thickened, with numerous large ulcers; the remainder of its mucous surface plastered with pseudo-membrane. Nos. 288 and 289, Medical Series, are successive portions of the colon in this case. Contributed by Assistant Surgeon William Thomson, U. S. A.

Private McD——, 39th Massachusetts Vols., was admitted to Douglas Hospital, Washington, D. C., from the Army of the Potomac, September 9th, 1864. He had suffered from frequent attacks of diarrhœa during the summer, and had also had intermittent fever. For three weeks prior to his admission, he had been in field hospital. On admission, he was emaciated and feeble; conjunctiva yellow; tongue furred; pulse 80; abdomen flat and tender, especially over the course of the colon; frequent stools; slight cough. Death, September 30th. Autopsy: Pleuritic adhesions on both sides; peritonitis; the pelvic cavity filled with thin pus; the viscera coated with patches of yellow lymph; small intestine normal; large intestine greatly thickened, with extensive irregular ulcers. No. 400, Medical Series, is a portion of the colon of this patient. Contributed by Assistant Surgeon W. F. Norris, U. S. A.

Private S——, 2d New York Heavy Artillery, was admitted to Douglas Hospital, Washington, D. C., from the Army of the Potomac, September 9th, 1864, with chronic diarrhœa. At the time of his admission, he was much emaciated, with jaundice and frequent bilious vomiting. Abdomen flat and tender; stupor; low delirium; involuntary stools; and death on the 17th. Autopsy by Assistant Surgeon E. Curtis, U. S. A.. Emaciation; jaundice; thoracic organs healthy; small intestine normal; mucous membrane of colon greatly thickened, with large irregular ragged ulcers; a perforation the size of a dime in the caput coli; peritoneal adhesions, principally between right lobe of liver and colon; numerous metastatic foci in liver, especially in right lobe. No. 448, Medical Series, is a piece of the ulcerated colon. No. 449, a section of the liver. The small yellow foci scattered through the liver consisted of granular matter and the debris of normal tissue, but contained no pus. The condition was similar to what is often observed in pyæmia due to gunshot wounds. Contributed by Assistant Surgeon W. F. Norris, U. S. A.

Corporal C——, 160th Pennsylvania Vols., æt. twenty-four, was admitted to Columbian College Hospital, Washington, D. C., October 30th, 1864, for chronic diarrhœa. There was great emaciation, frequent pulse, and five or six loose stools daily. November 11th. Attention was drawn to a dry cough at night, with frequency of respiration. Death, November 18th. Autopsy: A large abscess was found in upper part of right lobe of liver. It had burst through the diaphragm into right pleural cavity, which contained a gallon of sero-pus. The fifth, sixth, and seventh ribs on this side were denuded of periosteum by the burrowing of the pus. The lower parts of the ileum and colon were thickened, with follicular ulcers, and coated with patches of pseudo-membrane. The mesenteric glands enlarged. No. 435, Medical Series, is a portion of the liver in this case, exhibiting the abscess cavity. Nos. 436 and 437 are successive portions of the ulcerated colon. No. 434, the collapsed right lung, coated with pseudo-membrane. No. 435, the seventh rib of the same side, its inner surface denuded of periosteum, and presenting several new formations of bone. Contributed by Surgeon Thomas Crosby, U. S. Vols.

Private R——, 1st Regt. Veteran Reserve Corps, aged forty-one, was admitted to the Post Hospital, Fort McHenry, Md., September 30th, 1865. He had suffered from chronic diarrhœa for several months, and was much emaciated; stools, from eight to ten daily. October 18th. He complained of a violent pain, which appeared to have its seat in the kidneys. Death, October 21st. Autopsy: Hypostatic congestion of the posterior parts of both lungs; four ounces of bloody serum in right pleural cavity; the right lobe of the liver, adherent to the abdominal walls, presented three abscesses, each containing about four ounces of thick flaky pus; spleen very large and soft; colon ulcerated from one extremity to the other; some of the ulcers very large, and penetrating to the muscular coat. No. 668, Medical Series, is the liver from this case. Contributed by Brevet Major De Witt C. Peters, Assistant Surgeon U. S. A.

The arrival of recent specimens at the Museum has afforded good opportunities for making drawings representing the appearance of the preparations immediately after their removal from the body. Accordingly a series of careful water-color drawings has been made, which show most of the typical forms of camp diseases. The drawings are the work of Mr. Hermann Faber, and are faithful to the minutest detail. Some experiments have been made which show that they can be reproduced with reasonable fidelity by chromo-lithography.

The chromo-lithograph here presented will, it is hoped, give an idea of the capabilities of this kind of illustration. (See plate opposite.) It represents a portion of intestine, taken from near the middle of the ileum, of a patient who died in the Third Division General Hospital, Alexandria, Virginia, December 11th, 1864. His disease is given in the mortality report of the hospital as typhoid fever. He stated on admission, however, that he had suffered from diarrhœa for several months before the febrile symptoms set in. On the autopsy, the ileum was found to present considerable vascularity, with patches of congestion. The solitary follicles were enlarged to the size of pin-heads. The patches of Peyer slightly thickened, with pigment deposits, giving them the shaven-beard appearance. There were a few small ulcers of the solitary follicles near the ileo-cœcal valve. The colon was thickened, with numerous follicular ulcers, especially in the cœcum and sigmoid flexure. In the transverse colon, several of the ulcers were in the different stages of cicatrization. The portion of ileum here represented is No. 465 in the Medical Series of the Museum. No. 466 is a portion of the transverse colon, showing the cicatrizing ulcers. This case belongs to the class in which typho-malarial fever supervenes in the course of chronic diarrhœa. The drawing here presented is equally characteristic of the uncomplicated cases of the malarial form of this fever. The plate represents the portion of ileum slit up along its mesenteric attachment, and spread out for examination. The blush of congestion in the lower part of the piece, the injected condition of the vessels, the pin-head tumors formed by the enlarged solitary follicles, the shaven-beard appearance of the small Peyer's patch near the top of the piece, and of the larger one near the bottom, are all shown with reasonable accuracy. It is desired to publish in the Medical History of the War about thirty plates, in this style, to illustrate the most important phases of the anatomical lesions in camp fevers and camp diarrhœa.

The *Microscopical series* of the Museum consists already of about 1400 specimens, of which 400 have been obtained by purchase and the rest have been prepared

ILEUM IN MALARIAL FORM
OF
TYPHO MALARIAL FEVER.

in the Museum. The Microscopical series grew out of the attempt to conduct exact investigations into the minute anatomical changes characteristic of the several camp diseases, and especially of fever and diarrhœa. The great mortality of these affections has already been intimated, and the vast practical importance of the present study will therefore be at once understood, when it is recollected that no intelligent efforts to prevent or cure diseases can be made without a reasonable comprehension of their nature, and that this must rest as a basis upon a just knowledge of their pathological anatomy. Unfortunately, in the United States, pathological anatomy is but little studied, and especially the application of the microscope to this branch of investigation has not received the attention it deserves, so that there appeared little probability that an exact study of the pathological anatomy of our camp diseases would be attempted, if it were not undertaken in the Army Medical Museum, and it became an imperative duty to make an effort in this direction. The result of this effort is the microscopical series, which, although small when contrasted with some of the European collections, is the only considerable micro-pathological collection in the United States.

The majority of the specimens thus far placed in the cabinet are sections illustrative of the normal histology of the intestines, and of the changes they undergo in fever and diarrhœa; but the actual number of specimens preserved indicates only a small part of the work done. Investigations have been continually made into pathological processes, in which want of time and of a sufficient number of assistants have not permitted the preservation of specimens. And this branch of the Museum has also been frequently consulted in questions of adulterations, etc. requiring microscopical investigation for their solution; a duty of considerable importance, which, of itself alone, would more than repay the trifling cost of the establishment of this branch of the Museum.

The greater number of the preparations hitherto made in the microscopical branch of the Museum are the work of Brevet Captain Edward Curtis, Assistant Surgeon U.S.A., whose patience and dexterity are deserving of high praise, and to whose intelligent assistance I owe much of the success attained in this direction. In addition, Acting Assistant Surgeon J. C. W. Kennon, who has recently been assigned as an assistant in this branch of the Museum, is preparing a series of very beautiful minute injections, which will form an important part of the collection. It would be wholly impossible to present here a detailed account of the results arrived at by the microscopical work performed. This must be postponed to its appropriate place, in the discussion of the pathological anatomy of our camp diseases in the Medical History of the War. It may, however, be noted, as a matter of interest, that the general results attained are not only of value in connection with camp diseases, but have an important bearing on the general comprehension of normal structure and of morbid action, as must in fact be the case with all studies honestly and earnestly directed to any one series of pathological lesions. In a general way, it may be said that the results of the investigations made in the Museum accord, in many respects, with the ideas of the modern Berlin school of pathological anatomy, are contradictory of the doctrine of exudation, taught so generally in the older medical text-books in use in this country, and at variance also in several particulars with the views of Dr. Lionel Beale, lately so favorably received in England.

The best means of making the results of our microscopical studies available for the information of medical men in America has exercised my most serious thought. Much can be done by good drawings executed with the aid of the camera lucida. Some valuable work in this direction has been executed by Mr. H. Faber, the artist before referred to. Such drawings, however, have always attached to them more or less suspicion of being in part at least ideal; and for this reason numerous attempts have already been made, both in Europe and America, to photograph objects as seen with the microscope. Among the experiments in this country, I may especially mention those of Prof. O. N. Rood, of Columbia College, New York, of Mr. L. M. Rutherfurd, of the same city, and of Dr. J. Dean, of Boston. The first two of these gentlemen directed their attention to test objects, and have obtained results which show the practicability of the idea. Dr. Dean has recently published a paper on the anatomy of the spinal cord, illustrated with photo-lithographs from micro-photographs of sections seen with low powers. This is the first attempt made in America to reproduce micro-photographs by photo-lithography, a method which, if successful with high powers, would be highly satisfactory, since no doubt could be entertained as to the fidelity of the picture. It was therefore resolved to attempt the photographic reproduction of the microscopical preparations necessary for the comprehension of the subjects under consideration, and, after some preliminary experiments made at the Douglas Hospital by Brevet Major W. Thomson, Assistant Surgeon U. S. A., on preparations furnished by the Museum, the necessary apparatus was constructed, and Assistant Surgeon E. Curtis was directed to undertake the labor of preparing the necessary illustrations. The task was by no means an easy one. The subject of micro-photography is comparatively new, and the processes still require much improvement. On the whole, however, the results attained by Dr. Curtis have exceeded the expectations formed when the experiment was undertaken, and justify the hope that they will eventuate in the satisfactory preparation of all the illustrations required.

With low powers, no serious obstacle was encountered in obtaining excellent photographs of properly selected preparations. The higher powers offered difficulties, most of which, however, have been overcome. In experimenting with the higher

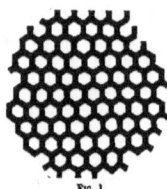

Fig. 1.

powers, the lined diatomaceæ were selected as test objects on account of their definite and well-known structure. With these the utmost success has been realized. A photograph of Gyrosigma angulatum (Navicula angulata) has been obtained, for example, magnified about 7000 diameters, in which the hexagons appear of the same size and nearly as distinct as in the cut, which was made by transferring to wood a tracing from the original photograph. In fact, any of the markings on diatoms that are visible with the microscope can be photographed with the utmost clearness and ease, and the time has arrived when the inability to photograph alleged markings will throw doubts on the correctness of the observers who have supposed they saw them.

The plan employed in the photographic work, hitherto executed with high powers, is as follows: The direct rays of the sun, reflected in a constant direction from the mirror of a Silbermann's heliostat (loaned for the purpose by the Coast Survey), are condensed by a large lens upon the plane mirror of the microscope, whence they are reflected through the achromatic condenser in the usual way. Before reaching the achromatic condenser, however, the rays pass through a cell containing a solution of the ammonio-sulphate of copper of sufficient density to absorb nearly all the rays except those at the violet end of the spectrum.* The light used, therefore, is essentially monochromatic, and contains, with enough illumination for agreeable vision, the greater part of the actinic force of the sun's rays. The heating rays being chiefly at the other extremity of the spectrum are of course excluded, and great actinic force is obtained, therefore, without any danger to the preparations or the balsam cementing of the object-glasses. The object-glass employed in the photograph of Gyrosigma above alluded to was a one-eighth of an inch, by W. Wales & Co., of Fort Lee, New Jersey. This glass is so constructed as to bring the actinic rays to a focus. At the bottom of the draw-tube was placed an achromatic concave lens—the amplifier of Tolles (of Canastota, N. Y.), and an ordinary medium eye-piece completed the optical apparatus. The eye-piece extremity of the microscope was thrust into one end of a long camera box, the connection made light-tight by means of a black silk hood, and the image, received on a piece of plate glass, observed by means of a focussing glass, while the focal adjustments were made. As with the very long camera used, the arm of the observer cannot reach the milled head of the fine adjustment of the microscope, this head was grooved, and connected by a band with a grooved wheel at the end of a long steel rod, the other extremity of which is near the observer, who, by means of it, can focus accurately with any required length of camera. There is nothing peculiar in the chemicals employed, and, with ordinary collodion, and the high power above spoken of, from thirty to forty seconds' exposure was quite sufficient.

Of the foregoing devices, most importance is to be attached to the employment of monochromatic light (the violet end of the spectrum), and the use of an object-glass constructed with special reference to the actinic rays. Both these points were suggested to me by Mr. L. W. Rutherfurd, of New York, so well known by his connection with telescopic photography, who has thought much, and made many satisfactory experiments in this direction. I believe, however, that the apparatus, as above described, loses some of its advantages by the use of the eye-piece, which I propose to substitute by a lens of proper magnifying power, corrected, like the object-glass, in such a way as to bring to a focus the actinic rays. Such a lens is now in process of construction for further experiment.

The pathological photographs hitherto satisfactorily executed in the Museum have chiefly been made with moderate magnifying powers, twelve to fifty diameters, though some experiments with higher powers justify me in the belief that with the improvements above described, all that is desired in this direction can be attained. Among these experiments, I may particularly mention a view, magnified about four hundred diameters, of the polygonal cells and flat cholesterin tables of a cholesteatoma, which was found on the inner surface of the frontal bone of a soldier who died of epilepsy in the neighborhood of Washington.

---

* Einleitung in die Höhere Optik, von Dr. August Beer. Braunschweig, 1853, p. 48.

For the preservation of these photographs for study, glass positives have been printed, and mounted with a piece of ground glass behind them to serve as a background. These are held between the eye and the light, and present, when thus examined, a faithful image of the field of the microscope in every particular except color.

To render these photographs available for the general illustration of the subjects to which they refer, especially of the minute pathological anatomy of camp diseases, it was attempted to reproduce them by photo-lithography, instead of copying them by any other method of drawing or engraving. After trial, however, I was reluctantly obliged to conclude that, in its present undeveloped condition, photo-lithography is inadequate to represent the objects in question, which are among the most delicate and beautiful within the range of microscopical observation, and all the details of which are fully preserved in the photographs. Although I much regret this failure, and am not without hopes that, at an early day, improvements in heliographic methods of lithographing or engraving will give a process adequate to copying even the most difficult photographs, I regret it the less because I have been fortunate enough to find in Mr. H. Faber, the artist already mentioned, an engraver perfectly competent to make faithful copies of the photographs to be reproduced. As an illustration of what may be expected in this direction, I present on the opposite page the reproduction of a photograph of a perpendicular section of ulcerated colon, from the form of Chronic Diarrhoea or Dysentery described on page 143. The blood-vessels were not injected in preparing this section. The picture is not exaggerated, and is a good representation of the original photograph, which, with the specimen, is preserved in the Army Medical Museum, where both can be seen by any one desirous of comparing them with the engraving. The

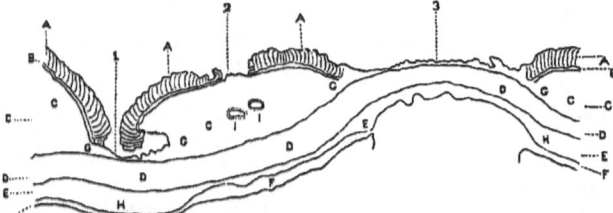

FIG. 2.—Outline of the plate on opposite page. A A A A. Follicles of Lieberkühn. B B. Muscle of Brücke. C C C C. Submucous connective tissue. D D D D. Circular muscle of the colon. E E E. Longitudinal muscle, cut transversely; at H H, two of the longitudinal bands of this layer. F F F. Peritoneal layer. G G G G. Points of very active cell multiplication. I I. An artery and vein cut through transversely. 1. A deep follicular ulcer, extending to the muscular layer. 2. A small superficial ulcer, which has penetrated to the submucous connective tissue. 3. An ulcer of greater size, penetrating nearly to the muscular layer, which is covered with granulations.

wood-cut here introduced gives an outline of the plate opposite, and is lettered for the purposes of description. The section was cut perpendicularly through the colon transversely to its length, and presents three points of ulceration, marked 1, 2, 3 in the figure.

To render this representation more intelligible, it may be remarked that two forms of ulceration have been observed in the colon in these cases of Chronic Diarrhoea. In the first, the process begins in the closed follicles; in the second, in the intestinal epithelium or the glandular layer. In the first form, the closed follicles enlarge by multiplication of their cellular elements till they project as little tumors above the surface, as shown in Fig. 3, in which [1] is the enlarged solitary follicle. This figure is

PERPENDICULAR SECTION OF
ULCERATED COLON – CHRONIC CAMP DIARRHOEA
CUT TRANSVERSELY.

an outline transferred to wood from a tracing of the original photograph, which is quite as beautiful and detailed as that represented in the plate. It is lettered like Fig. 2. The tumor, having enlarged to a certain extent, ruptures, its cellular elements escape, and a minute ulcer is formed, as shown in Fig. 4, in which [1] is the ruptured follicle with the minute ulcer; the letters represent the same parts as in the two previous figures. The cells or corpuscles of the connective tissue surrounding the enlarged follicle now multiply, and the ulcer spreads by the superficial cells floating off into the intestinal cavity, while a new base is continually formed by the multiplication of the subjacent cells.

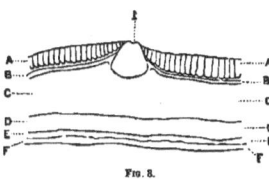

Fig. 3.

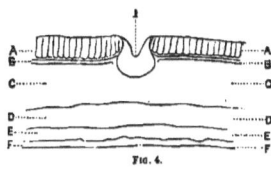

Fig. 4.

If the plate be carefully observed (especially with a lens), it will be noticed that the connective tissue layer presents a finely granular aspect, in which each granule corresponds to what, with a higher power, is recognized as a connective tissue cell or corpuscle. In the neighborhood of the edges or base of any of the ulcers, it will be seen that these corpuscles are more numerous, giving the tissue a more granular aspect. Whether the corpuscles in question are true cells, with distinct cell walls, as argued by Virchow and the Berlin school, or mere masses of germinal matter without distinct parietes, as Beale would have us believe, is a question which cannot here be entered upon, on account of the space necessary to explain and justify the views entertained. In either case, it must be admitted that it is through the multiplication of these corpuscles by division that the greater number of elements is produced, and not by the equivocal generation of new cells, as has been so generally held. The Museum contains preparations which illustrate all the stages of this multiplication, and it is believed that these can be satisfactorily photographed for the Medical History of the War. The multiplication of the cells or corpuscles of the submucous connective tissue is accompanied by the marked thickening of the intestine so common in the disease under consideration. The ulcers shown at the right and left of the section represented in the plate (and in Fig. 2, [1] and [3]) show different stages of the excavation thus produced.

The second form of ulceration begins by an abrasion or denudation of epithelium at some point which does not correspond to the position of a solitary follicle. The follicles of Lieberkühn are next destroyed, and the ulcer spreads in the connective tissue by the process which has just been described. The central ulcer of the plate (Fig. 2, [2]) is of this variety. Such ulcers are much rarer than those of the first kind, and probably are always secondary to them. It is not possible to go into further details in this direction at present, but it is hoped that a careful and fully illustrated account of the minute anatomy of these diseases will be presented to the medical profession in the Medical History of the War.

HOSPITAL ORGANIZATION AND CONSTRUCTION.

The material bearing on hospital construction, organization, and administration is extremely rich and complete. It consists of numerous reports in connection with the subject, and of plans and descriptions of all the principal hospitals which have been organized during the war, furnished by the surgeons-in-charge to the Surgeon General, or by the medical inspectors to the Medical Inspector General. In addition, the records of the general hospitals in existence during the war have been turned in to the Surgeon General's Office.

From this lavish material, it will be possible to prepare a complete and faithful history of the hospital system and of its transformations, both as to construction and administration. Such a history will be of inestimable value in future wars, and is full of most important applications to the hospitals of civil life. Never before, in the history of the world, was so vast a system of hospitals brought into existence in so short a time. Never before were such establishments, in time of war, so little crowded or so liberally supplied. They differed, too, from the hospitals of other nations, in being under the command of medical officers. Instead of placing at the head of establishments, intended for the treatment of disease and wounds, officers of the line, who, whatever their other accomplishments, could not be expected to understand the requirements of medical science, and who, with the best intentions in the world, might seriously embarrass the action of the surgeon, as was sadly the case in the Crimean war, and has been since in the English hospitals, our Government, with a wiser discretion, made the surgeon the commandant of the hospital, and thus, while holding him responsible for the results of its management, put it into his power to do much to make those results favorable. The medical staff can point with pride to the consequences of this liberal course. Never before, in the history of the world, has the mortality in military hospitals been so small, and never have such establishments so completely escaped from diseases generated within their walls.

The hospital buildings used in the beginning, and on occasions of emergency throughout the war, had been erected for other purposes; public buildings, school-houses, churches, hotels, warehouses, factories, and private dwellings being fitted up, as circumstances required. But gradually wooden pavilions, erected for the purpose, came into extensive use, and ultimately the majority of the general hospitals belonged to this class. The introduction of these pavilion hospitals was not the work of any one man. Originally suggested by European experience, they were erected in all parts of the country, under the direction of various medical officers, some by order of the Surgeon General, others by the authority of local commanders. The necessities of the service and increasing experience suggested numerous alterations from time to time, and it was not until the summer of 1864 that a circular order was issued directing uniformity in certain essential points. To trace out this gradual evolution of hospital construction is, of course, out of the question here; but as the Circular of July 20th, 1864, gives in a few words an idea of the system as fully developed, it is here reproduced:

HOSPITAL ORGANIZATION AND CONSTRUCTION. 153

WAR DEPARTMENT, July 20th, 1864.

The following instructions are promulgated for the information of officers charged with the construction of general hospitals, and will be deviated from only in cases of imperative necessity: Buildings will not be taken or occupied for hospital purposes until after full examination and approval by a medical inspector, or other officer of the Medical Corps detailed for this purpose; and all alterations will be made in accordance with plans submitted by him and approved by the Surgeon General.

E. M. STANTON,
Secretary of War.

Site.—The site of the hospital should be a well-drained plain, with a sub-soil of gravel, and sufficiently extensive to accommodate the buildings. The situation should be elevated; as remote as possible from marshes or other sources of malaria, and must have a convenient supply of pure water.

Plan.—General hospitals will be constructed on the principle of detached pavilions, each ward being in a separate building, with beds for sixty patients. Besides the wards, there will be detached buildings for each of the following purposes: General Administration Building, Dining-Room and Kitchen for Patients, Dining-Room and Kitchen for Officers, Laundry, Commissary and Quartermaster's Store-House, Knapsack-House, Guard-House, Dead-House, Quarters for Female Nurses, Chapel, Operating-Room, and Stable. The wards, administration building, kitchens, dining-rooms, and chapel are to be connected by covered walks which will have floors, but no sides.

No general plan for the arrangement of the buildings can be directed, as the varying character and dimensions of sites render an uniform adherence to any one impracticable. Wards may be arranged "en echelon" in two converging lines, forming a V,—in this case, the administration building should be at the apex of the V, the other buildings between the wings; or as radii from the periphery of a circle, ellipse, or rounded oblong,—in this case, the administration building should be one of the radii, the other buildings within the enclosure; or parallel to each other,—in this case, the administration building should be in the centre of the row, the other buildings in the rear. Other plans may be rendered necessary by the special features of the ground. In any case, the important points to be observed are, to place the buildings far enough apart (at least thirty feet should intervene between two parallel buildings), and to locate them in such a manner that no one shall interfere with the ventilation of another. It is preferable to locate the wards so that the long diameter may run north and south, or nearly so.

Each *ward* will be a ridge-ventilated pavilion one hundred and eighty-seven by twenty four (187 × 24) feet. At each extremity, two small rooms nine by eleven (9 × 11) feet, one on each side of a passage, six (6) feet wide, will be partitioned off. The space remaining for patients will be one hundred and sixty-five by twenty-four (165 × 24) feet (see Figure 5, A), which gives the location of the beds and position of the doors and windows. The small rooms are occupied as follows: Figure 5, *a*, chief nurse; *b*, closet for medicines, etc.; *c*, bath-room; *d*, closet for close stools. Figure 6 is the side elevation.

The wards will be fourteen (14) feet high from floor to eaves—the pitch of the roof to vary in accordance to the materials composing it. The floor to be elevated at least eighteen (18) inches from the soil, with free ventilation beneath it. A ward thus constructed will accommodate sixty (60) patients, allowing more than one thousand (1000) cubic feet of air-space to each. The number of wards will be regulated by the number of patients the hospital is intended to accommodate. A hospital of twelve hundred (1200) beds will require twenty (20) wards.

20

Administration Building.—For a hospital of six to twelve hundred (600 to 1200) beds, this will be a ridge-ventilated building, thirty-eight by one hundred and thirty-two (38×132) feet, and two stories high; the first fourteen (14) and the second twelve (12) feet high in the clear. This building contains the general office, office of surgeon in charge, linen and store rooms, dispensary, chaplain's office, lodging rooms for officers, etc.

Dining-Room and Kitchen for Patients.—The dining-room will be a ridge-ventilated building, large enough to seat a number equal to two-thirds the number of beds. The most convenient form is a long parallelogram, into which the kitchen opens in the centre of the long side. The kitchen will be divided into two unequal parts—the larger for the preparation of ordinary diet, the smaller for the extra diet—the cooking in both to be done on ranges. Where there is an engine, steam may be advantageously used for boiling.

Dining-Room and Kitchen for Officers.—A small building for this purpose will be situated near the administration building.

Laundry.—A building two stories high, with lodging for the laundresses on the second floor. The roof should be flat, with posts for stretching clothes-lines.

Commissary and Quartermaster Store-Room.—A small two-story building, furnished with boxes and shelves for the various parts of the ration,—having an ice-house connected with it for the preservation of meats and other perishable articles, and a room for clothing. The second story to contain lodging-rooms for the cooks.

Knapsack-House.—A building to receive the effects of the patients while in hospital. It will contain as many pigeon-holes, each two (2) feet square, as there are beds in the hospital.

Guard-House.—A detached building to lodge the guard, with a guard-room for prisoners.

Dead-House.—A small building containing two apartments, located so as not to be observed from the wards, and lighted by sky-lights.

Quarters for Female Nurses.—A detached building containing lodging-rooms, dining-room, and kitchen for the female nurses.

Chapel.—A detached building, fitted for the purpose of religious services, so arranged as to be used also as a library and reading-room.

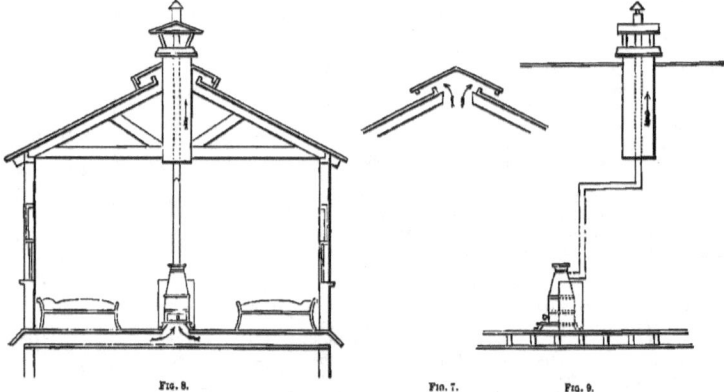

FIG. 8.   FIG. 7.   FIG. 9.

Operating-Rooms.—Two rooms, each fifteen (15) feet square; one well lighted by sky-lights, the other by windows. The first for surgical operations, the second for discharge-boards, etc. It should be situated near the administration building.

Stable.—For ambulance and officers' horses.

Water Supply.—Where practicable, a large tank will be erected and kept supplied from wells or springs by pumps worked by a steam-engine. The engine, if possible, will be situated near the kitchen and laundry, in which case the steam may be made serviceable in cooking, and the power may be employed in working the washing and mangling machines.

Sinks.—Where the supply of water is adequate, water-closets may be constructed in one of the small rooms in each ward; but where this is not the case, privies will be built at a convenient distance from the wards, furnished with water-tight boxes, which must be emptied every night.

Ventilation.—During warm and mild weather the wards will be ventilated by the ridge (Figure 7), but during

HOSPITAL ORGANIZATION AND CONSTRUCTION. 155

winter the ridge will be closed (Figure 8), and ventilation by shafts substituted. Four stoves will be allowed to a ward, each partly surrounded by a jacket of zinc or sheet-iron, with an air-box opening beneath it to furnish the supply of fresh air. At eight (8) feet from the stove will be a shaft, properly capped, through which the stove-pipe will ascend. Figure 8 gives a section and Figure 9 a side view of the arrangement. The shaft should be eighteen (18) inches square, and should not come below the tie-beams.

A conception of the character and extent of the large pavilion hospitals can be perhaps still better obtained from a description of some one of them than from the foregoing circular. A description of the Lincoln Hospital, one of the hospitals of Washington, D. C., is therefore here presented. This hospital was constructed in the latter part of 1862, and first occupied in January, 1863. The original plans for its construction were furnished to the Surgeon General's Office by the writer of this paper. Several modifications and improvements were, however, subsequently made by the successive surgeons in charge.

The following description was furnished by Brevet Lieutenant Colonel J. C. McKee, Surgeon U. S. A., for a long time surgeon in charge.

Lincoln Hospital, Washington, D. C., is located about a mile east of the Capitol Building. Its site is a gently-undulating, uncultivated plain, without shade-trees. East and south of the hospital, the plain declines towards the Eastern Branch of the Potomac, which is about half a mile distant. The soil is a light sandy loam, resting on a deep stratum of gravel. The hospital covers an area of thirty acres of ground, and consists of twenty detached pavilion wards, arranged en echelon in the shape of the letter V, the apex of which looks westwardly. The administration building is at the apex of the V. The buildings for kitchen, dining-rooms, etc. are in the space between the two sides of the letter. The whole is surrounded by a picket-fence, five feet high, between which and the wards is a wide road for ambulances. (See Figure 10 and the plate opposite to it.)

The *Wards* are pavilion barracks, built of rough boards, white-washed, with roofs of boards covered with tarred paper; they are twenty (20) in number, ten on each wing. Each ward is 187 feet by 24, 16 feet to the eaves and 20 to the ridge, at which there is the usual ridge-ventilation the whole length of the ward. They are plastered on the inside for about eight feet above the floor. At the west end of each are four rooms, occupying fifteen feet in length. These are used for clothing, baths, nurses, and sinks. Each ward contains thirty-four windows and four doors, one at each end and two in the middle, opposite each other. Four ventilating gratings, at regular distances in the floor of the ward, communicate by wooden flues under the floor with the air outside, thus giving a full supply of fresh air whenever the weather requires the doors and windows to be closed. With sixty-two patients, there are 72 square feet of floor and 1447 cubic feet of air-space for each. Thirty-one beds are arranged on each side, with a chair and bed-side table between each pair. An avenue of eleven feet is left between the two rows of beds. The wards are lighted at night by kerosene lamps, and heated by stoves in winter. On the inner side of the two wings of the hospital, and running the whole length of each, is a raised covered walk or corridor, on which is laid a railway track two feet wide and 2156 feet long. Box-cars convey the food from the main and extra kitchens to each ward.

The *Administration Building*, at the apex of the triangle, is 184 by 38 feet, 22 feet to the ridge and 16 to the eaves. A hall, 8 feet wide, runs the entire length of the first floor. On the left side of the hall are the following rooms: office of surgeon in charge, 14 by 14; office of military assistant, 11 by 14 (employs two clerks); principal office, 56 by 14 (employs fourteen clerks); printing-office, 19 by 14 (employs two men); quartermaster's store-room for clothing, etc., 44 by 14 (employs two clerks); wardmaster's room, 13½ by 14; bath-room, 4½ by 14; post-office, 7 by 14 (employs a postmaster and assistant). On the other side of the hall, and on the right of the entrance door, are the office of the officer of the day, 15 by 14; office of the officer of the guard, 11 by 14 (four clerks); office of surgical records, 11 by 14 (one clerk); private office of surgeon in charge, 12½ by 14; office of medical inspector, 11 by 14; linen-room, 66 by 14,—all washed clothing and bed-linen is sent from the laundry to this room, and thence distributed to the different wardmasters; one clerk and four women are employed here, the latter in mending, etc. The medical store-room, 11 by 14, adjoins the dispensary, and is used for storing supplies. The dispensary, 25 by 14, usually employs four men; the medicines for the whole hospital are compounded here, under the charge of a hospital steward. Lastly, the laboratory, which adjoins the dispensary, is 22 by 14 feet, used for preparing tinctures, ointments, plasters, etc.

On the second floor of the Administration Building is the Knapsack-Room, 111 by 37 feet. The effects, accoutrements, etc. of the patients coming into hospital are deposited in this room for safe keeping. It employs two men, who receive the articles deposited, issue tickets for the same, credit them to depositors, and deliver them when the patients leave. There are 2184 boxes, arranged in parallel rows, reaching from the floor to the ceiling. Adjoining the Knapsack-Room is the extra-duty men's room, 50 by 37 feet, used as a sleeping-room by the men employed on extra duty, and a clerks' room, 25 by 23 feet, used by the clerks of the principal office for the same purpose.

Within the triangle, formed by the two wings, and east of the administration building, is the *Tank*, resting upon a platform 25 feet high, and holding 12,000 gallons of water. It is supplied from a well under the engine-room, and the water forced into it by the engine, which drives the machinery of the laundry. This tank supplies each ward with water by means of pipes. There are four other wells in the enclosure, used for drinking and culinary purposes.

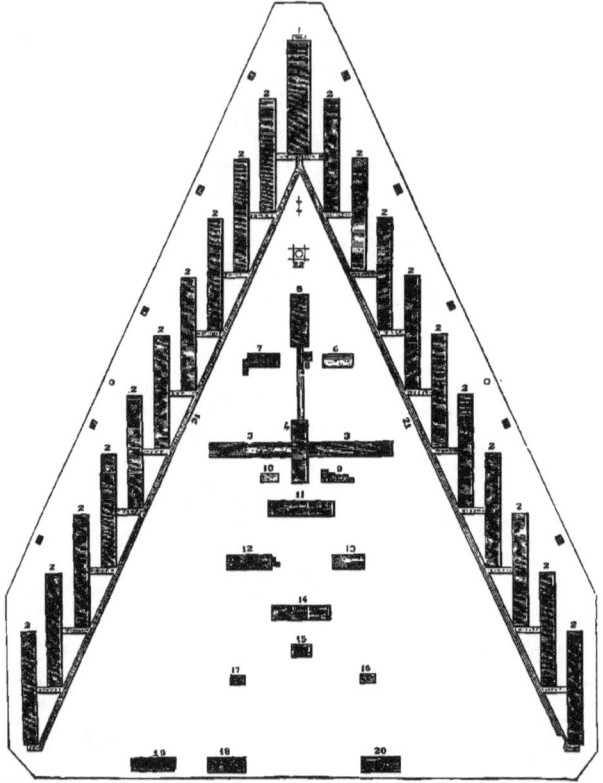

FIG. 10.—GROUND PLAN OF LINCOLN GENERAL HOSPITAL, WASHINGTON, D.C. Scale, 200 feet to the inch. 1. Administration building. 2 2 2 2. Wards. 3 3. Dining-rooms. 4. Kitchen. 5. Laundry. 6. Stewards' quarters. 7. Sisters' quarters. 8. Engine-house. 9. Meat-house. 10. Coal-house. 11. Commissary building. 12. Sutler. 13. Chapel. 14. Stable. 15. Freedmen's quarters. 16. Guard-house. 17. Dead-house. 18. Barracks for guard. 19 20. Officers' quarters. 21. Covered way. 22. Tank. The tents shown in the plate are not represented in this plan.

Twenty yards east of the tank is the *Laundry*, 61 by 24 feet. The building runs east and west, is two stories high, and has a platform for drying clothes on the roof. Seven men and twelve women are employed in its various departments. The washing is done by steam-power, as is also the drying and ironing. The average wash is 5000 pieces daily—has been pushed to 7000. On the first floor of the laundry is the washing apparatus, consisting of a mangle, steam-boiler, revolving drum for wringing, rinsing-boxes, roller and ironing-table; on the second floor is the steam drying-room, 36 by 12½ feet. This is in addition to the drying arrangements on the roof. Separated by a partition from the laundry on the first floor, is a sleeping-room for women, 22 by 24 feet; a kitchen for the same, 9½ by 17; a dining-room, 9½ by 18. The engine is in a building adjoining the laundry on the east; it is of six-horse power, and

BIRDS EYE VIEW OF
LINCOLN GENERAL HOSPITAL, WASHINGTON, D. C.
SEEN FROM THE REAR

employs one engineer and an assistant. It supplies power for the tank as well as for the laundry. The well which supplies the tank is 40 feet deep, with usually 4 feet of water; its diameter is 6 feet. The steam pump can raise 2000 gallons of water per hour.

The building for *Sisters' Quarters* is 23 by 51 feet, with a wing 16 by 28, forming a letter "L." It is divided into chapel, sitting-room, kitchen, etc. Twenty-eight Sisters of Charity were on duty, and I must bear evidence to their efficiency and superiority as nurses. The extra-diet kitchen is under the care of a sister, and one is detailed by the superior for each ward. They administer medicine, diet, and stimulants, are under the orders of the ward surgeon, and are responsible to him alone. They have been beloved and respected by the men.

The *Stewards' Quarters* are 18 feet north of the engine-room, are two stories high—contain dining-room, kitchen, sleeping-rooms, etc. Five stewards generally occupied this building.

The *Operating-Room* is 25 feet east of the engine-room. It is 17 feet square, and lighted by a sky-light on the north side of the roof. A revolving-table is in the centre of the room; also a cupboard for instruments, sponges, microscope, etc., with a sink in the northwest corner. The Examining-Room adjoining it is 17 feet 7 inches square, and communicates by a door with the operating-room.

The *Extra-Diet Kitchen* is under the same roof with the general kitchen. It is 18 by 24 feet—has in it a Harrison's European range, 8 feet front, 3 feet 6 inches deep. A room 18 by 12 feet adjoins on the south. This kitchen is under the supervision of a sister, who is generally assisted by from four to six men.

The *Main Kitchen* is 77 by 24 feet. It contains a cooking-range, 28 feet 10 inches long and 3 feet 2 inches wide; also three of "Peters' and Johnson's bake-ovens or roasters," two boilers for tea and coffee, each with a capacity of 120 gallons, five boilers or cauldrons for soup or hash (60 gallons each), and two for heating water (one 60 gallons, the other 22 gallons). Full diet is prepared here for all the men in the hospital.

On either side of the kitchen, opening from it north and south, are the *Dining-Rooms*, each 146 by 24 feet, with three tables running the whole length of each, capable of seating in all 860 men. At the distal end of each room a door opens on a corridor and raised walk, so that the patients are protected from the weather in coming to their meals. Cars, with cans fitted in them, are run around the corridors to the several wards with the food for those unable to come to the dining-room.

On the northwest corner of the kitchen is a room 30 feet long, 14 feet wide, and 10 feet high, used for washing dishes, roasting coffee, etc. From 40 to 50 men are usually employed in the various departments of the kitchen.

Opposite the centre of the northern dining-room, and distant to the west 30 feet, is the *Fire-Engine and Hose House*, 26 by 20 feet—contains one fire-engine, three hose-carriages carrying 1850 feet of hose, 34 ladders, 22 hooks, 278 axes, and 300 buckets.

Thirteen feet south of the kitchen is the *Meat-Shop*, 14½ by 23. In its centre is an ice-box, 3½ by 14½ and 4 feet deep, lined with zinc. The allowance of ice per day is one pound for each man.

East of the kitchen, and connected by a covered way, is the *Commissary Building*, which is two stories high,—the upper story is used to lodge attendants; the lower story, used for commissary store-room, is 82 by 23½, and is under a commissary steward. In the northeastern corner is the liquor-room, 8½ by 13, heavily planked and secured against marauders. All liquor is issued here on the orders of the ward surgeons. The vegetable-room is in the northwestern corner, and is 9 by 13½. An office, 9 by 15½, adjoins the liquor-room. The books and accounts are kept in this office. The store-room is provided with a counter 52½ feet long, and gives employment to one steward, one clerk, and two men. At the southern end is the bread-room, 14½ by 23, which employs two men cutting bread for the tables. Adjoining, on the east, is the bakery, 14 by 23½. The oven is 10 by 16 feet.

The *Chapel* is situated 63 feet east of the commissary building. It is a structure shaped like the letter "T," one story in height, with a cupola on top. The main building is 24 by 78 feet. The northern end is used during the week as a reading-room. The left wing, 18 by 26 feet, is used as a library; it contains 3000 volumes, contributed to the hospital from various sources. The right wing is the same size, and is used as a school for the freedmen employed in the hospital, who are instructed by two female teachers.

Twenty-four feet south of the chapel is the *Sutler's Store*, 24 by 68. The *Stables*, 25 by 101 feet, are 72 east of the sutler's shop; they contain 18 horses, 3 wagons, 3 ambulances, 2 carts and 1 night-cart. Thirteen men are employed as hostlers, drivers, etc. One hundred and twenty-one feet northeast of the stables is the *Guard-House*, 15 by 47 and one story high. South of this is the *Oil-Room* and *Freedmen's Quarters*, 29 by 69 feet. The oil and lamp room are in the northern part. Kerosene oil was used in lighting the whole hospital, and all the lamps were filled and trimmed in this room. A corporal and two men were employed. Ninety-one feet southeast of the oil-room is the *Dead-House*, 15 by 40 feet. It is divided into two rooms—the northern one used in making post-mortem examinations, and the southern for plaster-casts, etc. Thirty-two feet south of this room is the *Photographic Gallery*, 16 by 24 feet. An operator is employed at $100 per month, paid from the slush fund. Surgical cases, pathological specimens, etc. are taken; also likenesses of all men discharged on surgeon's certificate of disability, as a guard against fraud. On the base line of the triangle are the *Medical Officers' Quarters*, 63 by 24 and two stories in height; also, in the same line, the quarters for the *Veteran Reserve Corps*, a building two stories high, with an outside entrance-stairway to the second floor. Ninety feet further back, 100 hospital tents are pitched, placed four end to end, on substantial frames, with floors raised from the ground and a door at each end of the frame. The sides of these tents were always easily raised, and gave the best of ventilation; hence I selected some of them as gangrene wards, and, I think, with the very best results. In winter, each ward was heated by two stoves, with pipes running to a shaft in the centre. Each ward of four tents contained 20 beds. The length of the fence around the hospital is 1458 yards. The distance of the fence from the tents at the base of the triangle is 124 feet. Sinks were arranged around the whole line of fence. They had movable boxes, which were regularly emptied and limed. Policing was done by a gang of about 20 freedmen. The hospital could accommodate 1240 patients in the 20 barrack wards. Its total capacity in January, 1865, was 2575 beds, including those in tents and the branch barracks, a short distance off.

This hospital was opened December 23d, 1862, and closed August 22d, 1865. During this period the movements of patients were as follows:

	ADMITTED.			Returned from furlough and desertion.	AGGREGATE.	RESULTS.						
	Sick.	Wounded.	Total.			Returned to duty and mustered out.	Sent to General Hospital.	Furloughed.	Transferred to Veteran Reserve Corps.	Discharged.	Deserted.	Died.
White Troops	12,391	7,837	20,228	3,565	23,793	7,191	9,411	4,400	392	1,058	286	1,060
Colored Troops	13	5	18	......	18	......	18	......	......	......	......	......
Prisoners of War	174	959	1,133	......	1,133	......	924	......	......	45	3	161
Total	12,578	8,801	21,379	3,565	24,944	7,191	10,353	4,400	392	1,098	289	1,221

Deducting those sent to general hospital as cases not terminated, and considering that furloughed and deserted amounted to 4686, while only 3565 of these are reported as returned from furlough and desertion, we shall have the following statistics for the terminated cases of white troops treated.

Total to be accounted for, excluding those sent to other hospitals	10,817	
Returned to duty		6,389
Mustered out of service at the close of the war		852
Loss by desertion and failure to return from furlough		1,121
Discharged for disability		1,058
Transferred to Veteran Reserve Corps		392
Died		1,060
	10,817	10,817

These figures represent excellent results, but they are not more favorable than the general statistics of all the hospitals. Making proper corrections for transfers from hospital to hospital, there were over a million of patients treated in the general hospitals during the four years of the war, and the mortality, including both that from disease and that from wounds, was but one death to every twelve patients, or about 8 per cent.

Harewood Hospital, Washington, D. C., was constructed on a plan quite similar to that of Lincoln Hospital. The Hampton General Hospital, near Fortress Monroe, was also composed of wards arranged en echelon in the form of a V, but not overlapping

HOSPITAL ORGANIZATION AND CONSTRUCTION.   159

each other, as those of the two foregoing hospitals did. The hospital at Point Lookout, Maryland, at Jeffersonville, Indiana, and the Sedgwick Hospital, at Greenville, near New Orleans, La., may be mentioned as examples of constructions in which the pavilion wards radiated from a circular covered way. An idea of this form of construction can be obtained from the following brief account of the latter hospital, abstracted from the Inspection Report of Medical Inspector E. P. Vollum, U. S. A., dated July 10th, 1865:

Sedgwick Hospital is situated at Greenville, La., about seven miles above New Orleans, on the east bank of the Mississippi River. The site is flat, and drains back from the river into the swamp lands lying between the Mississippi River and Lake Pontchartrain. The soil is a rich, black alluvium. The grounds embrace about 30 acres, which have been for many years under cultivation as a plantation. At present, there is a fine vegetable garden sufficient for all the wants of the hospital. A large part of the premises is shaded by splendid groves of live-oak, pecans, and

FIG. 11.—GROUND PLAN OF SEDGWICK GENERAL HOSPITAL, GREENVILLE, LA. Scale, 120 feet to the inch. 1 1 1 1. Wards. 2. Administration building. 3. Guard-house, knapsack-room, and store-house. 4 4. Dining-rooms. 5. Kitchen. 6. Cistern. 7. Covered ways, through which a railway runs with hand-cars for carrying food to the wards.

oranges, with crape myrtles and the flowering shrubs peculiar to the latitude. The hospital is approached from the river front by a substantial road, and shell-roads and walks connect the several buildings and wind among the groves. The hospital is composed of fifteen one-storied pavilion wards, each 145 by 24 feet, and an administration building, 145 by

40, radiating from the periphery of a circular covered way, in the centre of which are the buildings for kitchens, etc. etc. The arrangement is shown in Figure 11, in which the part towards the bottom of the page is that facing the river front.

Outside the circle, at convenient distances, are detached buildings for chapel, cooks' and nurses' quarters, laundry, gas-house, bake-house, dead-house, reservoir, and stables. All these buildings are constructed of boards, set upright and battened; the roofs shingled, and open at the ridge for ventilation. They are raised 3 feet above the ground on brick piers. The covered way which connects them is twelve feet wide. The ward pavilions have two small rooms partitioned off at each end, leaving a space in the centre, 115 by 24 feet, available for patients. There are two beds between each pair of windows, as in the plan figured on page 153, but the number of beds is less—40 to each ward. The dimensions allow about 69 square feet of floor and 1200 cubic feet of air-space to each patient. Three of the small rooms mentioned are occupied as sleeping apartments for nurses. The fourth, which is one of those at the outer extremity of each ward, is divided into bath-room and water-closet. The administration building is two stories high, and contains the office, dispensary, officers' reception, lodging, and dining rooms, etc. etc. The hospital kitchen is shown in Figure 12, which explains its arrangement. The building is 80 by 30 feet. There is a patent steam cooking apparatus with boilers, etc., and a carving-table, the pans of which are kept warm by steam. There is also one of Myers, Sandford, Winslow & Co.'s challenge ranges, No. 10, for roasting and cooking extra diet. The railway, on which cars run to distribute food to the wards, passes through the centre of the kitchen. This kitchen is reported by Medical Inspector Vollum as having been "sufficient and in good condition" at the time of his visits. The laundry is situated on the river bank, and is furnished with a steam washing-machine, capable of washing for 1500 patients. Water for washing, etc. is obtained from a reservoir on the river bank, capable of holding 320,000 gallons, whence it is carried by pipes through the administration building, wards, kitchen, dining-rooms, and dead-house. For drinking purposes, rain-water is collected in a central cistern, which holds 150,000 gallons, and in smaller cisterns, holding 10,000 gallons each, at the end of each ward. The water for those cisterns is carried from the roofs of the buildings by zinc gutters and pipes. For the purposes of drainage, the grounds are graded from the centre of the circle towards the periphery with a descent of one inch to every 10 feet; the surface water flows at the periphery into brick sewers, which also receive the sewage from the water-closets, kitchen, etc. by pipes. The several sewers unite into a common trunk, by which the sewage is carried far to the rear of the hospital into the swamps which drain into Lake Pontchartrain. The water-closets throughout the hospital are furnished with patent pans, and discharge into brick sinks lined with cement and built up to the floor. These sinks, which are of some size, are connected with the sewers into which all the liquid parts drain. The hospital is heated by coal-stoves, and lighted with gas which is generated on the premises.

This hospital was opened for the reception of patients April 1st, 1865, and, at the time of writing, is still in existence. On the thirty-first day of October, 1865, which is the date of the last report, there were 97 sick and 8 wounded patients remaining under treatment. Prior to that date, the total number of admissions of white soldiers was 2163, of whom 1869 were sick and 474 wounded. The number of patients sent to other general hospitals was 673. Deducting this number and the remaining, we have 1385 terminated cases to be accounted for, the results of which were as follows:

Total to be accounted for, excluding those sent to General Hospitals and the remaining Oct. 31, 1865....	1385	
Returned to duty...		848
Mustered out of service at the close of the war...		210
Furloughed...		181
Discharged for disability..		56
Died..		90
	1385	1385

As one of the most recently constructed hospitals, I may mention the Hicks' Hospital, at Baltimore, Md.

The Hicks' Hospital is situated on the continuation of Townsend Street in the western suburbs of Baltimore, near the city boundary. It was opened for the reception of patients June 9th, 1865, and is therefore one of the most recently constructed hospitals. The plan was essentially the circular one already described, but many important improvements and additions were devised by Surgeon Thomas Sim, U. S. Vols., under whose supervision the details of the plan were prepared. The original design contemplated a circular hospital, built on the War Department

HOSPITAL ORGANIZATION AND CONSTRUCTION. 161

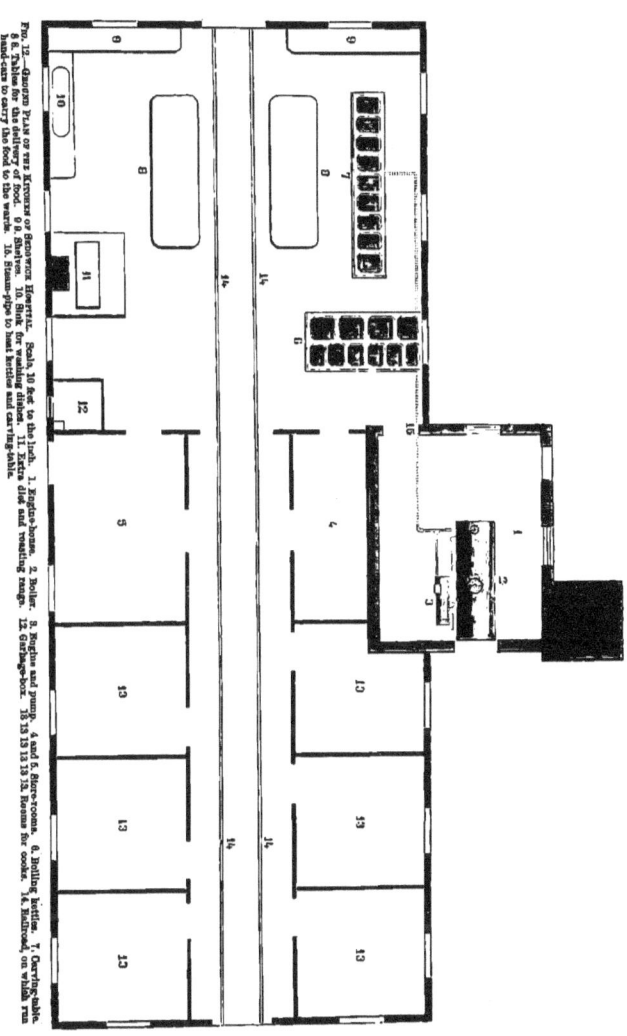

FIG. 12.—GROUND PLAN OF THE KITCHEN OF SEDGWICK HOSPITAL. Scale, 10 feet to the inch. 1. Engine-house. 2. Boiler. 3. Engine and pump. 4 and 5. Stove-rooms. 6. Boiling kettles. 7. Carving-table. 8 & 8. Tables for the delivery of food. 9 & 9. Shelves. 10. Sink for washing dishes. 11. Extra diet and roasting range. 12. Grilling-box. 13.13.13.13.13. Rooms for cooks. 14. Railroad, on which run hand-cars to carry the food to the wards. 15. Steam-pipe to heat kettles and carving-table.

plan, with thirty-six radiating pavilion wards, each to accommodate 60 patients. The approach of the end of the war, however, prevented this from being executed, and the hospital, as completed, is a semicircle, in which the wards radiate from a covered way, as in Figure 13. It is, however, both on account of the substantial character of the wooden buildings and the numerous conveniences which have been carefully supplied, one of the most complete of the hospitals built during the war.

The wards are built and ventilated as directed in the circular from the War Department. The administration building is 132 by 38 feet and two stories high; the first story contains offices for the surgeon in charge, executive officer, quartermaster, commissary and their clerks; it also contains the hospital library and printing-office. On the second floor are sleeping apartments for officers. This building is flanked on each end by a smaller one, 70 by 28 feet, one of which

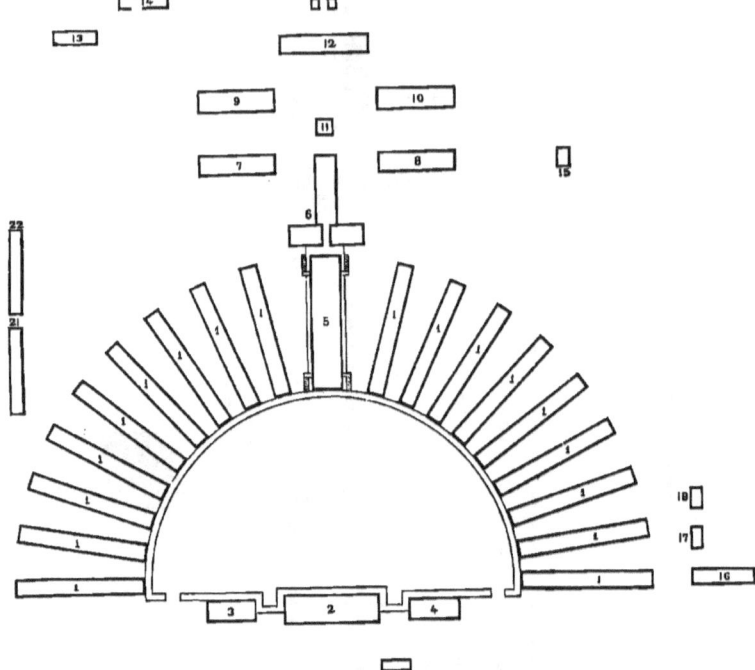

FIG. 13.—GROUND PLAN OF HICKS' GENERAL HOSPITAL, BALTIMORE, MD. Scale, 180 feet to the inch. 1 1 1 1. Wards. 2. Administration building. 3. Linen-room, etc. 4. Dispensary and operating-room. 5. Dining-hall. 6. Kitchen and laundry. 7. Ward for detailed men. 8. Knapsack-room. 9. Commissary store-house. 10. Quartermaster's store-house. 11. Tank. 12. Quarters for guard. 13. Stable. 14. Wagon-house. 15. Sutler. 16. Stewards' quarters. 17 18. Officers' houses (of which, also, there are several not in the figure). 19. Guard-room. 20. Guard-house, near entrance gate. 21. Workshop. 22. Contagion ward; this is farther distant than is represented in the figure. The wards, dining-room, and administration building are connected by a covered way, which is indicated by faint lines in the plan.

contains the linen-room and post-office, with the officers' dining-room, kitchen, and pantry. The other contains the dispensary, medical store-rooms, room of the discharge board, and an operating-room lighted by a sky-light. The dining-room building is 187 by 48 feet, and is two stories high. The dining-room, which is on the first floor, is capable of seating about 1200 patients. The second floor, which is accessible by stairs on the outside, is occupied by the chapel and by dormitories for female nurses. At the end of the dining-room is a T-shaped building for kitchen and laundry. The general kitchen, extra-diet kitchen, and bakery occupy separate apartments; the former two each contain a suitable range and steam fixtures, the latter two bake-ovens. The laundry has a separate room for drying by steam, and immediately adjoins the engine-room, which is at the extremity of the building. There are, besides the foregoing, separate buildings for knapsack-room, quartermaster's store-house, commissary store-house, quarters for

HOSPITAL ORGANIZATION AND CONSTRUCTION. 163

detailed men, barracks for guard, workshop, contagion ward, dead-house, stewards' quarters, and quarters for married officers. The buildings are plastered inside, are lighted by gas, to be warmed in the winter by stoves, and receive their water supply by pipes from the city water-works, besides which there is a tank for the purpose of keeping a stock of water constantly on hand in case of fire. For the purpose of extinguishing fire, there is abundant hose to fit the steam-pump. There are also water-buckets, axes, etc. At the distal end of each ward is a lavatory and bath-room and a water-closet. Each bath-room has in it a small stove, on which is a boiler for the supply of hot water. In the water-closets the excretions are received in troughs, into which a stream of water runs, and which are emptied by withdrawing a plug several times daily. They discharge into sewers constructed for the purpose, which carry all offensive matters entirely away from the hospital. A very beautiful model of the hospital in holly-wood has been presented to the Army Medical Museum by Surgeon Sim.

This hospital was opened for patients June 9th, 1865; and the total number of white soldiers received prior to November 30th, 1865, which was the last report up to the date of writing, was 1247, of whom 984 were sick and 263 wounded. Of these, 366 were transferred to other general hospitals, and 120 remained under treatment at the date of the last report. The number of terminated cases, therefore, was 761, who are thus accounted for:

Total to be accounted for, excluding those transferred to other hospitals and those remaining at date of last report	761	
Returned to duty		131
Mustered out of service at the close of the war		443
Loss by desertion and failure to return from furlough		52
Discharged for disability		89
Transferred to Veteran Reserve Corps		2
Died		44
	761	761

Besides the above, 280 colored soldiers were admitted, of whom 15 died.

All the hospitals hitherto described were situated near the base of military operations, and received therefore more severe cases than those at a distance. As an example of the more distant hospitals, the figures of the Lovell Hospital, at Portsmouth Grove, Narraganset Bay, R. I., may here be given.

This hospital, which is composed of twenty-eight fine wooden pavilion wards, situated on a tongue of land jutting out into the bay, was opened in July, 1862, and closed October 10th, 1865. During this period it received 11,696 white soldiers, of whom 8491 were sick and 3205 wounded. Of these, 2461 were transferred to other hospitals, leaving 9235 patients to be accounted for, as follows:

Total to be accounted for, excluding those sent to other hospitals	9235	
Returned to duty		4386
Mustered out at the close of the war		875
Loss by desertion and failure to return from furlough		961
Discharged for disability		2021
Transferred to Veteran Reserve Corps		716
Died		276
	9235	9235

On comparing the statistical reports of the hospitals in various parts of the country, we are struck by the fact that the number returned to duty and the ratio of deaths to terminated cases were greater in those hospitals which were nearest the seat of war. On the other hand, the number discharged the service for disability and transferred to the Veteran Reserve Corps was greater in the more distant ones. These facts, which naturally result from the reception of acute cases into the nearest hospitals and the frequent transfers thence to the more distant ones, must be remembered in all comparisons made between the results of treatment in different institutions. To give an idea of the vast extent of hospital accommodations demanded, the following list of general hospitals in existence in September, 1864, is here presented. The hospital system had at that time attained its maximum extent, there being 202 general hospitals and 136,894 beds for patients. The number of beds was gradually reduced till January, 1865, when there were 121,000, and about this number was kept on foot to the close of the war.

Hospitals in the Atlantic Region, September, 1864.

No.	Name.	Locality.	Beds.	No.	Name.	Locality.	Beds.
	Department of the East.				Brought forward............		43,051
1	David's Island	New York Harbor	3,000		*Middle Department—*		
2	Fort Columbus	New York Harbor	100		Continued.		
3	Ladies' Home	New York City	400				
4	St. Joseph's	Central Park. N. Y.	353	9	Tilton	Wilmington, Del.	352
5	Newark	Newark, N. J.	927	10	McKim's Mansion	Baltimore, Md.	300
6	Lovell	Portsmouth Grove, R. I.	1,644	11	Officers'	Annapolis, Md.	400
7	Knight	New Haven, Conn.	1,121	12	Camp Parole	Annapolis, Md.	2,000
8	Brattleboro'	Brattleboro', Vt.	1,097				
9	Marine	Burlington, Vt.	920		*Department of Washington.*		
10	Mason	Boston, Mass.	60				
11	Buffalo	Buffalo, N. Y.	150				
12	McDougall	Fort Schuyler, N. Y. Harbor.	1,228	1	Armory Square	Washington, D. C.	1,000
13	Augusta	Augusta, Me.	1,062	2	Augur	Near Alexandria, Va	971
14	Grant	Willets' Point, N. Y. Harbor.	1,172	3	Carver	Washington, D. C.	1,300
15	Sloan	Montpelier, Vt.	482	4	Campbell	Washington, D. C.	1,000
16	Albany	Albany, N. Y.	560	5	Columbian	Washington, D. C.	844
17	Elmira	Elmira, N. Y.	300	6	Douglas	Washington, D. C.	400
18	Rochester	Rochester, N. Y.	608	7	Ricord	Washington, D. C.	120
19	Officers'	Bedloe's Island, N. Y. Harbor.	80	8	1st Division	Alexandria, Va.	1,226
20	New York City	New York City	151	9	2d Division	Alexandria, Va.	1,800
21	Jews'	New York City	50	10	3d Division	Alexandria, Va.	1,500
22	Brooklyn City	Brooklyn City, N. Y.	100	11	Emory	Washington, D. C.	900
23	Sisters of Charity	Buffalo, N. Y.	200	12	Finley	Washington, D. C.	1,581
24	Readville	Readville, Mass.	610	13	Fairfax Seminary	Virginia	638
				14	Harewood	Washington, D. C.	2,000
	Department of the Susquehanna.			15	Judiciary Square	Washington, D. C.	610
				16	Kalorama	Washington, D. C.	454
1	McClellan	Philadelphia, Pa.	1,841	17	Lincoln	Washington, D. C.	2,575
2	Turner's Lane	Philadelphia, Pa.	310	18	Mount Pleasant	Washington, D. C.	2,000
3	Convalescent	Philadelphia, Pa.	806	19	Seminary	Georgetown, D. C.	325
4	Satterlee	Philadelphia, Pa.	3,819	20	Stone	Washington, D. C.	170
5	Mower	Philadelphia, Pa.	3,326	21	Freedmen	Washington, D. C.	98
6	Cuyler	Germantown, Pa.	700	22	Stanton	Washington, D. C.	420
7	Christian Street	Philadelphia, Pa.	299	23	U. S. General	Point Lookout, Md.	1,000
8	South Street	Philadelphia, Pa.	270	24	Louverture	Alexandria, Va.	500
9	Citizen's Volunteer	Philadelphia, Pa.	250	25	Claremont	Alexandria, Va.	364
10	Summit House	Philadelphia, Pa.	1,204	26	Giesboro'	Giesboro' D. C.	536
11	York	York, Pa.	2,200				
12	Haddington	Philadelphia, Pa.	1,225		*Department of Virginia and North Carolina.*		
13	Islington	Philadelphia, Pa.	60				
14	Officers'	Camac Woods, Pa.	64				
15	U. S. General	Pittsburg, Pa.	725	1	U. S. General	Near Fort Monroe, Va.	3,570
16	Broad Street	Philadelphia, Pa.	527	2	Balfour	Portsmouth, Va.	840
17	Chester	Chester, Pa.	1,167	3	Foster	Newbern, N. C.	475
18	Beverly	Beverly, N. J.	1,440	4	U. S. General	Beaufort, N. C.	230
19	White Hall	White Hall, Pa.	1,373	5	Mansfield	Morehead City, N. C.	300
	Middle Department.				*Department of the South.*		
1	National Hotel	Baltimore, Md.	400	1	Division No. 1	Beaufort, S. C.	295
2	Newton University	Baltimore, Md.	200	2	Division No. 2	Beaufort, S. C.	440
3	Convalescent	Baltimore, Md.	1,172	3	U. S. General	Hilton Head, S. C.	600
4	Jarvis	Baltimore, Md.	1,380	4	U. S. General	Jacksonville, Fla.	174
5	West's Buildings	Baltimore, Md.	422	5	Officers'	Beaufort, S. C.	20
6	Division No. 1	Annapolis, Md.	1,117	6	Cenot	St. Augustine, Fla.	783
7	Division No. 2	Annapolis, Md.	661	7	Field	Marietta, Ga.	2,115
8	Annapolis Junction	Annapolis Junction	290				
	Carried forward		43,051		Total Atlantic Region		78,550

HOSPITAL ORGANIZATION AND CONSTRUCTION.

Hospitals in the Central Region, September, 1864.

No.	Name.	Locality.	Beds.	No.	Name.	Locality.	Beds.
	Northern Department.				Brought forward......		32,170
1	Seminary	Columbus, Ohio	223		*Department of Kansas.*		
2	U. S. General	Camp Chase, Ohio	234				
3	U. S. General	Cleveland, Ohio	380				
4	Denoison	Camp Dennison, Ohio	2,500	1	U. S. General	Leavenworth, Kansas	240
5	West End	Cincinnati, Ohio	120	2	U. S. General	Fort Scott, Kansas	148
6	Washington Park	Cincinnati, Ohio	160				
7	Marine	Cincinnati, Ohio	122				
8	U. S. General	Evansville, Ind.	630		*Department of the Arkansas.*		
9	Madison	Madison, Ind.	2,096				
10	U. S. General	Indianapolis, Ind.	258				
11	Desmarres	Chicago, Ill.	150	1	U. S. General	Little Rock, Ark.	797
12	Marine	Chicago, Ill.	110	2	U. S. General	Fort Smith, Ark.	325
13	U. S. General	Camp Butler, Ill.	480	3	Colored Ward	Little Rock, Ark.	24
14	U. S. General	Quincy, Ill.	478	4	Officers'	Little Rock, Ark.	120
15	St. Mary's	Detroit, Mich.	460	5	U. S. General	Helena, Ark.	100
16	U. S. General	Gallipolis, Ohio	800				
17	Main Street	Covington, Ky.	300				
18	Seminary	Covington, Ky.	218		*Department of the Tennessee.*		
19	Grant, Officers'	Cincinnati, Ohio	50				
				1	Overton	Memphis, Tenn.	450
	Department of the Northwest.			2	Gayoso	Memphis, Tenn.	400
				3	Adams'	Memphis, Tenn.	500
1	Harvey	Madison, Wis.	585	4	Officers'	Memphis, Tenn.	100
2	U. S. General	Keokuk, Iowa	1,380	5	Old State (Post)	Memphis, Tenn.	200
3	U. S. General	Davenport, Iowa	200	6	Washington	Memphis, Tenn.	400
				7	Webster	Memphis, Tenn.	500
	Department of Western Virginia.			8	U. S. General	Mound City, Ill.	596
				9	Post	Near Vicksburg, Miss.	147
1	Frederick	Frederick, Md.	1,776	10	U. S. General No. 2	Vicksburg, Miss.	280
2	Cumberland	Cumberland, Md.	1,191	11	U. S. General No. 3	Vicksburg, Miss.	800
3	Parkersburg	Parkersburg, West Va.	412	12	U. S. General	Natchez, Miss.	144
4	Grafton	Grafton, West Va.	267	13	Jackson	Memphis, Tenn.	300
	Department of the Ohio.				*Department of the Cumberland.*		
1	Clay	Louisville, Ky.	970				
2	Brown	Louisville, Ky.	1,000	1	U. S. General No. 1	Nashville, Tenn.	900
3	Eruptive	Louisville, Ky.	348	2	U. S. General No. 2	Nashville, Tenn.	665
4	U. S. General	New Albany, Ind.	1,728	3	U. S. General No. 3	Nashville, Tenn.	800
5	Ohio	New Albany, Ind.	300	4	U. S. General No. 8	Nashville, Tenn.	540
6	Jefferson	Jeffersonville, Ind.	2,802	5	U. S. General No. 1	Nashville, Tenn.	720
7	No. 15	Jeffersonville, Ind.	110	6	U. S. General No. 10	Nashville, Tenn.	280
8	Nelson	Camp Nelson, Ky.	600	7	U. S. General No. 15	Nashville, Tenn.	176
9	Nelson (Eruptive)	Camp Nelson, Ky.	100	8	U. S. General No. 21	Nashville, Tenn.	180
10	Convalescent	Camp Nelson, Ky.	500	9	U. S. General No. 19	Nashville, Tenn.	620
11	U. S. General	Lexington, Ky.	463	10	Cumberland	Nashville, Tenn.	2,400
12	U. S. General	Bowling Green, Ky.	128	11	Field	Bridgeport, Ala.	408
13	U. S. General	Ashland, Ky.	273	12	U. S. General	Gallatin, Tenn.	108
14	Corps d'Afrique	New Albany, Ind.	82	13	U. S. General	Murfreesboro', Tenn.	730
15	Tottes	Louisville, Ky.	1,150	14	U. N. General	Tullahoma, Tenn.	100
16	Joe Holt	Jeffersonville, Ind.	1,350	15	U. S. General No. 1	Chattanooga, Tenn.	672
17	U. S. General	Knoxville, Tenn.	1,247	16	U. S. General No. 2	Chattanooga, Tenn.	1,131
18	Officers'	Knoxville, Tenn.	54	17	Field	Chattanooga, Tenn.	1,247
19	Holston	Knoxville, Tenn.	656	18	U. S. General No. 14	Nashville, Tenn.	750
20	Officers'	Louisville, Ky.	33	19	Sherman	Nashville, Tenn.	430
21	Branch "A."	Bowling Green, Ky.	88	20	U. S. General	Lookout Mountain, Tenn.	800
22	Branch "B."	Bowling Green, Ky.	40	21	Officers'	Lookout Mountain, Tenn.	250
				22	Provisional	Chattanooga, Tenn.	100
	Department of the Missouri.				*Department of the Gulf.*		
1	Marine	St. Louis, Mo.	208	1	St. James	New Orleans, La.	300
2	Small-pox	St. Louis, Mo.	236	2	University	New Orleans, La.	500
3	U. S. General	Benton Barracks, Mo.	575	3	Marine	New Orleans, La.	600
4	U. S. General	Jefferson Barracks, Mo.	1,700	4	U. S. Barracks	New Orleans, La.	1,200
5	U. S. General	Jefferson City, Mo.	134	5	St. Louis	New Orleans, La.	600
6	U. S. General	Springfield, Mo.	200	6	Charity	New Orleans, La.	350
7	U. S. General	Rolla, Mo.	120	7	U. S. Convalescent	Baton Rouge, La.	400
8	U. S. General	Kansas City, Mo.	160	8	Corps d'Afrique	New Orleans, La.	1,700
9	Prison	St. Louis, Mo.	300				
	Carried forward		32,170		Total Central Region		58,266

Hospitals in the Pacific Region, September, 1864.

No.	Name.	Locality.	Beds.	No.	Name.	Locality.	Beds.
1	Wright	Presidio, San Francisco, Cal.	40	2	Barnes	Benicia Barracks, Cal.	28

RECAPITULATION.

Atlantic Region	98 Hospitals.	78,560 Beds.
Central Region	107 "	58,206 "
Pacific Region	2 "	68 "
Total	292 "	136,894 "

In addition to hospital construction, it is important that the system of hospital administration should be faithfully described. The hospital fund and its management, the slush fund, hospital cooking and diet tables, nurses, the question of female nurses, the hospital records and reports, are all subjects on which there are abundant data for a complete historical investigation.

In the foregoing remarks, my intention has been simply to give an idea of the nature and extent of the data for a Medical History of the War to be found in the part of the office under my direction. Many matters of interest have not been touched upon, for a full discussion of which abundant material exists; as, for example, the comparative health of the colored troops, of the prisoners of war held by us, of those of our own men who were unfortunate enough to fall into the hands of the rebels, etc. Moreover, there is much material in other branches of the Surgeon General's Office the consideration of which is necessary to a full understanding of the medical administration of the army.

In conclusion, I may express the opinion that, with the utmost brevity and care, it may be hoped to digest the material above sketched, not including surgical cases, into three quarto volumes, of about the size of the volumes of the Medical Statistics heretofore published. The prominent subjects in these volumes would be the medical statistics of the several armies, with the principal facts in their medical histories; the medical statistics of the several general hospitals, with descriptions of their construction and administration, illustrated by a sufficient number of ground plans and perspective views to give a just idea of them; and lastly, an account of the causes, history, symptoms, pathology, and treatment of the principal diseases of the troops, based upon statistical facts, contributed papers, histories of cases and autopsies, and observations made in the medical and microscopical sections of the Museum. This part of the work it is proposed to illustrate with such colored plates of morbid conditions and representations of the microscopical anatomy of the chief diseases as may be necessary to preserve, for the future study of medical men, a faithful account of the costly experience of the Medical Department during the war. Of the subjects thus indicated, about one-half of the statistical matter is compiled, and most of the material required for the remaining portion of the work is collected, and can be prepared for the press with reasonable rapidity. Almost all the necessary drawings are made, and ready for the lithographer; a large number of the wood-cuts are actually executed, and the material for the microscopical illustrations is in a forward condition.

I have the honor to be,
Very respectfully,
Your obedient servant,
J. J. WOODWARD,
*Assistant Surgeon and Brevet Major U. S. A.,
In charge of the Record and Pension Division, Surgeon General's Office,
and of the Medical Section, Army Medical Museum.*

www.ingramcontent.com/pod-product-compliance
Lightning Source LLC
Chambersburg PA
CBHW021734220426
43662CB00008B/840